The World University Library is an international series
of books, each of which has been specially commissioned.
The authors are leading scientists and scholars from all over
the world who, in an age of increasing specialisation, see the
need for a broad, up-to-date presentation of their subject.
The aim is to provide authoritative introductory books for
university students which will be of interest also to the general
reader. The series is published in Britain, France, Germany,
Holland, Italy, Spain, Sweden and the United States.

Frontispiece Half a century after.
Frans Masereel's woodcut 'Hommage
à Verhaeren', 1955.

John Willett

Expressionism

World University Library

Weidenfeld and Nicolson
5 Winsley Street London W1

Photoset by BAS Printers Limited, Wallop, Hampshire
Manufactured by LIBREX, Italy.

Contents

1 The Expressionist puzzle

Warning

Anybody rash enough to open a book about an artistic or literary -Ism needs to make some reservations. For one thing, such groupings and movements always sound more clear-cut than they really were. People who talk or write about the arts like to use them as convenient pigeon-holes, but in many cases the individuals now held to have taken part in them had no idea or intention of doing anything of the sort; they may not even have heard of the particular -Ism under which posterity has filed them. Also, each individual changes all the time, so that even if he did at a given moment consciously adhere to an -Ism his works both then and later may reject it. They, not he, are what finally matters, and any work of art is entitled to separate consideration. The fact that it can be put in the context of a wider movement, however intriguing that movement may seem, is of primary interest only to critics and historians. Once you start treating a work as something more than a specimen pinned to a board both -Ism and individual ought to drop into the background.

A further point is that a movement is by no means like a marching army, even though the military metaphor of the 'avant-garde' often seems to imply that it is. It is more like a current in the sea. Shapeless, it is at the same time continually changing shape; it has no outlines, just marginal areas where nobody can say which way it is going or if it is moving at all. Thus it cannot be lined up and numbered off from the right, let alone divided between a 'front rank' (another convenient critical term borrowed from the military) and the rest. Though it is full of fish of different sorts and sizes, they may be swimming with it or against it, each in his own individual direction. The fish can be caught separately and enjoyed in themselves, irrespective what current they are in. Nobody, however, can catch the current. It may be detected by a series of observations made at particular times and places, but there is only one way to appreciate it as a whole: by mapping the larger ocean through which it moves.

The meanings of Expressionism

These considerations apply to Expressionism more than to most movements. For Expressionism was never, like Futurism or Surrealism, a conscious grouping which can be related to a common programme (however loosely worded) or to certain collective demonstrations and publications. It is one of those rarer concepts which get used more or less retrospectively to describe something already felt to be happening, or else a permanent basic element in all art which the times seemed to have brought to the surface. Thus it is not one of the easiest -Isms to nail down. Some of the very people whom any outsider would at once associate with it became the keenest to disown it; thus the late Kurt Wolff, who from 1912 on was the principal publisher of the writers and artists we now think of as constituting German Expressionism, hated being associated with this word and held that it meant giving those writers 'a common stamp which they never in fact possessed'. Similarly the painter Ernst Ludwig Kirchner, who in many opinions was the Expressionist artist *par excellence,* told a critic in 1924 that he found it 'more degrading than ever ... to be identified with Munch and Expressionism'. The poet Gottfried Benn, perhaps the movement's outstanding survivor, was likewise shaken in 1955 to find that his work was being presented as Expressionist, and queried many of the assumptions underlying this definition.

If this applies among the persons most closely involved with the movement at the time, how much more difficult must it be for any outsider to situate the individual artist or writer in it. Gromaire and the early Chagall, for instance, are both painters whom it seems reasonable to term expressionist, yet they have before now been authoritatively classed as surrealists, while Utrillo and Modigliani, who have little visible or historical connection with the German and Flemish movements, have been placed in art books and exhibitions among the expressionists. On the other hand the chief Belgian expressionist review, André de Ridder's *Sélection,* could say in 1924 of the Surrealist Manifesto that 'leaving aside the special German use of the term, it strikes us that this surrealism is very little different from the *expressionism* which we have propagated from the outset', (i.e., since *Sélection*'s foundation in 1920). To complicate matters further, creative artists are often reluctant to admit anything that might seem like dependence on such a movement; their sense of their own individuality is too strong. Those who actually called themselves expressionists, once the term had become at all current, were often the less important figures.

All the same it does seem possible to give certain fairly clear meanings to the term, even if these differ according to the context (and to some extent the country) in which they are used. Expressionism then is normally

1 a family characteristic of modern Germanic art, literature, music and theatre, from the turn of the century to the present day.

2 a particular modern German movement which lasted roughly between 1910 and 1922.

3 a quality of expressive emphasis and distortion which may be found in works of art of any people or period.

Whenever the experts use it – experts in this connection being specialists in modern German art and literature, or those who themselves played a part in the movement – they usually mean Expressionism in the second, or most restricted sense. Outside the German-speaking world it is more generally used to mean the first, and not always in a specially complimentary way; thus 'expressionism' was one of the criticisms levelled at Brecht's Berliner Ensemble when it first performed in Moscow. The third meaning may crop up almost anywhere, though unlike the others it usually relates only to the visual arts: to the expressive aspect, for instance, of Fayum portraiture, or negro sculpture, or early Cézanne, or late Jackson Pollock. It then becomes one of those universal terms like 'realism' or 'classicism', carrying no suggestion of a coherent movement.

However, the German Expressionism referred to in the second meaning is central to the subject, and we shall distinguish it by spelling it with a capital E. Here was an intense, all-embracing movement which so swept central Europe immediately before, during and after the First World War that much of the reaction away from it in the later 1920s still looks more or less expressionistic to the non-German. Within that area it was for ten years or so quite simply the Modern Movement; that is to say, for the Germans it was in effect Fauvism, Futurism, Cubism (not to mention Orphism and Unanimism and other obscurer offshoots) rolled into one, absorbing ideas and elements from them all and transmuting them in a recognisably expressionist way. There was, for example, no such thing as a German cubist, though the impact of cubism can be seen in the work of one Expressionist after another. This is perhaps the major reason why for the next thirty years the movement was ignored by French critics and by the whole art world centred on

Paris. In the visual arts at least it at first seemed natural for non-Germans to judge its outstanding members not by the features which these had in common with one another but by the elements which they had obviously borrowed from elsewhere, so that Kirchner could be dismissed as a lesser Fauve, Marc as a lesser Futurist, Feininger as a lesser Cubist and so on. In so far as such people had added some further component of their own it was German and to be regretted.

To grasp the real meaning of expressionism we must try to discover what it was in the national and international background that was so expressionist (in the first or third senses) as to make the modern movement in Germany take the form it did, at the same time recognising how this differed from the various other modern movements on which it drew. For expressionism is above all else that particular element which the different senses of the term have in common. It was brought to a focus, certainly, by the special circumstances of the younger German artists and writers in the last years of William II's empire, when intellectual exchanges with other countries were a great deal easier and more informal than they are now, yet the weight of conservative nationalism often seemed quite stiflingly oppressive. It is this conflict of atmospheres which gave the movement its extraordinary manic-depressive quality: visions of universal brotherhood alternating with the blackest despair. And the reason why that movement is now of such interest to the historian is that it interlocks with other, better-known manifestations of the same conflict: the First World War, the collapse of the Socialist International, the fragmentation of eastern Europe – those great explosions, in short, to which we owe our present uneasy world.

Scope of the inquiry

This combination of a highly-charged core with ill-defined margins means that we must make our survey fairly wide, at any rate a good deal wider than the 'Expressionist decade' on which Gottfried Benn looked back a few months before his death in 1956. Even within that decade attention has been too largely concentrated on the opening years, on pioneers, precursors and origins, and too little on the processes by which the movement became established. So far as its less important members were concerned, and the general public, and any art requiring institutional support, Expressionism was mainly a post-war phenomenon and a product of the German revolution of November 1918. Though this may not have been the period of its purest and intensest works, two things need to be borne in mind. First of all, one of the remarkable features of German Expressionism as against any other avant-garde movement before the Second World War, was that its conventions became so widely accepted. It provided, as other such movements generally do not, a framework within which second- or third-grade writers and artists could work effectively; the distance between leaders and led was not so great as in other cases, (though it can be argued that this was because even the best of them were less outstanding). Secondly, and as a result of this, it seemed to permeate the whole cultural life of the Weimar Republic in a way for which there was no parallel elsewhere.

The structure of the movement's success deserves study quite as much as its aesthetic origins, not least because of the ruthless demolition process which followed. The reaction against Expressionism did not come, as most of its historians imply, with the slackening of the German movement proper in the early 1920's, for many of the developments which followed – the work of Grosz and Beckmann, for instance, or even that of Brecht – reflect the same influences and assumptions, and still lie a good deal closer to Expressionism than to any previous movement. What killed it rather was the all-out attack launched by the (democratically elected) Nazis in the mid-1930's against the whole twentieth-century aesthetic revolution: an attack that was to some extent paralleled by the reactionary art policies simultaneously instituted in Russia, much to the confusion of left-wing anti-Nazis ever since. Yet this too was far from being the end of the Expressionist story, for the almost total extinction of this movement between 1933 and 1945 was itself a main factor in the revival of German cultural life after the Second World War. In all age groups and on many different levels people felt a self-evident challenge to pick the threads up.

We shall start our survey, then, around the beginning of the century, with some reference to the particular influence exerted by certain earlier artists and writers (exemplifying expressionism in the third sense), and try to trace developments up to the present day. We shall centre the inquiry on Germany, where this influence was most strongly felt, but will aim first to give the general European setting and show how it produced proto-Expressionist works in other countries, returning again to the wider scene once we have followed the German movement to its climax, then finishing off after the Nazi interlude with a consideration of expressionist influence both inside and outside Germany during the past twenty years. We shall hope to deal fairly with all the arts, for this is an -Ism which, like romanticism but unlike any other, applies alike to literature, the theatre and the visual arts, and in a lesser degree to music and architecture too. It is not a mere name which the different arts have in common (as is the case, say, with classical art and classical music), but stands to a great extent for a shared heritage, a common spirit, a close working relationship and direct personal links.

One of the remarkable things about the German Expressionist movement was that it represented such an extraordinary concentration of artistic effort from a number of different fields. Sometimes this kind of fusion, taking place often at white heat, helped the individual to surpass himself: to give more than anybody thought he had got, more indeed than he ever had again. At others it did not, either because, like Klee, the man was a complete original or because the heat became too much for him, as it did at times for the poet Becher. This is where any student of such movements must be careful not to let his appetite for specialised knowledge dictate his standards. For the ultimate importance of an artistic or literary movement, judged critically and not committedly, lies in the element of stimulation or mis-direction which it offers to its members. However fascinating it may be to follow, however topically relevant its history, however impressive its theoretical justifications, however intense its effect on men's lives, the works which flow from it must be judged on their own merits and not on the movement's reputation. Perhaps this does not exactly apply to the illustrations in the present book, which are meant only as a kind of shorthand notation for the works themselves, so many pointers inserted in the text. But it must apply to both author's and reader's approach to the originals, and to other actual works of the period. In these days of art historical expertise and scholarly specialisation the temptation is always to treat them as better than they really were.

2 The European setting

A change of centuries

A certain imaginative effort is required in order to understand how the European cultural horizon was tilted some seventy years ago, and how many of the earlier landmarks we now see in it were missing. The critic Julius Meier-Graefe, who more than any other man helped to give Germany a balanced view of nineteenth-century French painting, could look back in 1914 and say that

in 1890 the inside of our heads looked like an emergency railway station in wartime.

It is impossible to conceive how riddled with holes our mental communication system was. Toulouse-Lautrec, Vallotton, Odilon Redon, Axel Gallén, Vigeland, Beardsley, Gauguin and Munch, Puvis de Chavannes and Whistler were our main sources of awareness apart from the German romantics ... I knew Bonnard before I knew Manet, Manet before I knew Delacroix. This confused state of mind explains many of our generation's subsequent mistakes.

At that date Cézanne, Van Gogh and to a great extent Rimbaud were virtually unknown; the plays of Büchner, the poems of Hölderlin and the paintings of Daumier were recent discoveries; Bosch, Brueghel, El Greco and the blacker side of Goya were almost entirely unappreciated. Gauguin's one-man exhibition of November 1893 and his auction of February 1895 were both flops.

Paris in those days was the absolute cultural capital of the world, and it is astonishing even now to see how many later developments were anticipated there, in ways that have been largely forgotten even in France. That the well-intentioned official makers of taste – like Brunetière in literature, or Léonce Bénédite in painting – now mean nothing to us is perhaps not surprising; but there were also figures of genuine, if limited, interest and originality who tend to be dismissed either because they rose (like Puvis de Chavannes) to the ranks of the Establishment or because the trends to which they contributed were not those (such as surrealism or cubism) which subsequent critics have felt to matter. Zola and the Naturalist school, Mallarmé and the Symbolists and Anatole France were in their various ways big enough to remain as landmarks even if their work is not entirely in fashion today. Others, for instance the artists Redon, Gustave Moreau and Eugène Grasset, went into limbo, then were brought out again as critical fashion began to change. But people like Carrière, with his cloudy, smoky paintings of mothers and children (*Maternités*: dozens of them in the cellars of the Louvre alone) or Cottet, with his solemnly melancholic scenes of the life of poor Bretons, are now not on our horizon at all. We must put them back there, if only in imagination, if we are to visualise the background against which the essential discoveries and reactions took place.

There were three main elements in the atmosphere of those times, and because they would now seem to us contradictory they made a special mixture without which the Expressionist movement a decade or two later is hard to grasp. First of all there was a revival of mysticism, partly as a reaction against nineteenth-century materialism and the current laicising tendencies in both France and Germany, partly no doubt out of a sense that a great century was dying. This development, which can be felt throughout the French and Russian Symbolist movements and particularly in the paintings of Watts and Moreau and the Belgian Xaver Mellery, found its purest expression between 1892 and 1897 with the series of Salons de la Rose Croix organised by Joséphin (the Sâr) Péladan, who hoped to kill off Realism in favour of myth, allegory, Catholic mysticism and 'the interpretation of oriental theogonies except those of the yellow races'. Probably the most important single work shown there, among much rubbish, was the Swiss Ferdinand Hodler's 'Die Enttäuschten' (now in the Berne Museum), a large figure composition not unlike a toughened-up Puvis de Chavannes. It was the moment when Dostoevsky's novels were starting to be read outside Russia, eight of his novels appearing in French translation between 1884 and 1890. Schopenhauer's philosophy, with its oriental emphasis, was at last being widely studied, for instance by the poet Jules Laforgue (who died in 1887) and by the group of artists around Gauguin at Pont-Aven. Madame Blavatsky had founded the theosophical movement a decade earlier, and in 1889 the Alsatian Eduard Schuré, best known for his championship of Wagner's music in France, published *Les Grands initiés,* a study of outstanding mystics which made a particular impression on the young group of 'Nabis' around Bonnard, Vuillard, Paul Sérusier and Maurice Denis.

At the same time the 1890s in France were a decade of Anarchism. Given the relative insignificance of the Anarchists even now, when their movement is again reviving among students and intellec-

'L'Anarchiste'. A wood engraving of 1892 by Félix Vallotton, one of the ancestors of the German Expressionist woodcut.

tuals in a number of countries, it is easy to forget what a major force they then seemed. Particularly in the arts their ideas had an appeal if anything greater than that of Socialism; thus the whole Neo-Impressionist movement in painting (Seurat, Signac, Pissarro, Luce, etc.) was politically Anarchist, while the literary reviews and the new humorous weeklies were largely dominated by more or less anarchist sympathies. One of the most curious things about the change of centuries is that, after the wave of Anarchist outrages in the 1890s (such as President Carnot's assassination in 1894) and the tremendous consolidation of left and liberal sympathies brought about by the Dreyfus case, the Anarchist movement became so ineffective. But anybody who looks at old numbers of *La Revue Blanche,* which ran from October 1891 to 15 April 1903, will see how naturally its ideas fitted with other advanced notions of the times. Felix Fénéon, now best remembered as a supporter of Seurat, was the magazine's secretary (except when in gaol for his Anarchist views); Maurice Denis its main art critic; Jarry, Verhaeren, Verlaine, Paul Adam, Apollinaire, Léon Blum among its contributors; Nietzsche, William Morris, Munch and Hamsun among those whose work or ideas it introduced to France. Whatever the violence and muddle of Anarchism's practical activities, in such contexts as these it stood for utopianism, anti-militarism, contempt for authority, a sense of international brotherhood and a common feeling that social injustice was not only unethical but unaesthetic.

With this went something of which we are now a good deal more suspicious: what Misia Natanson, wife of the *Revue Blanche*'s director, called 'the rising tide of humanitarianism'. This was a great wave of feeling, sometimes true and passionate, sometimes phoney and conventional or plain dishonest, which swept Europe and North America between (approximately) the death of Victor Hugo in 1885 and the outbreak of the First World War. At one end of the scale it embraced Van Gogh's letters, which marvellously communicate both the convictions, Christian and social, and the earlier models (such as Millet's peasant paintings) that underlay it; at the other are those stock figures of workers and peasants who are even

14

L'ANARCHISTE.

now to be found decorating Mairies and ministries built under the Third Republic or – a sad hangover – constituting the new established art of eastern Europe in our time. Christian Socialism itself dates from the encyclical *Rerum novarum* of 1891, Tolstoyanism from a few years earlier, when the novelist wrote such works as *Confession* and *What I Believe* (published together in Geneva in 1888); Oscar Wilde's *The Soul of Man under Socialism* appeared in *The Fortnightly Review* in February 1891; the first Hague Peace Conference was held in 1899. Those were the years when the Belgian Constantin Meunier became recognised as the outstanding sculptor (and painter) in the humanitarian tradition, while theatres like Antoine's Théâtre Libre (founded in 1887) or Lugné-Pöe's Théâtre de l'Oeuvre (1893) or Brahm's Freie Bühne in Berlin (1889) became the home of the new social and human drama of Bjørnson and Ibsen and Gerhart Hauptmann. Closely associated with the same trend was a wide movement for popular culture deriving from Fourier's utopian Socialism and the doctrines of Morris and Ruskin, who were then influential throughout Europe. Among its

15

dozens of manifestations (from the Proletkult and the Belgian Maisons du Peuple to Britain's Everyman's Library and the Berlin Volksbühne) were the English Garden City movement and the French attempts (starting at Bussang in the Vosges and Belleville in the Parisian East End) to create a People's Theatre.

In addition to all this there were two new forms of lower-level communication which from our present point of view were more significant than the overpowering *Gesamtkunstwerk* of Wagner, then regarded as the outstanding example of a virtually new medium. These were the literary cabaret or *chansonnier*, starting in 1881 with the Chat Noir, where the waiters dressed as French Academicians and the director Rodolphe Salis wore a *sous-préfet*'s uniform; and the comic illustrated weeklies such as the *Gil Blas Illustré* (founded in 1891), *Le Chambard* (1893), *La Feuille* (1897) and *L'Assiette au Beurre* (1901), in which the line block replaced wood engraving as a means of reproduction, while the rotary press made possible large printings and a low selling price. The characteristic men of this new cultural half-world were the French-Swiss draughtsman Théophile Steinlen and the singer-poet Aristide Bruant, whose black hat and red scarf are well known from Toulouse-Lautrec's poster. Bruant, in the words of Anatole France, was the first person to 'express the pathos of filth', while Zola described him in fictionalised form in *Paris*, as the author of songs in which 'the whole disgusting sore of our social inferno shouted and spat out its sickness in revolting words, full of blood and fire'. Steinlen, who illustrated many such texts by Bruant, was the most skilled and prolific socialist artist of the time, combining a humane penchant for social (or low-life) subject matter with a sharp expressiveness not unlike Toulouse-Lautrec's. He was then at the height of his influence, and when a public banquet was given for him in 1895 the speakers included not only Anatole France but also the Belgian Socialist leader Emile Vandervelde, and Frantz Jourdain, the subsequent founder of the Salon d'Automne.

Disturbing influences

Into this now slightly unfamiliar climate a number of fresh winds had begun blowing, some of them bracing, some positively chilly. They came from all sorts of different directions: France itself, Germany, Vienna, Belgium, Norway, Russia, the United States, Spain, though not so much from Italy or from England, whose main contribution had already taken place through the Pre-

Munch's lithograph 'The Cry' from *La Revue Blanche*, 1894.

Overleaf Constantin Meunier's drawing 'Le Retour des Mineurs' (Meunier Museum, Brussels) and H. G. Ibel's lithograph for the programme of Hauptmann's *The Weavers* at Antoine's Théâtre Libre, 1892-3, with Steinlen's lithograph of Aristide Bruant from *Gil Blas* 12 June 1892 opposite.

Raphaelites and their followers and, even more tellingly, through Charles Darwin. If Paris was the focal point there was an extraordinarily free and natural system of cultural exchanges over the whole continent, particularly between France, Germany and the Low Countries. Painters from all over the world arrived to work in France, like the young Picasso in 1900, though a number of the Russians, like Kandinsky in 1896, preferred to work or study mainly in Munich. Dieppe, where Wilde went after his release from prison, was then the meeting place for the French Impressionists and Symbolists and the English of the *Savoy* and the *Yellow Book*. Ibsen based himself for years in Germany; while the Munich publisher Albert Langen took Steinlen to see Bjørnson in Norway in 1895. For those who could afford to travel, all doors were open. In those days there were no formally organised 'cultural relations' between the European countries. Nor were passports needed in

LES TISSERANDS

Drame en cinq actes, en prose

PREMIER ACTE

Dreissiger	MM	Pons Arlès
Pfeifer		Renard
Banker		Dupal
Bæumert		Desmarets
Reimann		Henrich
Heiber		Renaudot
Neumann		Reynold
Une Femme	Mᵐᵉ	Reynold

Tisserands, Femmes de tisserands, un Commis, un Enfant.

SECOND ACTE

Bæumert	MM	Gémier
Jæger		Arquillière
Ansorge		Levane
Auguste		Verse
Fritz		Le Petit Ma
Mère Bæumert	Mᵐᵉ	Leverçand
Emma		Jeanne Dur
Bertha		Hellem
Une Femme		Reynold

Tisserands

TROISIÈME ACTE

Jæger	MM	Arquillière
Backer		Dupal
Wittig		Henrich
Kutsche		Desmarets
Un Commis-voyageur		Argus
Hornig		Michelet
Welzel		Pinard
Wiegand		Le Van
Ansorge		Levane
Bæumert		Gémier
Un paysan		Vrisse
Un tisserand		Renaudot
Madame Welzel	Mᵐᵉ	Glézavet
Anna		Totven

Tisserands

QUATRIÈME ACTE

Dreissiger	MM	Pons Arlès
Kittelhaus		Laudres
Le Commissaire		Dupal
Pfeifer		Renard
Kutsche		Desmarets
Weinhold		Henrich
Jean		Verse
Jæger		Arquillière
Backer		Dupal
Ansorge		Levane
Bæumert		Gémier
Wittig		Henrich
Madame Dreissiger	Mᵐᵉ	Ines Pesaro
Madame Kittelhaus		Viset

Tisserands, Femmes de tisserands

CINQUIÈME ACTE

Hilse	MM	Antoine
Gottlieb		Etinant
Bæumert		Gémier
Banker		Dupal
Jæger		Arquillière
Wittig		Henrich
Hornig		Michelet
Schmidt		Argus
Mère Hilse	Mᵐᵉ	Barny
Louise		Na
Mielchen		La Petite Suzanne Sem

Tisserands, Femmes de tisserands

de la part de M. Gerhart Hauptmann

Paris, Imp. Eugène Verneau, lith. rue de la Folie-Méricourt.

La Vigne au Vin

Vieille Chanson recueillie et chantée par ARISTIDE BRUANT

De vigne en fleur
La voilà, la joli' fleur!
Fleur, fleurons, fleurons le vin,
La voilà, la joli' fleur au vin!
La voilà, la joli' fleur!

De fleur en grappe
La voilà, la joli grappe?
Grappe, grappons, grappons le vin,
La voilà, la joli' grappe au vin!
La voilà, la joli' grappe!

De grappe en cueille
La voilà, a voit' cueille!
Cueill'-cueillons, cueillons le vin,
La voilà, la joli cueille au vin,
La voilà, la joli' cueille!

De cueille en hotte,
La voilà, la joli' hotte!
Hott'-hottons, hottons le vin,
la voilà, la joli' hotte au vin!
La voilà, la joli' hotte!

De hotte en cuve
La voilà, la joli' cuve?
Cuv'-cuvons, cuvons le vin,
La voilà, la joli' cuve au vin?
La voilà, la joli' cuve!

De cuve en presse
La voilà, la joli' presse!
Press'-pressons, pressons le vin,
La voilà, la joli' presse au vin,
La voilà, la joli' presse!

De presse en tonne!
La voilà, la joli' tonne!
Tonn'-tonnons, tonnons le vin,
La voilà, la joli' tonne au vin,
La voilà, la joli' tonne!

De tonne en cruche,
La voilà, la joli' cruche!
Cruch'-cruchons, cruchons le vin,
La voilà, la joi cruche au vin,
La voilà, la joli' cruche!

De cruche en verre,
La voilà, la joli' verre?
Verr'-verrons, verrons le vin?
Le voilà, le joli verre au vin,
La voilà, le joli verre!

De verre en bouche,
La voilà, la joli' bouche!
Bouch'-bouchons, bouchons le vin,
La voilà, la joli' bouche au vin,
La voilà, la joli' bouche!

De bouche en ventre,
Le voilà, le joli' ventre!
Ventr'-ventrons, ventrons le vin,
La voilà, le joli ventre au vin,
Le voilà, le joli' ventre!

De ventre en pisse,
La voilà, la joi' pisse!
Piss'-pissons, pissons le vin,
La voilà, la joli' pisse au vin,
La voilà, la joli' pisse!

De pisse en terre,
la voilà, la joli' terre!
Terr'-terrons, terrons le vin,
La voilà, la joli' terre au vin,
La voilà, la joli' terre!

De terre en vigne,
La voilà, la joli' vigne!
Vign'-vignons, vignons le vin,
La voilà, la joli' vigne au vin,
La voilà la joli' vigne!

(Dessin de Steinlen.)

order to travel from one to the other.

The seeds which blew hither and thither across Europe before 1910 were those not only of Expressionism in its German form but also to a great extent of life as we know it, a life filled with vast technical possibilities and at the same time with cruelties and uncertainties such as few could then even guess at. The aeroplane, radio, cinema, popular press, motor car, airship, chemical warfare, submarine, steam turbine and countless other fundamental inventions for better or worse made their appearance in those years, and their impact on writers and artists everywhere can hardly be overrated. To such great technological surprises must be added the impact of Nietzsche, Bergson and (a little later) Freud, of Strindberg and Munch, of freer sexual relations and of the feminist movement, of Verhaeren, Whitman and Rimbaud (whose works were scarcely available before the mid-1890s), of Daumier, Van Gogh, Cézanne and the new vogue for El Greco, of the linear vitality associated with Art Nouveau and the brilliant flatness evolved by Gauguin and the Synthetists and passed on by them via the Nabis to the Fauves. What distinguished the majority of these artistic and intellectual impulses and made them contrast so startlingly not only with the placid optimism of early twentieth-century Europe but with the new technological advances too, was their element of savagery and passion. 'Fauves', or wild beasts, the label stuck on Matisse and his friends in 1905, was a prescient name for a tendency so rooted in the primitive and irrational: in the Breton and Polynesian environments sought out by Gauguin, in the negro sculpture discovered for themselves by Matisse, Derain and Picasso in 1905-6, and ultimately in the sub-rational drives revealed by anthropologists and psychologists from about 1860 onwards and appreciated in the light of evolutionary theory. 'The time for gentleness and the amateur approach is past', wrote the novelist Charles-Louis Philippe in 1897. 'Now we need some barbarians ... The age of passion begins today.' A year later the *Mercure de France* started issuing Nietzsche's complete works.

Today Nietzsche's appeal has faded, since so many of his ideas have become discredited by misinterpretation, crude popularisation (Superman) and the political abuses to which they have led or been put. It is difficult for us to hear the word 'bejahen' without a shudder, while the pseudo-Biblical rhetoric of *Also sprach Zarathustra* (published in parts between 1883 and 1891) often falls into pretentiousness where that of Whitman and Claudel only totters. At the time however the force of Nietzsche's ideas was immense throughout Europe, particularly among writers and artists, and far more so than other less passionately-written philosophies of irrationalism: Bergson's with its concept of the *élan vital* or the near-anarchist Sorel's brilliant *Réfléxions sur la violence* with their emphasis on political myth. One after another of the figures in our story was swept off his feet by Nietzsche's aggressive affirmations of life, its Dionysian aspects, its unbounded instincts and potentialities and hazards. Thus Paula Modersohn-Becker, for instance, in 1899, on finishing *Zarathustra:*

With his new values Nietzsche is really a man of gigantic stature ... It was a strange experience for me to find latent feelings of my own, still unclear and undeveloped within me, now being clearly formulated. I rejoiced to find myself once more a modern being and a child of my time.

A few years later Sorge, the first Expressionist playwright, wrote a poem 'Christus und Nietzsche', putting the two figures side by side, while for Gottfried Benn, Nietzsche was quite simply 'the world-scale giant of the post-Goethean era'.

Strindberg and Munch lay closer still to the Expressionist movement, for the two Scandinavians helped to shape not only its ideas and attitudes – its concern with extreme despair, with human relationships at the point of highest tension, and, in Strindberg's case, with dreams and visions of the Beyond – but also its actual artistic forms. Munch indeed is often spoken of as an Expressionist himself, for although he was in Paris for three years from 1889 (during which time he is supposed to have seen the work of both Gauguin and Van Gogh) his reputation dates from his subsequent sojourns in Germany, and between 1892 and 1914 he was virtually part of the German movement. Similarly Strindberg may at the turn of the century have been an accepted figure in Paris; thus he wrote his play *Father* in a French version in 1887, and this and other of his earlier, more or less naturalistic drama were performed by the Théâtre Libre and the Théâtre de l'Oeuvre in the 1890s. But he too came to find his chief interpreters and his most enthusiastic public in Germany, particularly after his change to a more symbolic, metaphysical kind of dramaturgy after 1900. Max Reinhardt alone staged seventeen of his plays, while Georg Müller of Munich published the only complete edition of his works outside Sweden, where he long had difficulty in getting them performed at all. Indeed, the plays of Strindberg's fifties, notably *To Damascus* (with its

The apocalyptic city. 'View of Toledo' (Metropolitan Museum, New York), by El Greco, a rediscovery of the 1900s.

three parts), and *Dream Play* (1903), were virtually Expressionist dramas, with their unidentified characters (The Officer, The Unknown, The Beggar), their loose sequence of 'stations' rather than acts and scenes, their desperate search for spiritual calm, their self-dramatising monologues (particularly in *Damascus*) and their conception in terms of an almost bare stage. At the time they were compared with Goethe's *Faust*.

At the other pole, Verhaeren represented a more forceful revival of the social-humanitarian tradition in the arts. Taking over from Whitman (who only began seriously to penetrate France through the biography and translations of Léon Bazalgette around 1908) and the Hugo of *Pauvres Gens,* he was at the same time in touch with the Symbolists and Neo-impressionists and with the Socialist Maisons du Peuple. He was not much of a formal innovator, though Stefan Zweig, no doubt with Art Nouveau in mind, wrote of the 'wild, boldly curving lines' of his free verse. But he brought to the slightly jaded humanitarianism of those days a new awareness of modern industrial and city life, and a passion which convinced many of his contemporaries (but not Claudel, who thought him 'flatulent'), even if it seems a bit suspect to the modern reader. 'Verhaeren's poetry is the communication of an ecstasy', wrote Zweig, who thought it important that he was a Belgian, like his contemporaries Maeterlinck and Henri van de Velde and the thirty-year older Meunier. For although from 1899 on he lived in Paris he seemed to have a 'Teutonic perception', derived from 'the laws of his blood'. And indeed his awareness of Europe, his utopian visions of

> Those times when, fixedly, the simplest ethics
> Will proclaim humanity to be peaceful and harmonious.

– his concept of a larger social entity where the individual is begged to

> Défais
> Ton être en des millions d'êtres,
> Et sens l'immensité filtrer et transparaître.
>
> (Dissolve
> Your being among thousands of beings,
> And feel how immensity percolates and manifests itself.)

– his vocabulary, with such terms as *halluciner, fou, hagard,* or *colossal, tumultueux, tumultuaire* (to take some of the words which struck his friend Henri Guilbeaux as most typical of him); finally his conviction that

> Nous apportons, ivres du monde et de nous-mêmes,
> Des coeurs d'hommes nouveaux dans le vieil univers.
>
> (Intoxicated by the world and by ourselves we bring
> The hearts of new men to the old universe)

– all point forward to certain aspects of the Expressionist movement.

A similar concern with the mythical City, a subject which recalls the Apocalypse of St John and the work of William Blake, even then being revived in England, is common to many obscurer writers of the same period, such as the anarchist André Ibels, brother of the draughtsman, whose 'Prophetic Book' *Les Cités futures* came out in 1895. Here, under epigraphs from Nietzsche and Bakunin, Lao-tse and Schiller, is a cosmic picture of *l'Homme* with a capital H, who 'surgira d'un Astre inconnu de nos Terres', while Humanity is to set forth 'vers les plaines Où nous voulons bâtir les Cités étoilées.' In 1908 again, Anatoly Lunacharsky, subsequently Commissar for Education under Lenin, wrote his play *Faust and the City*, a vastly ambitious development of the last act of Goethe's play, in which Faust aims to build 'a paradisial land'. There is a link here too with those French men of letters – Duhamel, Romains, Vildrac, René Arcos, Luc Durtain – who tried to found their own form of communal life at the Abbaye de Créteil, expressing a quasi-religious belief in humanity and its future. For Verhaeren had envisaged Man becoming God; Gorki ended his *The Lower Depths* (one of Reinhardt's earliest and most successful productions) with a great monologue on Man as being something greater than any individual or his needs; Lunacharsky and Bogdanov hoped by means of the Proletkult to make this notion of the Man-God into a Socialist substitute for religion: an ambition ruthlessly deflated by Lenin in *Materialism and Empiriocriticism* and satirised by Norman Douglas in *South Wind*. Now Jules Romains, in his long and astonishingly evenly written didactic poem 'La Vie unanime', developed his own concept of Unanimism, a collective soul within which apparently without misgivings)

> Nous consentirons à la joie
> Lasse et femelle d'être agis
>
> (We shall accept the passive, feminine
> Pleasure of being worked by others)

This sense of fusion with a larger entity is traced through the recruits in a barracks, the audience in a theatre, the crowd at a great political demonstration. The opening words are 'O ville ...'.

The wild beasts

So far as is now known, the earliest printed appearances of the word 'expressionist' were a reference to 'the expressionist school of modern painters' in *Tait's Edinburgh Magazine* in July 1850; an allusion to 'the expressionists, those who undertake to express special emotions or passions' in a lecture on modern painting given by Charles Rowley in Manchester on 23 February 1880; and the title given to a group of writers, 'The Expressionists', in the novel *The Bohemian* (1878) by the *New York Times* critic Charles De Kay, who was American consul-general in Berlin between 1894 and 1897. In 1901 at the Salon des Indépendants in Paris, a now totally obscure painter, Julien-Auguste Hervé, showed some pictures which he called *Expressionismes,* and continued using this term each year until 1908. Conceivably he might have put the word into the head of some artist or critic who noticed them among the several thousand works in that unselective show. Kandinsky, Gabriele Münter, Pechstein, Curt Herrmann and the sculptor Bernhard Hoetger were among the German artists showing there in the same years, while the *Figaro* critic Louis Vauxcelles, who has been credited with fathering this -Ism as well as the expressions 'cubism' and 'les Fauves', might well have noticed the catalogue entries, even if the pictures (which seem never to have been reproduced) were not very striking.

Inconclusive as this is, it seems symptomatic of the visual arts' primacy in bringing the movement to a recognisable head. The key figures here initially were five artists of different periods whose paintings only began to be at all widely appreciated, and in some cases at all adequately shown, around the turn of the century. Van Gogh's great posthumous assault on the eyes and hearts of our age began with his retrospective at Amsterdam in 1893, three years after his suicide, and the publication of some of his letters in the *Mercure de France,* whose short-lived critic Albert Aurier was the first (in 1890) to praise his work in print. Cézanne, whose work had to all intents and purposes not been seen in Paris since 1877, held his first one-man show at Vollard's new gallery at the end of 1895. Daumier's paintings (as opposed to his well-known drawings and prints) were shown in force for only the second time at the Paris Exhibition of 1900, twenty years after his death. The revaluation of El Greco dates

AUTI TE PAPE.

from much the same time; in 1901 Mrs Havemeyer bought the 'View of Toledo' now in the Metropolitan Museum, while five years later Durand-Ruel the dealer was able to buy the 'Assumption of the Virgin' and resell it to the Art Institute of Chicago at a profit of 200 per cent; Cossio's pioneering study of his work appeared in Madrid in 1908.

The connection of all these men with Expressionism seems self-evident. It has become common to echo Theodor Däubler's view that Van Gogh was the first Expressionist, while Johannes R. Becher found the 'View of Toledo', with its apocalyptic storm, 'like a summing-up of all my opinions'. Daumier made an immediate impact on Rouault, and Cézanne too is a much more passionate artist than might be thought from the controlled mastery of his pictures or the intense patience with which he worked. Not only were his distortions as drastic as those of more consciously expressive painters, but such early works as 'La Madeleine ou la Douleur' or 'Le Nègre Scipion', painted before he had acquired these gifts, help to explain what it was in his later 'Bathers' and other works that the German Expressionists found congenial. None of these four great pioneers, however, was so instantly important as Gauguin, whose special mixture of primitivism and symbolism was the real starting point for the German movement. In Brittany in the later 1880s with

Emile Bernard and others he had worked out the principles of Synthetism, using simplified forms and large flat surfaces of more or less unmixed colour. When he left for Tahiti, where he passed the greater part of the 1890s, the Nabis, led by his disciple Paul Sérusier, developed their own versions of this approach. They were much milder temperaments, leaning to the Japanese (Bonnard), the humorous (Vallotton), the domestic (Vuillard), the domestic-cum religious (Denis), or the satirical (Henri Ibels), but they were important for their work in the applied arts and even in the theatre – e.g. Lugné-Pöe's – and also for the direct links which we shall find between Sérusier and Verkade, and possibly the woodcuts of Vallotton too, and the new movement in Germany.

Their group broke up in 1903, like the *Revue Blanche* and for that matter like Gauguin's own life, though his book *Noa-Noa* with its proto-Expressionist woodcuts was still to come. The same year saw the foundation of the Salon d'Automne, a new exhibiting society which was to be less crowded and indiscriminate than the Indépendants while retaining many of its best exhibitors. Among the latter was Henri Matisse, then an astonishingly gifted painter in search of a style, who after sending to the first two shows spent the summer of 1905 in Collioure. Here the sculptor Maillol, a close associate of the Nabis, took him to see Henri de Monfreid, who had at his house the bulk of Gauguin's Tahiti paintings. Largely under their impact Matisse now changed to a style of simplified drawing and flat surfaces and, in big works like the Barnes Foundation's 'La Joie de Vivre' (1905-6), 'Le Luxe' (1907, Musée de l'Art Moderne) or the 'Baigneuses à la tortue' of 1908 formerly in Essen, symbolic groupings like those found in Hodler or late Gauguin. This shift, which formed the basis of his later work and to a great extent of his reputation abroad, coincided with his emergence as leader of the Fauves, a group of allies including Vlaminck, Derain, Rouault and Van Dongen, who made a common front between 1903 and 1907 and were given their nickname at the 1905 Salon d'Automne. Three years later, at the suggestion of such new patrons as the Stein family, Matisse opened a school for foreign pupils, with Hans

A German rediscovery of the 1900s:
Matthias Grünewald.

His 'Crucifixion' from the Isenheim
Altar in the Colmar Museum.

Purrmann as his chief aide; they included the Germans Rudolph Levy and Oscar Moll, the Norwegian Per Krogh, the Swedes Isaac Grünewald, Sigrid Hjertén, Leander Engström and Einar Jolin, the Hungarian Béla Czóbel, the Englishman Matthew Smith and the American Max Weber. Hans Hofmann, who was to make his reputation much later than any of these, seems also to have had some contact with the master, though without attending the school; a stipend from a German patron allowed him to work in Paris from 1904 to 1914. In the winter of 1908 Purrmann took Matisse to Berlin for the latter's first big show at Cassirer's gallery. He said at the time that 'what I am looking for above all is expression'. But the difference between him and the younger Germans in Dresden and Munich was that he conceived of this 'expression' in painterly rather than literary or theatrical terms:

Expression, for me, is not to be found in the passion which blazes from a face or which is made evident from some violent gesture. It is in the whole disposition of my picture.

Although Matisse did a good deal of the formal spadework for the German Expressionists there were less influential artists who were temperamentally nearer to the Expressionist outlook. His fellow-student Rouault was one of them, telling Schuré, for instance, that he felt 'seized to the depths of my entrails by an immeasurable pity' for people under their appearances, as his early drawings and gouaches effectively confirm. Picasso too in his 'blue' and circus pictures (painted prior to the Salon d'Automne's Cézanne retrospective of 1907) was expressive with a kind of attenuated sentimentality in the humanitarian symbolist tradition then followed by his Catalan friends like Isidro Nonell, but even as a Cubist he was at first regarded in Germany as a slightly secondary figure, and if his blue paintings were seen there at all at this time (which is doubtful) they left no mark. There was also Rodin, who in the first years of the century was at the height of his reputation. The very expressive 'Balzac', first shown publicly in 1898, was among a group of his works at the Düsseldorf International Art Exhibition in 1904; Meier-Graefe considered it one of the summits of French art. Through Rilke, who became his secretary, and Rilke's wife Clara Westhoff, Rodin was accessible to Paula Modersohn-Becker and the sculptor Bernhard Hoetger, both working in Paris, while Count Harry Kessler introduced his work to Weimar, with the slightly unfortunate results which will be recorded in the next chapter.

Unless one considers the monumental Hodler as such, the true proto-Expressionists outside Germany, other than Munch, were in Belgium, where the Brussels societies Les xx and La Libre Esthétique were from our point of view the most interesting of all exhibiting bodies before the Salon d'Automne. The deaf, nearly blind artist Eugène Laermans was one of them; thus his characteristic 'La tribu errante', which was in the Dresden Grosse Kunstausstellung of 1904, takes a theme common to Daumier, Goya, Meunier and a dozen other artists, and renders it in a naive style half-way between Van Gogh's 'Potato Eaters' and the Flemish Expressionism of ten to fifteen years later. He is now largely forgotten, though he was a much more obviously 'modern' artist than the better-known painters and sculptors of the first Laethem-Saint-Martin group such as Georges Minne. Ensor, however, who is generally seen as one of the forefathers of the movement, was still being rejected by the Brussels societies as late as that year, though his first 'masks' had been painted in 1881, at a time when Van Gogh had barely begun painting. In 1899 a special issue of the Paris Symbolist review *La Plume* was devoted to him – relations between France and Belgium have never been closer than in the heyday of Symbolism – with articles by Verhaeren and Octave Maus of Les xx, while in 1908 the first book on him appeared in Brussels, with a text by Verhaeren. 'Something of that sort had to exist', noted Klee when introduced to his work (presumably the etchings) by a Munich friend in 1907. But although Ensor was undoubtedly a factor in the development of German as well as the later Flemish Expressionism – exerting an evident influence on Nolde around 1909 – he is far too solitary and idiosyncratic, and above all far too complicated an artist to be categorised as an expressionist himself. He was simply an original, of immense technical and painterly gifts: one of the supreme artists of the whole modern movement.

France and Germany

Before we cross the frontier and look at the same years and similar ideas from within the German-speaking area, there is one other factor which should be briefly mentioned. This is the broader question of the intellectual relationship between France and Germany in the years before the First World War. It should not be forgotten that it was France who was defeated in 1871, and that the loss of Alsace-Lorraine in particular helped to develop a spirit of nationalism among such writers as Barrès and Maurras, who came to see even French-speaking Belgians as intruders into traditional French culture. Already before the Dreyfus case (1894-9), which gave this spirit a certain anti-semitic gloss, even to get Wagner's gifts acknowledged had been something of a battle. Thus when Romain Rolland began publishing his Franco- German novel *Jean-Christophe* in 1902 (in the *Cahiers de la Quinzaine* which he edited with Péguy and Suarès) the very idea of conveying to French readers the background and make-up of a great German composer – which is what Jean-Christophe is, with traits drawn from Hugo Wolf as well as from Beethoven – was hazardous. Rolland's hero was meant to be more than a German and more than a merely psychological study; he was what the author called 'an arch over the Rhine, linking Germany and France and showing how they complement one another'. And the success of the book, which gave Rolland a unique position in both countries, was above all a success for this unfashionable conception.

Rolland was utterly French; he could not speak German, and up to that point he seems to have had surprisingly few German friends. His sympathy for their country centred on its music, and in other respects was far from uncritical; thus he felt that the German bourgeoisie was 'servile and sheep-like' and wrote in 1899 to Malwida von Meysenbug that

In contemporary German thinking I find a concentrated barbaric force of undeniable power, but also seeds of madness: a delirious pride and a sick will, for all its heroic jerkings. Nietzsche dominates even those who fight him. It is a terribly dangerous ocean for the present-day German soul.

For him the concept of reconciliation was above all one of principle, and that principle one that reflected not only his attitude to the Dreyfus case but his whole belief in fraternity as preached by Tolstoy and Whitman, together with the sense of equality which made him between 1900 and 1904 one of the chief champions of a *Théâtre du Peuple*. He was a socialist, but primarily on moral and philosophical grounds: he felt that his job was 'to reintroduce the Divine into the social revolution'. But above all he was a consequential republican in a way that so many in the Third Republic were not, and this meant that his vision did not stop short at frontiers. Looking back in the light of later knowledge, it now seems symbolic that he should have reacted to the centenary of the French Revolution by sitting down at his piano to play through the last movement of the

Choral Symphony with its elevatedly optimistic words by Schiller, and then writing in his diary: 'I believe in the Republic of the future, which will embrace all the earth.' Much may be said against Rolland both as a writer and as a political figure, but, as we shall see, without that hopeful internationalist creed the course of the modern movement in Germany would have been very different.

3 The German mixture

The outward look

Whatever the symptoms of nationalism in other aspects of German life in those years before the First World War, there was in the arts a remarkable readiness to look abroad, and particularly towards France. The contrast with England's persistent insularity was striking. By 1910, when Roger Fry organised the first Post-Impressionist show in London, not only Berlin but several of the big provincial cities in Germany had seen the works of Cézanne, Gauguin and Van Gogh, which had been shown a number of times by artists' societies and taken up by the most enterprising dealers. For several years the great French innovators had been finding their way into private and public collections; thus the Berlin National Gallery came by its first Cézanne in 1897. As for Munch, the abrupt closing of his room at the Verein Berliner Künstler in November 1892 had led to a one-man show in Berlin in January 1893 after which his pictures had toured Düsseldorf, Cologne, Breslau, Dresden and Munich. His first one-man exhibition in England was at the London Gallery in October 1936.

It is sometimes said that this exceptional open-mindedness was due to the Jewish element in the big German cities, but there were after all influential Jews in other countries too, and of those most responsible for it a number were no more Jewish than Fry. Leaving aside literature and the theatre for a moment, the people who brought modern French art to Germany were in the first place Max Liebermann the painter, Meier-Graefe whom we have already mentioned, Count Harry Kessler (later the Weimar Republic's first ambassador to Poland), the collector Karl Ernst Osthaus from Hagen in Westphalia, and Hugo von Tschudi who became director of the Berlin National Gallery in 1896. To these must be added the many young German artists who either studied in Paris, like Purrmann and his group of friends at the Café du Dôme, or went there for prolonged visits to find out what was going on. There were also the dealers, such as Arnold and Richter in Dresden, Thannhauser in Munich, Miethke in Vienna and, above all, Paul Cassirer, who

36

The first Cézanne to enter any public collection. 'Moulin sur la Couleuvre à Pontoise', which was given to the Berlin National-Galerie in 1897, and is still there.

opened his Berlin gallery in the Viktoriastrasse in 1898 with a show of Liebermann, Meunier and Degas, and held a big Van Gogh exhibition in 1908 in addition to the Matisse show. Nor is it entirely irrelevant that Picasso's subsequent dealer Daniel-Henry Kahnweiler was of German origin. He launched his Paris gallery in 1907 with an exhibition of work by the Fauves, and can later be found occasionally writing on modern art for German publications under the name Daniel Henry.

Liebermann spent many years working abroad, both at Barbizon and with the Hague school, where he came across the tracks of Van Gogh, then turned to Impressionism in the 1890s under the influence of Manet and Degas. In 1896 he accompanied Tschudi to Paris (where Tschudi bought Manet's *La Serre* for his gallery), and in 1900 became the first president of the Berlin Sezession, one of several such breakaway artists' societies formed around the time: (Munich Sezession 1892, Vienna Sezession 1897, Düsseldorf Sonderbund 1907). Meier-Graefe, after training to be a mining engineer in Liège, spent the first half of the 1890s in Berlin, where he helped write a monograph on Munch (1894) and founded the review *Pan*; his literary friends there included Strindberg, the misogynistic Polish novelist Przybyszewski, author of *Homo Sapiens* (which Klee described as a 'banal delirious monster') and the poets Richard Dehmel and Otto Julius Bierbaum. In 1896 he returned to Paris, where he remained for some years, working briefly for Bing's Art Nouveau and publishing a number of influential works: on Vallotton in 1898, on Manet and on Impressionism in 1902, on Hogarth in 1907, on Hans von Marées – an artist sometimes considered important for the evolution of Expressionism though it is difficult for the non-German to see why – in 1909-10, and above all his remarkable *Entwicklungsgeschichte der modernen Kunst*, the first edition of which appeared in 1903.

Osthaus, a young art historian who inherited a fortune from his industrialist grandfather, decided to use it to make his own museum in the minor industrial town of Hagen. He brought Henri van de Velde to design the building, which was opened under the nordic-sounding title of Folkwang-Museum in 1902. Van de Velde also introduced him to the painter Christian Rohlfs, who became in effect the museum's resident artist. Besides making the astonishing series of purchases listed in the table, in 1906 he went to see Cézanne at Aix and selected two works, of which the 'Bibémus Quarry' is now in a private collection in New York. Also in 1902 Count Kessler, co-founder of *Pan* and a collector with a penchant for the work of the neo-Impressionists and the Nabis, became the director of the Weimar Museum and, through his connection with the Grand-Ducal Chamberlain, a kind of cultural adviser to the Weimar Court. He had already managed to get Van de Velde appointed to supervise design matters throughout the duchy, and now the Belgian was put in charge of the new *Kunstgewerbeschule,* whose buildings he designed and which later became the Bauhaus. Among the exhibitions organised by Kessler were shows of Monet, the Neo-

Notable purchases by the Folkwang-Museum before 1910. Works still in the museum's collection are marked with an asteris.

Artist	Work	Price	Date
Renoir	'Lise'		1901
Gauguin	'Die Woge'	2500 frs	1903
	'Ta Matete'	2000 frs	1903
	*'Contes barbares'	4500 frs	1903
	*'Tangsammler am Strand der Bretagne'	1800 frs	1904
	'Das Mädchen mit dem Fächer'	1800 frs	1904
	'Die Reiter am Strand'	3000 frs	1904
Van Gogh	'Tête de garçon' (portrait of Armand Roulin)	1000 mks	before 1905
	'Vallon de Saint-Rémy, avec moissonneur'	3000 mks	before 1905
	'Garten'	1300 fls	1905
	*'Irrenhausgarten Saint-Rémy'		1905
	'Felsen mit Bäumen'	1200 fls	1905
	'Les oliviers'		1905
Hodler	'Der Auserwählte'		1906
	'Frühling' (from museum's Hodler show)		1905
Rodin	'L'age de bronze' and two others		by 1905
Daumier	*'Ecce homo'		
Munch	'Landscape'	1200 mks	1907
Matisse	'Still-life with asphodels'	1300 frs	1907
	'La Berge'	864 frs	1908
	'Baigneuses à la tortue'		
Van Dongen	'Sada Yacco'		

Note: Osthaus, the museum's patron and director, kept some works in his own house, including a Vuillard, a ceramic frieze by Matisse and the statue 'Sérénité' by Maillol.

impressionists, Rodin and Gauguin, while books produced by Morris, Walter Crane and Cobden-Sanderson were also on view. In 1904 he brought Munch to the city, which for a time was the artist's principal German base. Unfortunately the load on the grand-ducal understanding became too much, and there was a blazing scandal when a nude drawing given to the museum by Rodin proved to be inscribed 'Hommages respectueux de Aug. Rodin au Grand-Duc de Weimar'. The result of this piece of presumed lèse-majesté was not only Kessler's enforced resignation but an increasingly unfavourable situation for van de Velde and his school.

Another fruitful source of outside influences in the same years was the world of the cabaret and the illustrated weekly press, which largely followed the Paris model. As in that city the two institutions were closely related, especially in Berlin and Munich, where members of the playwright Frank Wedekind's 'Elf Scharfrichter' cabaret, such as Bierbaum and Wedekind himself, contributed to the former's anthology *Deutsche Chansons* and also to the illustrated papers. Among these, *Pan* (with Meier-Graefe, Kessler and Bierbaum) was followed in 1896 by the Munich papers *Jugend* (associated with Art Nouveau) and *Simplicissimus* (published by Langen and best known for Wedekind's verses and the comic drawings of Th.Th. Heine, Bruno Paul and Olaf Gulbransson), then by *Das Narrenschiff* in 1898 and *Die Insel* (Bierbaum and others) in 1899. These magazines, whose would-be Gallic approach infected older papers like the Berlin *Ulk* and the Munich *Fliegende Blätter*, not only brought in French writers and artists (such as Vallotton and Toulouse-Lautrec) but printed much of the liveliest German writing of the day. The particular style of drawing which they encouraged, with its slightly trembling line, flat Fauve-like surfaces and exaggerated perspectives and foreshortenings, is at once recognisable in the work of those young draughtsmen who grew up under its influence: Pascin, Rudolf Grossmann and George Grosz. Ernst Barlach and Käthe Kollwitz both drew for such journals before 1910, while Lyonel Feininger's case is particularly interesting, since his comic illustrated work, so much at the root of his later watercolours, was virtually international. He was a German-American who, after some ten years cartooning for the Berlin papers, worked for the Paris *Le Témoin* between 1906 and 1908. He was in touch with the group at the Dôme, and for nearly a year provided the grotesquely quaint comic strips for the *Chicago Tribune*, 'The Kin-der-Kids' and 'Wee Willie Winkie's World'.

Artist and patron.
Right Rodin's memorial to Balzac,
1898 (now in the Musée Rodin, Paris).
Below The offended Grand-Duke
Wilhelm Ernst.

As for literary influences in the same period, they came thick and fast. We mentioned Strindberg's position in the German theatre; by 1906 some thirty of his works had appeared in Emil Schering's translation. The collected German Dostoevsky, in a translation by Moeller van den Bruck (the subsequent author of *Das Dritte Reich*), began coming out in 1907. Rimbaud was translated by Karl Klammer the same year, then later by three poets associated with the Expressionist movement proper: Theodor Däubler, Alfred Wolfenstein and Paul Zech. Whitman had already been translated by Johannes Schlaf and at least six other German writers when the anarchist Gustav Landauer began publishing his translations (and a critical essay, stressing Whitman's principle of 'In the Beginning was the Emotion') in 1916-17. Stefan Zweig's study of Verhaeren, with its influential chapter on 'the new emotionalism', *das neue Pathos*, appeared as part of a three-volume selection of his poetry in 1909; later Zweig was also to edit two volumes of Verlaine. Baudelaire's *Les Fleurs du Mal* was admirably translated by Stefan George, himself a member of Mallarmé's circle from 1889; Laforgue by the critic Paul Wiegler in 1905 and by Franz Blei and Max Brod a few years later.

The younger French writers were translated mainly by Blei, who was a close associate of the equally Francophil Carl Sternheim and edited the Munich magazine *Hyperion* with him between 1908 and 1910, incidentally rejecting some of Klee's early drawings. Gide, Suarès and Claudel were among those whom he recommended to German publishers or editors; he also visited Péguy in Paris about 1908. 'Just before the war', wrote Benn retrospectively, 'we were reading Claudel and Gide, Bergson and Svarez'. Of these Claudel was perhaps the most important, not only for the characteristic mélange of Whitman, Rimbaud and the Bible which seems to underlie his work, as it did likewise that of certain Expressionists who aspired to a similar dynamism, but also because of his plays. Thus *L'Echange* and *Partage de Midi* were published by Kurt Wolff before 1914 in Blei's translation, while *L'Annonce faite à Marie*, translated by Jakob Hegner the publisher, was given at the garden city of Hellerau outside Dresden in 1913. Moreover Claudel himself after his return from China in 1909, though he seems to have remained aloof from the German scene, was posted successively to the French consulates in Prague, Frankfurt and Hamburg. One other case is of particular interest, that of the Strasbourg-born poet Ernst Stadler who translated the verse of Péguy and of Francis Jammes. For in those

The mediators.
Right Count Harry Kessler, painted by Munch in 1906 (Staatliche Museen, Berlin).
Below Karl Ernst Osthaus, whose Daumier 'Ecce Homo', *overleaf*, is still in the Folkwang-Museum which he founded.

hopeful days Stadler was on the way to becoming a genuinely international figure – pursuing his studies in comparative literature at Strasbourg, Munich and Oxford (where he was a Rhodes scholar) before getting a lectureship at Brussels. With his friend René Schickele, the Alsatian who was to succeed Blei in the editorship of *Die Weissen Blätter,* he helped to root the beginnings of German literary Expressionism in a European soil.

The inward tradition

The particular mixture in which the German movement grew was only up to a point a general continental one. There was also a crucial, distinctively German element which was part of a very much older and more deep-seated tradition. This had, and still has, a number of components which are seen as characteristically 'Teutonic' not only by the outside world but also by many German critics: darkness, introspection, a concern with the mysterious and uncanny, massive metaphysical speculation, a certain gratuitous cruelty and a brilliant linear hardness, expressed sometimes by the most extravagant convolutions. At its head, influencing both artists and poets in our period, stands the sixteenth-century painter Matthias Grünewald, whom Meier-Graefe called 'the greatest artistic figure ever born this side of the Alps', and whose magnificent Isenheim Altar in the Musée d'Unterlinden at Colmar first struck Huysmans in 1905 'as a kind of typhoon of unrestrained art, which carries you off as it passes … you leave it in a state of lasting hallucination'. What was so special about such German and Swiss artists of the Renaissance was not only their persistently Gothic quality, evident in their use of expressive distortion and their apparent indifference to classical 'beauty', but also their peculiarly graphic gifts. Indeed only Grüne-wald and Cranach painted pictures to equal the really astonishing woodcuts and etchings which continued to pour out of Germany right into the seventeenth century. These represent something which was to be a marked feature of the Expressionist movement too: an inborn gift for harnessing free expression to the laborious demands of wood carving, whether in the lump or in the block. Kirchner, who possessed it to an outstanding degree, was to see in the work of Cranach and Hans Sebald Beham in the *Brücke* artists' first 'points of art historical reference', while Ludwig Meidner in 1918 cited a tradition of drawing going back to Bosch, Brueghel, Callot, Hogarth, Schongauer, Dürer, Altdorfer and Urs Graf, the last of whom seems particularly to anticipate certain features of his own floridly apocalyptic work.

Max J. Friedländer's two-volume study of Grünewald appeared in Strasbourg in 1907-11; studies of El Greco by W. Weisbach and A. L. Mayer in 1909 and in 1911; monographs on Goya in 1903 (Von Loga), 1907 (Oertel) and 1910 (Von Loga again). Meier-Graefe's book on Hogarth was published in 1907; Brueghel and Bosch too were now coming into fashion. The revelation of such artists to the reading public was one basic step in preparing for Expressionism. Another was the rather solemn new concern with caricature; thus Ernst Fuchs, author of a standard work on Daumier's paintings, published three studies of caricature between 1901 and 1906, while in 1911 the Munich firm of Piper brought out *Das Teuflische und Groteske in der Kunst* by Wilhelm Michel, the Dionysiac critic and Hölderlin scholar, who took an early but unfruitful interest in Klee's work. Not only was all this concentration on expressive fantasy and distortion itself very German but so was a great part of the historical material: the wealth of grotesque woodcuts and broadsheets, for instance, of the Counter-Reformation, or the brilliant but sometimes disturbingly sadistic nineteenth-century children's illustrations of *Struwwelpeter* and Wilhelm Busch.

As for German literature, its association with similar ideas of darkness and exaggeration was common enough in nineteenth-century England, as Siegbert Prawer has pointed out:

Of the seven 'horrid' novels mentioned in *Northanger Abbey*. . . . two are actual translations from the German, and four others set their scene in Germany. 'Had my title borne *Waverley, a romance from the German*', writes Sir Walter Scott, 'what head so obtuse as not to image forth a profligate abbot, an oppressive duke, a secret and mysterious association of Rosicrucians and Illuminati, with all their properties of black cowls, caverns, daggers, electrical machines, trap-doors and dark lanterns?' The works of 'Monk' Lewis could be characterised, by the *Monthly Review,* as 'the direful croaking of this German raven'; Maturin could announce his intention of writing a horrific novel by saying that he would 'out-Herod all the Herods of the German school'; and far into the nineteenth century the appearance of a German-

sounding name in the title of a book made the right reader thrill with anticipation. *Kruitzner (The German's Tale)* ... *Wieland, or the Transformation* ... *The Ghost of Count Walkenried. ... Frankenstein, or the Modern Prometheus* ... *Dr Heidegger's Experiment* ...

Even on this admittedly trivial level there are comic anticipations of *The Cabinet of Dr Caligari*; while on the more serious side the romantic tradition of Kleist, Hölderlin, Grabbe, Büchner and other previously neglected nineteenth-century writers became a conscious part of the heritage of the Expressionist movement. Further back still, the great mystics also came to seem important: Eckehart, whom Gustav Landauer translated into modern German in 1903, Johannes Tauler (listed along with Eckehart in the bibliography of Hermann Bahr's *Expressionismus* of 1916), and Jakob Boehme. Here too it was significant that classicism had been so relatively slow to establish itself in Germany, for the linguistic richness of German writing persisted up to the early eighteenth century. Becher for instance could cite such extraordinary lines as these by his favourite Andreas Gryphius:

Ach und weh!
Mord! Zeter! Jammer! Angst! Kreuz! Marter! Würme! Plagen! Pech!
Folter! Henker! Flamm! Stank! Geister! Kälte! Zagen!
    Ach vergeh!
    Tief und Höh!
Meer! Hügel! Berge! Fels! Wer kann Pein ertragen!
Schluck, Abgrund, ach schluck ein! die nichts denn ewig Klagen

    (Oh, the cry!
Murder! Death! Misery! Torments! Cross! Rack! Worms! Fear!
Pitch! Torture! Hangman! Flame! Stink! Ghosts! Cold! Despair!
    Oh, pass by!
    Deep and high!
Sea! Hills! Mountains! Cliff! Pain no man can bear!
Engulf, engulf, abyss! those endless cries you hear.

More even than by the twisted and grotesque, the Expressionist
movement was to be characterised by such uncontrollable cries of
pain.

At the same time there was in it a strong utopian-symbolist
element which found its models not only in Whitman and Verhaeren
but in Schiller's 'Ode to Joy' (the text of the last movement of the
Choral Symphony) and the second part of Goethe's *Faust*. This
latter, which had long been regarded as unstageable, was given one
of its first full-scale productions by Reinhardt in Berlin in 1911, and
thereafter influenced a number of Expressionist dramas by Unruh,
Werfel, Kornfeld and other young writers. Another who derived a
considerable part of his thinking from *Faust II* or from Goethe's
scientific writings was the anthroposophist Rudolf Steiner, likewise
cited by Bahr as one of those who, like the great Jewish anarchist-
expressionist mystic Martin Buber, were preparing profound
changes in the nature of Mankind. Steiner had come to Germany in
1888 to work on the Weimar edition of Goethe's works, became
secretary of the new Nietzsche-Archiv in the same town, and from
1902 was the leader of the German Theosophists; Schuré translated
his *Le Mystère Chrétien* into French. He was a tireless lecturer, a
powerful educational theorist, a very bad but influential water-

Finale furioso.

colourist in the symbolist tradition, and perhaps the most interesting amateur architect of the century: altogether a phenomenal man, whose traces will more than once be visible in what follows.

Bahr, an Austrian critic and playwright, was also much impressed by Johannes Müller's *Über die phantastischen Gesichtserscheinungen*, a book on visions written likewise under Goethe's influence and published in 1862. Accordingly he saw Goethe as lying to a great extent at the root of the Expressionist movement. At the same time some of the other, less humanist irrational philosophies which became influential in the early years of the century were not without their bearing on it either. Not only Nietzsche, whose impact is traceable throughout the movement, but other ambiguous or easily abused figures like Wagner's son-in-law Houston Stewart Chamberlain, the philosopher of race, (whom Bahr quotes as witness to Goethe's essentially Aryan nature), and the vitalist, anti-intellectual 'characterologist' Ludwig Klages helped create its peculiar climate.

49

Klages indeed, with his interest in the gestural aspects of expression (*Die Probleme der Graphologie,* 1910, *Grundlage der Wissenschaft vom Ausdruck, Ausdrucksbewegung und Gestaltungskraft*, 1913, and a number of subsequent books on handwriting and speech), surely deserves quite as much as the more reputable Wilhelm Worringer (*Abstraktion und Einfühlung,* 1907), to be considered, for better or worse, as one of the unconscious prophets of modern German art.

Towards Expressionism

By 1910, which is when the Expressionist movement proper may be said to begin, the new European influences in literature, the theatre, music and the visual arts had interacted with the German background to produce certain works which can reasonably be called pre- or proto-Expressionist, and are indeed often included (by critics or anthologists or exhibition organisers) as part of the movement. This is evident above all in painting, where the foundation of such groups as *Die Brücke* in Dresden and the *Neue Künstlervereinigung* in Munich brought together a number of the leading Expressionists-to-be. To some extent it also applies in the theatre, since the plays of Strindberg and Wedekind remained an important part of the German repertoire throughout the life of the movement proper. In poetry, by contrast, there was little that could be called Expressionist before 1910, though there were one or two poets who later became associated with the younger Expressionists, while certain established writers had begun to anticipate particular Expressionist themes and techniques. Though there was at that time a school of fantastic prose writers – it was after all the age of *Dracula* – perhaps the strongest example for the new generation lay in the novels and stories of Thomas Mann's older brother Heinrich. This was due to nothing particularly expressive or grotesque in his style and subject matter, but rather to his sense of commitment and attacks on the German bourgeois attitude of mind.

In music and in architecture before 1910, links with the general Expressionist movement were more tenuous. In music, as we shall see, this was because there was not such a clear distinction between the pre-Expressionist phase, which is where Schoenberg's outlook was largely formed, and later developments; also perhaps because to talk of Expressionism at all in connection with so expressive an art is rather nonsense. In architecture, on the other hand, although there were to be various Expressionist experiments around the end

50

of the First World War they were marginal to the general development of the modern movement, in which Germany played so important a part. Thus the pioneers of the first decade of the century – Adolf Loos, Otto Wagner, Peter Behrens and, on the social planning side, Hermann Muthesius the founder of the *Werkbund* which many of them supported – have to be seen as part of something altogether larger than any -Ism, while even the idiosyncratic Hans Poelzig, who headed the Breslau Kunstgewerbeschule from 1903 to 1916, is worth remembering more for his contributions after that date than for any identifiably expressionistic features of his early industrial buildings. With only Van de Velde at Weimar to recall the swirling extravagances of Art Nouveau, the advanced German and Austrian architecture of those years, culminating in the Cologne Werkbund Exhibition of 1914, was quite startlingly sober.

Writers and the performing arts

By comparison with such figures as Hauptmann, Thomas Mann, Rilke and Hofmannsthal, the poets who did most to pave the way for the Expressionists are now almost unknown outside Germany. In 1913 many of them were grouped together in an interesting *Anthologie des lyriques allemands contemporains depuis Nietzsche* selected and translated by the Belgian-educated editor of *L'Assiette au Beurre* Henri Guilbeaux, with a preface by Verhaeren. Guilbeaux's interest lay in what he called 'la poésie dynamique'; that is to say, he saw Nietzsche as 'le principal renovateur de la lyrique allemande' and 'lyrisme' itself as 'l'expression de la vie totale'. Quite rightly he centred his selection on Richard Dehmel, who seemed to him, as to many of the younger generation, the most substantial and independent-minded of the living German poets. With its love poems, its lyric verse (some of it quite light), its poems of industrial civilisation and the big city, its translations of Verlaine and Stevenson, Dehmel's work contrasted forcefully both with the high aestheticism of the Stefan George circle and with the bourgeois prejudices of Imperial Germany. His friend Detlev von Liliencron (whose 'Durch die Nacht' carries certain anticipations of the early Eliot), Frank Wedekind in his light but often cynical ballads, Julius Hart with his poem 'Berlin', the difficult, symbolic or mystical free verse of Alfred Mombert: all prefigured different aspects of the movement to come, while remaining on the whole within a conventional technique, like Dehmel's own 'Mountain Psalm' with its Verhaerenesque lines:

Oskar Kokoschka: Poster for his first play *Mörder, Hoffnung der Frauen* at the Vienna Kunstschau of 1908. (Historisches Museum der Stadt Wien).

> Was weinst du, Sturm? Hinab, Erinnerungen!
> dort pulst im Dunst der Weltstadt zitternd Herz!
> Es grollt ein Schrei von Millionen Zungen
> nach Glück und Frieden …
>
> (O storm, why weepest thou?—Be gone, you memories
> There in the mist the city's heart pulsates!
> A million tongues roaring a million cries
> for peace and happiness …)

Freer forms derived from Whitman can be found in the work of Johannes Schlaf and his massively ambitious collaborator Arno Holz, who came to pivot his irregular lines, many of them very long, on a central axis on the page. Holz, whose sixtieth birthday in 1923 was celebrated by a portfolio of prints by many of the leading Expressionist artists – those of the Brücke having been among his early admirers – was the chief linguistic experimenter of the decade before Futurism, comparable in some ways to Hopkins in England.

The Triestine Theodor Däubler, later to become a kind of immense uncle to the Expressionist poets and painters, author of what Kurt Pinthus called 'cyclopean hymns of immanent metaphysics and ethics', was then working on his magnum opus the long poem *Nordlicht*. Barlach said of him cynically but not inaccurately that 'he does not bleed for humanity, but he blows humanity full of significance'. Else Lasker-Schüler, who is included in all the Expressionist anthologies although her sometimes rather archly exotic fancy-dress verse seems in many ways remote from the movement, married Herwarth Walden in London around 1900 and published her first book of poems *Styx* in 1902. Walden himself was an unsuccessful musician (and admirer of Liszt) who in 1903 organised a society called the Verein für Kunst in Berlin, with lectures and readings by his wife, Wedekind, Dehmel, Mombert, Van de Velde, the science-fiction novelist Paul Scheerbart (inventor of a perpetual motion machine) and the young doctor Alfred Döblin, who in those years was writing fantastic stories in the style of a latter-day Hoffmann or Poe. As with the later and better-known 'Sturm'

circle, the actor Rudolf Blümner was a key figure in its manifestations. In 1908 and 1909 Walden went on to edit a number of short-lived periodicals, and when his last employers wished to dismiss him was able to obtain testimonials from Meier-Graefe, Behrens, Heinrich Mann and Max Brod. Difficult though he may have been to work with, he was to become one of the outstanding *animateurs* of modern art.

The great theatrical figure of the early part of the century was Wedekind, whose plays *Erdgeist* (1895) and *Büchse der Pandora* (1904) provided the libretto for Alban Berg's subsequent opera *Lulu*. Actor, poet, cabaret singer and producer, his twenty or so plays have never become established outside the German-language area, yet their concern with the life of the instincts, their stylised dialogue, their fantastic characters and sometimes episodic construction lie at the root of many later developments in the European theatre. Kokoschka's short play *Mörder, Hoffnung der Frauen*, remarkable not only for its gratuitously savage treatment of relations between man and woman but for its concern with atmospheric lighting, is sometimes cited as the first Expressionist drama but was certainly of much less importance; it was performed in Vienna during the Wiener Kunstschau of 1908 with the actor Ernst Reinhold (the sitter for Kokoschka's portrait 'The Trance Player' in the Brussels Musée Royale) in the leading part. Another important factor was the appointment of Max Reinhardt to succeed Brahm in in the direction of the Deutsches Theater in Berlin in 1905. For though Reinhardt was on the whole remote in spirit from the Expressionists it was he who most effectively realised the plays of Strindberg, which he virtually introduced to Sweden itself by his tours of 1911 and 1917, while in 1912 he staged a whole Wedekind cycle. His greatest contribution to the movement perhaps lay in his mastery of comparatively new techniques such as the revolving stage (introduced at the Munich opera in 1898) and the use of spotlights. What he and his designers were to do with these was partly influenced by the theoretical writings of the Swiss Adolphe Appia (*La mise en scène du drame Wagnérien*, 1895) who helped Jaques-Dalcroze

develop the festival theatre at Hellerau and himself designed some of the settings for the 1912 festival. An even stronger example was that of the Englishman Edward Gordon Craig, who like so many innovators of that period was taken more seriously in Germany than in his own country. He held a number of exhibitions of his work there in 1905, when the Deutsches Theater gave *Venice Preserved* in his settings, and he maintained his German contacts for a number of years.

Among the musicians, Mahler, who died in 1911, was of interest in our context both for his outlook – from the introspective melancholy of *Kindertotenlieder* to the Faustian finale of the Eighth Symphony – and for his marriage to Alma Schindler, subsequently the wife first of Walter Gropius, then of Franz Werfel, as well as (for a time) Kokoschka's great love. One might cite also Scriabine, whose Symbolist compositions *Poème de l'Extase* (said to be theosophically inspired) and *Prometheus* (with its synaesthetic use of a colour organ and its instructions such as *comme un cri* and *dans un vertige*) are very much akin to certain notions of Kandinsky's. But the composers more commonly regarded as Expressionist were the subsequent dodecaphonists Schönberg, Berg and Webern, who were then in course of feeling their way away from tonality towards the new twelve-note system. Debatable as it is whether the establishment of this system was in any way part of the Expressionist movement and not just coincidental with it (as were so many other major artistic innovations), much of the taste and later outlook of its three leading exponents was formed in the immediate pre-Expressionist period. This is evident in their choice of texts for setting. Rilke, George (*Das Buch der hängenden Gärten* and several songs by Webern), Peter Altenberg, O.E. Hartleben, the French symbolist Albert Giraud (*Pierrot Lunaire*), the Dane Jens-Peter Jacobsen (*Gurre-Lieder*) and one or two otherwise obscure lady writers (e.g. the librettist of *Erwartung*): these, not the Expressionists, were the poets they turned to, even in later years. The only exception is Webern's Trakl songs, written between 1917 and 1921; and Trakl, as we shall see, was only Expressionist up to a point.

The visual arts

The picture in the visual arts is clearer. To begin with, there was Munch, who was largely based in Germany in the mid-1890s and again between 1904 and 1909; he showed a group of twenty-eight paintings at the Berlin Sezession in 1902, painted murals for Reinhardt's new Kammerspiele at the Deutsches Theater in 1906 and had a one-man exhibition at Cassirer's the following year. Meier-Graefe and others of his Berlin friends (who included Dehmel, Przybyszewski and Scheerbart) brought out a monograph on his works as early as 1894, and although he seems to have had little personal contact with German artists it would have been difficult for them to be unaware of such intensely expressive works as his lithograph 'The Cry' of 1895 or his many paintings on morbid, sexual or vitalistic themes. Then there was a still largely unknown pre-Expressionist artist in the shape of Paula Modersohn-Becker, granddaughter of a former Rector of Odessa university, who died aged thirty-one in 1907 leaving an extraordinary legacy of deep-felt, uncompromising, somewhat Gauguinesque still-lifes and portraits of women (often herself) and children; about the only man she painted was Rilke. She had settled nine years earlier in Worpswede, a village in the flat country north of Bremen, whose artist colony (notably Fritz Mackensen, Heinrich Vogeler and her husband Otto Modersohn) painted mainly sombre and rather symbolic landscapes or peasant subjects, in a spirit analogous to that of the first Laethem-Saint-Martin group in Belgium. However, she offset this atmosphere by a number of more or less prolonged visits to Paris, where she came under the influence of Cottet, the Nabis, Rodin and, against all her previous principles, the Impressionists, whose example lightened her palette without disturbing her marvellous seriousness. Unlike most of her compatriots in the Expressionist movement she was a painter, not a graphic artist. One of her last regrets was at missing the Cézannes in the 1907 Salon d'Automne. She sold two pictures in her life.

Käthe Kollwitz and Ernst Barlach both came early under the influence of Steinlen. The former, a Berlin doctor's wife, was an outstanding social draughtsman and print-maker, from her first cycle of etchings 'Weberaufstand' ('Weavers' Revolt') of 1894-8, right up to the Communist posters which she produced some thirty years later; she relates to the Expressionists above all by her later bronzes and her rather forcedly expressive (or sentimentalised) woodcuts, which also had a powerful influence in other parts of the

Overleaf The Brücke. Emil Nolde's 'Abendmahl', 1909, formerly in the Halle Museum from 1913 till its confiscation in 1937 and now in the State Museum, Copenhagen; Kirchner's 'Three Nudes in the Forest', 1908, from the Stedelijk Museum, Amsterdam; and a general view of the group's 1909 exhibition at the Galerie Richter in Dresden.

globe. Barlach at this time was just finding his style and his footing in the Berlin art world after a very difficult struggle to establish himself there. The turning point for him was a visit of 1906 to Kharkov, where one of his brothers was working. The hunched, earthy figures of Russian peasants which he modelled and showed in the following year's Sezession led to membership of that body and a contract with Cassirer. In 1909 he won the Villa Romana prize which Kollwitz had held two years earlier, and went for a year to Florence, where he met Däubler, thenceforward a good friend and an important critical ally. Barlach had also long been writing descriptive fragments and stories – the most substantial of those published in his posthumous prose works deal with ghosts, witches and storms – and in 1907 he began *Der tote Tag*, the first of the plays which, from 1912 on, were to make one half of his dual reputation as sculptor and writer.

Except in so far as these two artists can be called Expressionist (and both of them were too independent to be wholly that) the Berlin climate at this time was unpropitious for such people. This was largely because the Sezession was dominated by the best of the German impressionists – Liebermann, Slevogt, Corinth – so that even the young Beckmann, who won the Villa Romana prize a year before Kollwitz and whose 'Grosse Sterbesszene' had been praised by Munch, made his early reputation within their tradition. It was different in Vienna, where the whole current evolution in the visual arts derived from a refined and sophisticated form of Art Nouveau, together with a subtle (Freud) if sometime wrong-headed (Otto Weininger) interpretation of individual psychology and the relations between the sexes. In that city there was a natural progress from the glowing, intensely mannered fin de siècle decorative painting of Klimt to the work of Egon Schiele and Oskar Kokoschka. Schiele, who anyway died young, never came into contact with the greater savagery of the German Expressionist movement; Kokoschka, however, was to become one of its outstanding members, so that his early portraits, intense and febrile and of great beauty, are very relevant to it. At this time he was still to some extent in search of a

style; thus his book *Die träumenden Knaben* of 1908 for the craft centre called the Wiener Werkstätte is still tied to Art Nouveau, whereas his paintings of the same time lie closer to Schiele and to Van Gogh, of whom there had been an important exhibition at Miethke's gallery in Vienna in 1906. One, the *Stilleben mit Hammel und Hyazinthe* ('Still life with tortoise and hyacinth') of 1909, is strikingly akin to Ensor's 'La Raie' of 1892 in the Brussels Museum, though this seems more to reflect a similar balance of impressionist and expressionist elements in the artist than any contact with Ensor's work.

Prague at that time was administratively, and to a great extent culturally, an Austrian city, and many of the Viennese avant-garde, including Kokoschka, were of Czech or Prague-Jewish descent. So was Alfred Kubin, the fantastic draughtsman-novelist (his dream-like novel *Die andere Seite* appeared in 1908), who worked mainly in Munich. He came to know both Klee and Kafka, and is sometimes linked with the Expressionists although his spindly and macabre pen drawings, like a feeble cross between Goya and Arthur Rackham, have neither the force nor the skill of the best Expressionist graphics and do not export well. There was also a sometimes forgotten group of artists in Prague itself, which exhibited in 1907 under the name *Osma*, or 'The Seven', and included Emil Filla, Bohumil Kubišta, Antonín Procházka, Otakar Kubin (who later settled in France and changed his name to Coubine) and Kafka's friend Friedrich Feigl. These artists, who were to become the nucleus of the Czech cubist movement, were at first influenced by Daumier and Munch, who had a Prague exhibition in 1905; Filla wrote that the latter 'stood at the beginning of our path'. The Fauves by contrast seemed too gay and superficial for their purpose, which was 'to express again the neglected inner state of man'.

The centres of the movement proper, however, were Dresden and Munich, the capitals respectively of the then kingdoms of Saxony and Bavaria. In Dresden in 1905, a group of architectural students began meeting together to read and discuss and paint in an old shoemaker's workshop in the Berliner Strasse. Ernst Ludwig Kirchner, the eldest, came from Chemnitz (now Karl-Marx-Stadt), where his father taught the technology of paper-making, and had spent two terms at art school in Munich. Erich Heckel and Karl Schmidt-Rottluff had been at school together at the Chemnitz Realgymnasium, some three years behind Kirchner, and all three had met at the Technische Hochschule in Dresden. It was the year of the Galerie Arnold's first Van Gogh exhibition. In 1906 they wrote to several like-minded artists elsewhere, proclaiming that

As believers in evolution, in a new generation of both creators and art lovers, we call together the whole of Youth, intending, as youth upon whose shoulders the future rests, to win freedom of life and action against the entrenched forces of age.

– a somewhat vaguely worded programme. They followed this by holding a first show in an electricity showroom, which got a favourable review from their contemporary Paul Fechter in the *Dresdner Neueste Nachrichten*. Four new members joined, of whom only the young Dresden artist Max Pechstein was their contemporary; Emil Nolde being an as yet unremarkable artist of thirty-nine from the Danish border; Axel Gallén-Kallela a Finn based in Berlin, where he had come under Munch's influence; and Cuno Amiet a Swiss of thirty-eight who had worked at Pont-Aven with Emil Bernard and Sérusier and shared four rooms with Hodler in the Vienna Sezession of 1904. In 1907 a second show of paintings was held, this time in

Richter's Kunstsalon, including work by the new recruits and the Hamburg painter Fritz Nölken, who later left to study with Matisse. Kubišta from Prague briefly joined the group; Nolde left it after a year; Kees van Dongen the Dutch-born Fauve was invited by Pechstein to show with it, though it is not clear whether he was ever a member. In the winter of 1908-9 Pechstein, who at that time was considered to be the Brücke's most promising and characteristic artist, shifted his base to Berlin, showing three pictures in the 1909 Sezession, of which one was bought by the industrialist Walter Rathenau. His colleagues remained in Dresden.

The nucleus of the Brücke, was no mere alliance for exhibition purposes but a community which, like the Nazarenes or the Nabis, aimed to establish a new approach to art and life. Readings of Whitman, Strindberg and Wedekind, a shared admiration for Nietzsche, joint summer holidays from 1909 to 1911 with their girls by the Moritzburg lakes, a common choice of themes (nudes in the

The Brücke's French precursors.
Left Derain's 'Les Baigneuses',
1907, bought by a group of Czech
artists in that year and now
in the National Gallery, Prague.
Right Kirchner's woodcut poster
for a Dresden Gauguin exhibition
of 1910.

Overleaf A 'fauve' Kandinsky.
'Murnau Landscape' 1909,
from Richard S. Zeisler's
collection in New York.

bath, the bed or the open air, often with more or less erotic emphasis, Dresden street scenes, groups of dancers or circus performers), the use of bright flat colours, thinned with petrol and quickly put on: it all adds up to a recognisable Brücke style. Till the end of 1909 this lacked the typical Expressionist angularity, and though it is often alleged that Kirchner discovered negro sculpture in 1904 it is not till 1910 that evidence of this is visible in their work. The influence of Gauguin (shown by the Galerie Arnold in 1906 and 1910) is clear; to a lesser extent also that of Van Gogh and Cézanne, whom Nolde in 1908 spoke of as the other 'great ice-breakers'; Vallotton and the Nabis are also echoed in some of the early pictures. Of all such examples Munch lay readiest to hand; indeed his main German patrons, the Esche family, were Chemnitz industrialists. If Heckel later claimed that none of the Brücke at that time had even seen reproductions of his work it can perhaps be attributed to their often misleading touchiness whenever their own originality was impugned.

65

Also from the Neue Künstlervereinigung: Alexei Jawlensky's 'Portrait of a Girl', 1909, now in the Düsseldorf Art Collections.

Pechstein (in the autobiographical note in the *Junge Kunst* booklet on him) said that he and Heckel and, above all, Kirchner were all Munch admirers.

But the main affinity of both the Brücke and the Munich Neue Künstlervereinigung was with the Fauves. Amiet was then developing along Fauve lines, while Kirchner is thought to have seen Matisse's Berlin exhibition. Pechstein too had been to Paris, where he spent the first half of 1908, met Purrmann and saw Matisse's work, of which 'Luxe, calme et volupté' particularly impressed him. At his instigation works by Van Dongen and several other Fauves were shown in the Brücke exhibition of that September. In Munich the ties with the French were closer still, not least because of the presence of so many relatively well-to-do Russian painters, who normally went abroad to study either in Munich or in Paris and not infrequently moved between the two. Thus Alexei Jawlensky, a retired infantry officer of thirty-two, came to study under Azbé in 1896, to be followed by his contemporary the ex-lawyer Wassily Kandinsky in 1897. Jawlensky went to Pont-Aven in 1905, and in

Munich a year later met the Nabi Jan Verkade, who had become a Benedictine monk at Beuron, centre of a school of religious painting that had a certain success at the 1905 Vienna Sezession; 'Our minds ran along similar lines', wrote Verkade, 'and we immediately became friends'. In the early part of 1908 Sérusier too came to work for three months in Munich, while Verkade was studying there. Kandinsky up to that time had been poised rather restlessly between a derivative impressionism and a slightly Bakst-like fairy-tale Russian illustrative art, but he had already displayed his gifts as a teacher and organiser, had shown his watercolours in the Salon d'Automne in 1904 and became a member of that body the following year – the year of the Fauves – when he and Jawlensky showed six paintings each. In 1906, together with his pupil Gabriele Münter, he had lived and worked in Paris for twelve months. He sent six woodcuts to the Brücke exhibition of 1907.

In 1908 in the Bavarian village of Murnau, where he and Münter were to buy a house and Jawlensky and his friend Marianne von Werefkin were already installed, Kandinsky began painting landscapes and buildings in a clearly Fauve style of brilliant colours and firmly outlined areas – something also found in Jawlensky's still-lifes and Matisse-like heads of the same period. At the same time they became influenced by Bavarian peasant paintings on glass, which had an importance comparable to that which others came to see in ikons or in negro art. Early in 1909 the four artists – Münter being a gifted painter also in the Fauve style, while Werefkin was a sombre and shapeless symbolist – decided to form their own group, the Neue Künstlervereinigung, with Alfred Kubin, Adolf Erbslöh, Alexander Kanoldt and other Munich painters, briefly joined also by Carl Hofer, a German artist then living in Paris. The chief significance of this body, which held its first exhibition at the Galerie Thannhauser in the first fortnight of December 1909, was that it gave birth to the *Blaue Reiter,* which was to become the Brücke's main counterpart. For Kandinsky in particular the Murnau period was important since he then discovered the direction in which he was to work for the rest of his life.

Geography and timing

There is just one more thing that is worth noting before we go on to the real explosion of the Expressionist movement in 1910, and that is the significance of time and place. It was a movement with many

The placing of Expressionism

Nolde

Munch

HAMBURG
Rote Erde 1919-23

WORPSWEDE

Paula Modersohn-Becker

AMSTERDAM
Le Fauconnier
Campendonk
Filla, Czobel
Van den Berghe, De Smet

HANOVER
Schwitters
Burchartz
Kestner-Gesellschaft
Steegemann-Verlag

ESSEN Folkwang Museum
from 1923

HAGEN Osthaus
Rohlfs

moved to
Essen 1923

OSTEND
Ensor

ANTWERP
Ruimte
Jakob Smits

Gromaire

LAETHEM

DÜSSELDORF Lindemann
Nauen, Pankok
Das junge Rheinland
Frau Ey, Flechtheim

ERFURT

Permeke
Servaes
Van den Berghe
De Smet

COLOGNE
Sonderbund 1912
Werkbund 1914
Macke

Dada

Beckmann
Kornfeld

Hellmer, Hartung, Weichert
FRANKFURT

Zuckmayer

DARMSTADT Edschmid
Die Dachstu
Das Tribunal

MANNHEIM

HEIDELBERG
Richard Weißbach
Ernst Blass

A
L
S
A
C
E

Stadler
Schickele
Goll
(Arp)
Isenheim Altar

STUTTGART

To PARIS

MUNICH

BEURON

MURNAU

DORNACH

Rudolf Steiner

Rolland
Masereel
Jouve
Guilbeaux
Arcos

Goll

BERN
Kessler
E. Bloch
Zeit-Echo

ZURICH
Ehrenstein
L. Frank
Die Weissen Blätter
Dada
Joyce

INNSBRUC
Trakl
Der Brenne

GENEVA

DAVOS
Kirchner
Van de Velde

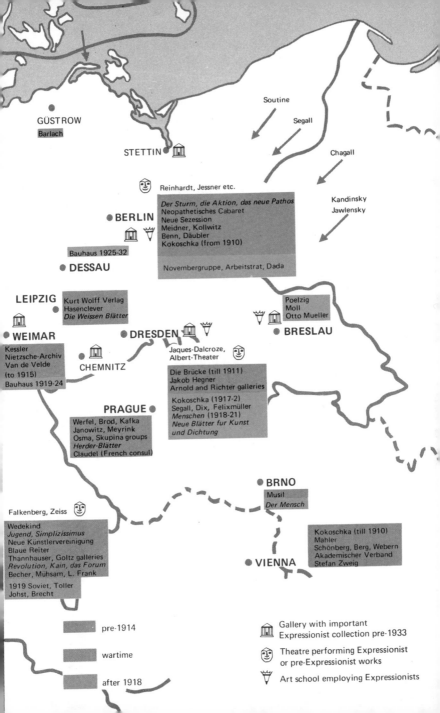

GÜSTROW
Barlach

STETTIN 🏛

Soutine

Segall

Chagall

Reinhardt, Jessner etc.

● BERLIN
🏛 ⚱

Der Sturm, die Aktion, das neue Pathos
Neopathetisches Cabaret
Neue Sezession
Meidner, Kollwitz
Benn, Däubler
Kokoschka (from 1910)

Novembergruppe, Arbeitsrat, Dada

Bauhaus 1925-32

● DESSAU

Kandinsky
Jawlensky

LEIPZIG
●
Kurt Wolff Verlag
Hasenclever
Die Weissen Blätter

🏛
● WEIMAR

Kessler
Nietzsche-Archiv
Van de Velde
(to 1915)
Bauhaus 1919-24

● DRESDEN 🏛 ⚱
CHEMNITZ 🏛

Poelzig
Moll
Otto Mueller
⚱ 🏛
● BRESLAU

Jaques-Dalcroze, 🎭
Albert-Theater

Die Brücke (till 1911)
Jakob Hegner
Arnold and Richter galleries

Kokoschka (1917-2)
Segall, Dix, Felixmüller
Menschen (1918-21)
*Neue Blätter fur Kunst
und Dichtung*

PRAGUE ●

Werfel, Brod, Kafka
Janowitz, Meyrink
Osma, Skupina groups
Herder-Blätter
Claudel (French consul)

● BRNO
Musil
Der Mensch

Falkenberg, Zeiss 🎭

Wedekind
Jugend, Simplizissimus
Neue Kunstlervereinigung
Blaue Reiter
Thannhauser, Goltz galleries
Revolution, Kain, das Forum
Becher, Mühsam, L. Frank

1919 Soviet, Toller
Johst, Brecht

Kokoschka (till 1910)
Mahler
Schönberg, Berg, Webern
Akademischer Verband
Stefan Zweig

● VIENNA

pre-1914

wartime

after 1918

🏛 Gallery with important
Expressionist collection pre-1933

🎭 Theatre performing Expressionist
or pre-Expressionist works

⚱ Art school employing Expressionists

centres, for in the German-speaking world there was no capital city with a cultural monopoly like those of Paris or London. Germany itself was a newly-unified empire of smaller states, each with its own capital, while Switzerland was a federation of independent cantons speaking four different languages and Austro-Hungary an increasingly ramshackle dual monarchy whose subject peoples (like the Czechs) had their own centrifugal cultures. Distances and axes of communication between these centres are not unimportant. Anybody who is unfamiliar with central Europe or finds it difficult to imagine it without its present division would do well to look at the map on pages 70–1. Prague, for instance, is just under halfway between Vienna and Berlin. Prague to Dresden is about 75 miles, Dresden to Berlin about 125 miles, with Leipzig some 60 miles to the north-west of Dresden. That was the main north-south axis of Expressionism, which can perhaps be better visualised by saying Kafka for Prague, Kokoschka for Vienna, the Brücke for Dresden, the Kurt Wolff Verlag for Leipzig and Walden for Berlin, with Munch and Strindberg off the map to the north. Across this runs an east-west axis on which distances are greater and travel correspondingly less easy: Budapest to Vienna about 160 miles, Vienna to Munich 200 miles, Munich to Basle 230 miles, Basle to Paris 300 miles.

The astonishing impact of the time can be judged by observing the ages of the leading Expressionists at the end of 1909. Most of those who made the movement were then quite young; thus Kokoschka and Gottfried Benn were 23, Kirchner 29, Pechstein exactly 28. But Barlach was already 39, Lasker-Schüler 40, Nolde 42, Kandinsky 43 and Rohlfs 60. If one reflects that Rimbaud, had he lived, would have been 55, Seurat 50 and Toulouse-Lautrec five years younger, it becomes plain that some of the Germans were slow developers to say the least. It must have taken some formidable upheaval in this area of the world to make so wide a selection of the creative artists in so many media coalesce in a common movement, often radically changing their style and their tempo of working.

4 Expressionism before 1914

1910

Nineteen-hundred and ten, said Benn some forty-five years later, 'was indeed the year when all the timbers started creaking'. The facts bear him out, even though the ideas which combined to disturb the existing structure were, as we have seen, not exactly new ones. It was as if all the major new influences of two decades, from Nietzsche and Van Gogh to Matisse and Freud, had been concentrating behind the scenery of Imperial Germany, with its pretentious triumphal perspectives and its smug bourgeois interiors, in order to come suddenly bursting on to the stage. In part this apparent damming-up of energies may have been due to a certain preliminary resistance to such extravagances in Berlin, whose publishers, editors, galleries and exhibition juries only now began to accept what had for some years been preparing itself in Munich and Vienna, in Dresden and Prague. In part, no doubt, it was a tribute to the thick-skinned imperviousness of the whole Hohenzollern apparatus, against whose materialism, militarism and anti-socialism the new movement was at first largely directed.

It now converged on the capital. In March Herwarth Walden in Berlin started a new weekly review called *Der Sturm* – a symbolic title – which rapidly became the leading organ for younger writers and (from May, when it began to print reproductions and full page woodcuts), artists from far and near. From the twelfth issue on it carried portrait drawings, largely of writers, by Kokoschka, who now broke away from Vienna, arriving to share a room with Blümner and hold first exhibitions at Cassirer's gallery and at the Folkwang Museum, which bought his portrait of the Duchesse de Rohan-Montesquieu. Cassirer paid him an income and he worked regularly in the *Sturm* office till 1911. Almost simultaneously a group of writers and students centred on Kurt Hiller's Neuer Club (formed a few months earlier) started to plan a *Neopathetisches Cabaret,* whose first performance was held on June 1. The moving spirits here were Hiller himself, who at twenty-five was the oldest member and the only one to have completed his studies, and the

The Neopathetisches Cabaret, Berlin. *Right* Its fourth programme.
Far right Drawing of Jakob van Hoddis by Ludwig Meidner, 1913, later
reproduced in *Menschheitsdämmerung*.

Nietzschean Erwin Loewenson, also known by his pseudonym Golo
Gangi. The programmes, nine in all over a period of almost two
years, consisted primarily of readings of their own poems by Hiller,
Ernst Blass, Georg Heym, Ferdinand Hardekopf, Robert Jentsch
and Hans Davidsohn (pseudonym Jakob van Hoddis). Selections
from Nietzsche, Wedekind, Meyrink and other older authors were
also read; Else Lasker-Schüler once or twice appeared as a guest
performer, and there was music by Walden, Schönberg (*Sechs
Klavierstücke*) and others. The central figure was certainly Heym,
who gave a solo evening in Cassirer's salon in May 1911 and whose
untimely death eight months later seems to have been the sign for
the group's dissolution. The most cited poem however was Van
Hoddis's 'Weltende':

> Dem Bürger fliegt vom spitzen Kopf der Hut,
> in allen Lüften hallt es wie Geschrei.
> Dachdecker stürzen ab und gehn entzwei
> und an den Küsten – liest man – steigt die Flut.

> Der Sturm ist da, die wilden Meere hupfen
> an Land, um dicke Dämme zu zerdrücken.
> Die meisten Menschen haben einen Schnupfen.
> Die Eisenbahnen fallen von den Brücken.

> (The bourgeois's hat leaps off his pointed head,
> the air all round is echoing with shouts.
> Tiles fall from the roofs, and break apart.
> Along the coast (I hear) the tide's in flood.

> The storm has come, its furious waves grow denser
> and burst through thick embankments as it rages.
> The bulk of us go down with influenza.
> The railways tumble off the railway bridges.)

This, like some of Heym's verses, first appeared in *Der Demokrat*,
a Berlin review edited by Franz Pfemfert. In January 1911 Pfemfert
left to found his own Expressionist-political weekly *Die Aktion*,

taking his line from Heinrich Mann's 1910 essay 'Geist und Tat', with its unflattering comparison of the situation of the 'committed' intellectual in Germany and in France. This paper became comparable in importance to *Der Sturm*.

The term 'Expressionism' seems to have made its appearance in Germany during 1910, though the evidence is uncertain and opinions vary. In the following year it was certainly used in the catalogue of the Berlin Sezession to describe a room of French Fauve and early cubist paintings, then picked up by the critic of *Der Sturm* in the July issue. Kurt Hiller applied it to himself and his friends in an article the same month, while Kurt Pinthus, the other leading literary impresario, wrote a few months later that it was a pictorial term which could be used of Heym. But an anecdote has it that it was first Germanised at a sitting of the Sezession jury, when one member, faced with a work by Pechstein, asked 'Is that *Impressionismus?*', to which Cassirer replied 'No: *Expressionismus*'. If this is true it must have taken place in the spring of 1910, when all the pictures submitted by Pechstein and Nolde (another new arrival in the capital) were refused, and the two artists organised their own show, together

75

Trier

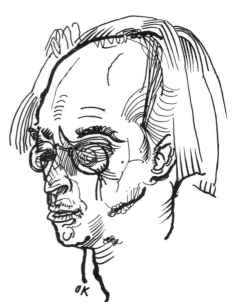

More landmarks of 1910.
Left Walter Trier's drawing of
Sturm readers at the Café
des Westens, Berlin.
Right Kokoschka's drawing of the
magazine's editor Herwarth Walden,
now in the Fogg Art Museum, Harvard.
Below left Kandinsky's near-abstract
'Study for Composition 2' from the
Guggenheim Museum, New York.

with contributions by the Brücke and some of the Neue Künstler-vereinigung, at the Macht gallery in the Rankestrasse. They called their group the Neue Sezession.

This body lasted till 1912, and until it split up it was the Brücke's Berlin shop window and the first centre of Expressionist art in that city. Its main moving spirits were Pechstein and the painter Cesar Klein. Of the other leading Expressionists, Nolde had completed his earliest characteristic works, the religious paintings which date from 1909. In Munich Kandinsky painted his first near-abstract 'Composition No. 1' and wrote his theoretical study *On the Spiritual in Art*. Barlach settled at Güstrow, near Rostock on the Baltic, where he was to spend the rest of his life. Altogether it was an eventful year.

Germany and the new vision

Between 1910 and 1912 the typically angular, distorted, violently emotional pictorial style of the Expressionists established itself, and the break with Fauvism became complete. This was due perhaps in part to a certain interaction with literary Expressionism as Brücke (starting in 1911) and other graphics began to appear in *Der Sturm*

77

Painters and writers.
Left Kirchner's portrait of
Alfred Döblin, 1913, (Busch-
Reisinger Museum, Harvard).

or to be used for illustrating the Expressionist writers, like Kirchner's brilliant woodcuts for two stories by Döblin, whom he met during 1912. But the general shift to sharper angles, more complex structures, less cheerful colours and a greater sense of dynamic movement was the result of two other artistic revolutions which had originated at very nearly the same time and now hit Germany with a year or so's delay. This virtual coincidence of the Expressionist movement with Cubism in France and Futurism in Italy is not just an indication that a great continental upheaval in the arts was now under way. It also meant that in Germany the Cubist and Futurist influences could be absorbed into Expressionism, which took what it wanted from them, not necessarily what they had inscribed on their programmes. As Kahnweiler later wrote in his book on Juan Gris,

one has to remember that there existed among the German painters a sort of feeling of *avant-garde* camaraderie ... Because they confused 'constructivist distortion' with 'expressionist distortion', they thought, albeit in good faith – that the cubists had the same aims as themselves.

It was very unlike the situation in Prague, where an indigenous

78

Right Meidner's portrait of
Max Herrmann-Neisse, 1913.
(Art Institute of Chicago).
Below Le Fauconnier's
portrait of Pierre-Jean Jouve,
1909, (Musée d'Art Moderne,
Paris).

cubism soon developed, or like Vorticism in England, which was inspired by the Futurists' attitudinising as much as by their actual works. The developments in Germany were within Expressionism itself.

Although Braque and Picasso were among the foreign artists who showed at the Neue Künstlervereinigung's second exhibition in September 1910, along with Vlaminck, Rouault and Van Dongen, they were less important to the Munich painters than were Henri Le Fauconnier and Robert Delaunay, of whom the former became a member of the group that year and wrote one of the catalogue forewords, while the latter married the ex-wife of the German critic Wilhelm Uhde. Together the two men hung the Cubist room in the 1911 Indépendants and sponsored Chagall in the following year's Salon d'Automne, and in Amédée Ozenfant's view their contribution to Cubism was subsequently much underrated, particularly by Apollinaire. Kandinsky asked Le Fauconnier to write on the Fauves for the planned Blaue Reiter almanac, and showed five works by Delaunay (including an 'Eiffel Tower' and an interior of Saint-Séverin, bought by Erbslöh), in the group's exhibition in December 1911. During the same year Le Fauconnier had a one-man show at the Folkwang Museum.

Delaunay's subsequent evolution towards a more abstract Orphism – a term coined by Apollinaire, whom he brought to Berlin to lecture for Walden in 1912 – was of considerable influence on the Blaue Reiter group, but the effect of his architectural scenes was certainly wider. 'He was the founder of the first of the many vulgarisations of the cubist idea', wrote Gertrude Stein (who very possibly never saw a German Expressionist picture in her life), 'the painting of houses out of plumb'. The responsibility may also in part be that of the Swiss-born poet Blaise Cendrars, who in 1910 found Delaunay laid up with a broken leg in a hotel looking on to the Eiffel Tower, and spoke to him encouragingly

of the amazing centres of industrial activity scattered across the earth's whole surface, of the new life taking shape, of the poetry of it all.

Another who helped to bring a similar Cubist vision to Germany was Feininger. He knew Delaunay, and on a brief visit to Paris in 1911

found the art world agog with Cubism – a thing I had never even heard mentioned before, but which I had already, entirely intuitively striven after for years.

His first important picture in this vein, 'High Houses 1', was completed the following year.

In March 1912 Walden opened his Sturm Gallery with an exhibition of work mainly by Kokoschka and the Blaue Reiter group, and from now on it, and the readings and performances which began in connection with it a year later, were as active as his flourishing paper. From 10 April to 31 May its second show was devoted to the Italian Futurists, whose paintings are said to have attracted up to a thousand visitors a day. This movement, formally proclaimed by the poet-impresario F. T. Marinetti in the *Figaro* in 1909, had been extended to painting by further manifestos issued in February and April 1910, and it shared many of the European origins of Expressionism: the Nietzschean notions, for instance, of dynamism and 'living dangerously', the elevation of instinct above reason, the unanimism of Romains, the free verse of Whitman, the new concern with modern industrial civilisation and even what one of its manifestos termed 'the dark manifestations of mediumistic phenomena'. Umberto Boccioni, who accompanied the show to Berlin after its earlier showings in Paris and London but knew no German, reported that Walden had given them four huge rooms, flanked by one containing Delaunay's 'Eiffel Tower' and two other Paris views, landscapes by Derain and Vlaminck and a Kandinsky 'Composition', with 'Braque, Herbin, Dufy, Kokoschka etc,' on the floor above. The paintings shown, by Boccioni, Carrà, Russolo and Severini, were suggestive above all in their concern with movement and simultaneity and the interpenetration and overlapping of events, features which were to be echoed by a number of German painters. Just how important they seemed to Walden, who had printed a number of the relevant manifestos in his paper, can be judged from the fact that he persuaded his backer, the banker Dr Borchardt, to buy twenty-four out of the twenty-nine pictures, subsequently touring them to other towns such as Vienna, Budapest, Munich, Zürich and Dresden.

During the following year Walden gave Delaunay a first one-man show of nineteen paintings (January-February), and also met Chagall, whose principal dealer he now became, selling his first major picture ('Golgotha') and then finally establishing his reputation with a one-man show in the summer of 1914. Chagall had been studying in Paris under Le Fauconnier, knew the Delaunays well, and had already developed his early penchant for the expressive and the mysterious – there is a surprisingly Munch-like 'Dead Man' of

Another expressionist Cubist: Robert Delaunay's 'Saint-Sévérin', 1909, from the Guggenheim Museum. A version of this picture was shown in Munich in 1911.

1908 – as well as for angular forms. 'Il pleut cette nuit, il fait noir', wrote his friend Cendrars in an allusive, almost Expressionist article on his work in 1912,

... Je touche partout au coeur défoncé de l'homme, ce coeur noir, défoncé, broyé par les pas lourds des peines, et qui pleure.
   Il pleure du sang.

A number of Russian painters at this time were likewise in contact with the German movement. Thus the Moscow group called 'The Knave of Diamonds' (Lentulov, Konchalovsky, Falk and Mashkov, whose 'Portrait of E.I. Kirkalda' of 1910 looks not unlike what Jawlensky was then doing) included work by Kandinsky and Jawlensky, Le Fauconnier (portrait of Jouve), Lhote and Gleizes at its 1910 exhibition. The Brücke artists too were represented in its second show in 1912, which Camilla Gray says was 'almost identical' with the Blaue Reiter show. Another group including Larionov and Goncharova developed from a primitivism faintly like that of Pont-Aven (her 'Picking Apples' of 1909) or Murnau through a Schmidt-

Le Fauconnier's pupil Marc Chagall's 'Half past three', 1911, formerly in Walden's collection and now in the Philadelphia Museum of Art. (Also known as 'The Poet').

Rottluff-like patch (observable in Goncharova's work around 1910-11, and in such paintings by Malevitch as the Stedelijk Museum's 'Woman with Buckets and a Child') to the splintery, Futuristic 'Rayonism' of 1911. Their Moscow exhibition of March 1912 under the title 'The Donkey's Tail' also included one Chagall. As for Kandinsky's Russian links, Vladimir Izdebsky of Odessa and the two Burljuk brothers, who had studied in Munich from 1903-5, were members or exhibitors with the Neue Künstlervereinigung, while Izdebsky in turn showed Kandinsky's and Münter's work in his own gallery and published the first, Russian, version of *On the Spiritual in Art*.

Establishment of Expressionist art

In showing the rapid development of the external background we have slightly anticipated that of the Expressionist movement, which was meanwhile finding something close to its final form. In 1911 the Brücke artists Kirchner, Heckel and Schmidt-Rottluff moved to

Berlin on the basis of encouraging reports from Pechstein, having recruited a new member in Otto Mueller, a specialist in not very good sentimental-angular paintings of gipsies. It was now that the negro influence began to assert itself, whether as a reminiscence of the Dresden museum or (more probably) under the impact of Gauguin and Derain. Their palette started to grow less brilliant, their forms splintered or fragmented; their themes, like Kirchner's Berlin streetwalkers, to approach some of the metropolitan literary interests of the time; they were also, it seems, reading Dostoevsky. Above all in their graphic work the tension between the laboriousness and natural angularity of the medium, the growing formal complexity of the design and the undiminished immediacy and passion of the artist's concept now gave birth to a tradition of print-making which is one of the great achievements of German, indeed of European art. This did not stop the group from almost immediately breaking up. First Pechstein drifted apart from the rest as a result of his greater success and immersion in Sezession politics, followed by his departure (like a sponsored Gauguin) for the South Pacific in the spring of 1914 – none of which however quite justifies his relative ostracism by the Brücke's historians. Then Kirchner's growing self-absorption irritated his friends, who so objected to the one-sided summary of the group's activity which he wrote for their supporters that they decided on its dissolution in 1913, though continuing to work in parallel directions.

In Munich too there was a regrouping. Two younger artists, Franz Marc and (rather more sceptically) August Macke, who had seen the 1910 show of the Neue Künstlervereinigung, came into contact with Kandinsky and proved useful allies, the former because of his energies and organising talents, the latter because of his wife's uncle the Berlin collector Bernhard Koehler. Among the new recruits that year were Le Fauconnier and a little-known follower of Gauguin, Pierre Girieud. During the summer of 1911, as relations between Kandinsky and the indigenous Munich painters in the group deteriorated, he and Marc planned an 'almanac', to be called *Der Blaue Reiter* and partly financed by Koehler, with outside contributions not only by Le Fauconnier but by David Burljuk, Schönberg. Pechstein and others. That autumn Kandinsky, Münter and Marc left the Neue Künstlervereinigung before its third show, got the Thannhauser gallery to give them half the space reserved for it, and, still with Koehler's backing, organised their own exhibition for the second half of December 1911 under the forthcoming almanac's name. Artists invited to show there by Kandinsky included Delaunay, the Burljuks and Schönberg (who painted after a fashion, in a mystic-symbolist way), while Marc brought in the two Rhinelanders Macke and Heinrich Campendonk, the second of whom had settled in the same Bavarian village as Marc and begun to evolve a style somewhere between his and

85

Chagall's. Klee was not in this show, but took part, along with the Brücke and several French, Russian and Swiss artists, in the graphic exhibition which followed in February 1912. Never an Expressionist, he was then a virtually unknown Munich draughtsman who had met Kandinsky for the first time only a few months before.

The life of the spirit may be graphically represented as a large acute-angled triangle, divided horizontally into unequal parts. ...

Thus Kandinsky's *On the Spiritual in Art* which, like the almanac, appeared in the course of 1912. During the previous three years he had been working out a kind of visual mysticism, possibly not un-influenced by the speculations of Rudolf Steiner, some of whose anthroposophical lectures he attended, and with synaesthetic features that recall Scriabin and the French Symbolists. This growing concern with what he called 'the inner element' had already resulted in a number of experimental stage works – from *The Yellow Sound* of 1909 to *Violett* of 1911 – followed by the set of abstract woodcuts which he labelled 'sounds' or *Klänge*. Now it turned him into an almost entirely abstract, if still very free and expressive painter. Macke, who can anyway hardly be termed an Expressionist, distrusted such thinking and kept nagging Marc about it; he particularly disliked the paintings of Schönberg, which he called 'greeneyed dumplings with an astral stare'. The result was that although from 1912 on Walden and his new Swedish wife became the group's most enthusiastic supporters, showing their work not only in their gallery but in other German and European cities, its members began to go their different ways. The only one who remained within the more figurative Expressionist movement as it was developing in Berlin was Marc, whose sentimental-Fauve paintings of figures and horses began around 1912 to break up into Cubist facets and angles, or Futurist lines of force (as in his 'Tierschicksale' of 1913 in the Basel Museum) or bright Delaunay-like disks and swirls.

For there were now the makings of a school which was larger than either the Munich groups or the Brücke, and was already being felt as such in many other centres. The Berlin artist-writer Ludwig Meidner, for instance, whose portraits of writers and other drawings were to appear in so many Expressionist publications, showed in 1912 (with Richard Janthur and Jacob Steinhardt) under the label *Die Pathetiker*. His 'apocalyptic landscapes' and the violently contorted paintings of that year – he damned 'all the Corots, Manets, Renoirs, Cézannes, Matisses' as being too frivolous and seductive – seem to have taken off from the last works of Van Gogh. He was also a close friend of the poet Ernst Wilhelm Lotz, with whom he moved to Dresden in the spring of 1914. He wrote later:

I imagine the most magnificent things – apocalyptic crowd scenes, Hebraic prophets and visions of mass graves – for the spirit is everything; I can do without nature. ... Monstrous buildings sag and shake out a suicide or two. Cathedral topples over leftwards into the landscape.

In Prague the Osma painters began to feel the appeal of cubism around 1910, well before the Germans, then merged in 1911 in a larger group called *Skupina výtvarných umělců* whose notable new members included the Čapek brothers, the playwright František Langer and the sculptor Otto Gutfreund, a remarkable pupil of Bourdelle's. For two or three years the 'cubo-expressionism' which was their characteristic style brought them close to the German movement; thus Kirchner, Heckel and Otto Müller visited Prague in 1910 or 1911; Brücke works were shown in the *Skupina's* 1912-13 exhibitions; while the Czechs in turn showed at the Neue Sezession in 1911 and the Sturm gallery in 1913. Likewise in 1911 a Swiss Expressionist group was formed, *Der moderne Bund,* with Gimmi, Kundig, Oscar Lüthy, the Alsatian Hans Arp and the German painter Walter Helbig; they too showed at the Sturm in 1913. In west Germany there were Heinrich Nauen from Crefeld, who had visited Laethem Saint-Martin in 1905, subsequently coming under the influence of Van Gogh, Matisse and early Picasso during five years in Berlin, and Wilhelm Morgner from Soest, whose religious paintings of 1912 were akin to those of Nolde. Further north Barlach was now producing some of his finest and most characteristic early sculptures - 'Der Einsame', 'der Spaziergänger', 'Panischer Schrecken', figures hacked out of wood and seemingly buffeted by elemental forces – as well as his first play *Der Tote Tag* with its twenty-seven lithographs, which Cassirer published in 1912.

The whole movement was set in perspective by two major exhibitions. The first was the *Sonderbund's* International Exhibition of 1912, at Cologne. In this exhibition, what the organisers called 'a conspectus of the movement which has been termed Expressionism', including both the Brücke and the Blaue Reiter artists, was accompanied by a vast review of the major modern influences, with Van Gogh at the centre and rooms (of twenty to thirty paintings each) devoted to El Greco, Munch, Cézanne, Gauguin and Picasso. The second was Walden's *Erster deutsche Herbstsalon* of September-November 1913, which with some 400 pictures represented a lone

attempt to organise a Berlin Salon d'Automne. Among the interesting points here were that the Brücke painters were not represented; that the Blaue Reiter were hung as individuals rather than as a group; that Bernhard Koehler offered to underwrite the show to the tune of 4,000 Marks; that Feininger showed for the first time with the Expressionists and sold his first picture 'High Houses I' (to Koehler); that there was a group of twenty-one works by Delaunay and that Marc showed 'The Tower of Blue Horses', a work whose combination of modified avant-garde forms with traditional sentiments were to make it perhaps the most widely popular of all Expressionist pictures.

Ernst Barlach: 'Die Vision', 1912. A four foot high oak carving later intended to be the model for Theodor Däubler's tombstone (see page 204) and now in the Nationalgalerie, West Berlin.

The new writing

Much the same imagery of twisted or toppling buildings, of death and disease or of everyday urban life is evident in the work of the Neopathetisches Cabaret and other young Berlin poets who emerged between 1910 and 1912. Sometimes there is also a marked concern with colour. Heym, for instance, who was strongly influenced by Rimbaud, Baudelaire and Verlaine, is very free with adjectives of colour (or pale and dark) either for their associations or for visual effect; similarly Kurt Hiller's own boozy 'Nacht-Schluss bei Bols' seems straight off a Kirchner canvas.

> Deine Fliederweste
> Du fahler Maler, küsst mich sehr; Bohême-girl,
> Dein Shawl glänzt ganz zitronen; du, System-Earl,
> Trägst statt des Schlips zerwalkte Himbeerreste
>
> (Your lilac waistcoat
> Kisses me well, you pallid painter; Chelsea girl
> Your shawl shines wholly yellow; you, racket-Earl,
> are wearing spattered raspberry, not a tie.)

What most distinguishes such poems from those of the later Expressionists is their clarity and, in some cases, dryness; there are no *Schrei*'s as yet, no rhetorical appeals. This does not prevent an underlying sense of desperation. Thus Ernst Stadler, writing just after Heym's death, could see him as a horrified visionary, soberly setting down in strong, clear strokes what he had agitatedly observed: a comparison that recalls the tension in contemporary Expressionist woodcuts and etchings. Alfred Lichtenstein too, whose poetry combines horror and neatness in an often very original choice of words, was told posthumously (by Alfred Lemm) that:

Possessed, you only needed the slightest wind to hear the world's whole structure cracking. ... Its crookedness and pointlessness were something that you could not depict too strongly in the utterly grey, utterly yellow light of every day, in family scenes and Sunday afternoons.

9. Abend: Mittwoch den 3. April 1912.

Architektenhaus, Saal C, Wilhelm-Straße 92-93, pkt. 8 Uhr.

❑

Hölderlin: Unveröffentlichte Gedichte und Briefe (R. J.)

Golo Gangi: Gedenkrede auf Georg Heym.

An Georg Heym (Gedichte von Robert Jentzsch, Fritz Koffka, W. S. Ghuttman.)

Martin Buber: Gleichnisse des Tschuang—Tse.

❑

GEORG HEYM: Gedichte aus dem Nachlaß, ungedruckte (R. J.; Gh.)

❑

Eduard Steuermann: Sechs Klavierstücke von Arnold Schönberg.

Ferdinand Hardekopf: Der Gedankenstrich.

Stanislaw Przybyszewski: Prosa (F. H.)

Robert Jentzsch: Hymnen.

Erich Unger: „Mit allen Wassern gewaschen" von Wedekind.

W, S. Ghuttman: Ein Herr.

Jakob van Hoddis: Gedichte (R. J.; Gh.)

Mynona. Novelle.

❑ ❑ ❑

Billets à 2 Mk. (numeriert) und 1 Mk. (unnumeriert) im Café des Westens
und an der Abendkasse.

❑ ❑ ❑

Geschäftsstelle des NEUEN CLUBS: Erich Unger, Sigmundshof 21.

❑

Im Verlage Ernst Rowohlt erschien soeben: Georg Heym: Der ewige Tag. 2. Auflage.

Demnächst erscheint: Die nachgelassenen Gedichte, und im Herbst 1912: Der Dieb, (Novellen).

Heym was drowned aged twenty-four in a skating accident on one of
the Berlin lakes in January 1912. His poems are not in any way
technically daring, but he felt himself, like Lenz, Kleist, Grabbe,
Büchner and Rimbaud, to be up against the society around him, and
he was profoundly marked by his first encounter with Van Gogh.
Accordingly besides his 'Berlin' sonnets and other poems about
modern urban life he wrote melancholy or morbid verses, heavy
with decay, or poems about physical or mental sickness, sometimes
with great perceptiveness, sometimes in a rather forced manner;
there are also strangely anticipatory poems like 'Gott', 'Der Krieg'
and 'Nach der Schlacht' which seem to indicate a positive longing

90

for the war which he did not live to see. None of the other Berliners had quite this attitude or quite this force. Van Hoddis, who used to walk the Berlin streets at night with Meidner before finally disappearing into a mental hospital in 1914, wrote poems with the widely leaping images that one finds in Pasternak (himself a student at Marburg just about this time). Ernst Blass and Ferdinand Hardekopf both wrote in the coolly ironical vein later associated with *Neue Sachlichkeit*; thus Blass's 'Abendstimmung':

> O komm!, o komm, Geliebte! In der Bar
> Verrät der Mixer den geheimsten Tip.
> Und überirdisch, himmlisch steht dein Haar
> Zur Rötlichkeit des Cherry-Brandy-Flip.
>
> (O come o come, my darling! In the bar
> The mixer gives away his secret tips.
> It's heavenly, unearthly how your hair
> Matches the red of cherry-brandy flips.)

While Hardekopf, a witty versifier and original prose stylist who worked as a parliamentary reporter, broke off a nocturnal 'Notiz' in free verse, descriptive of *Angst,* by suddenly saying:

By the way, I can always sharply interrupt such sensations in mid-stream, prescribe *Amerikanismus.* quite coolly light a cigarette and continue reading Henri Beyle's *Le Rouge et le Noir.*

The other outstanding Berlin poet was unknown until the publication in 1912 of a pamphlet of verse called *Morgue.* This was Gottfried Benn, a young doctor who had won a gold medal the previous year for his work on epilepsy in adolescents, and was now practising as a skin specialist and venereologist. He had never read either Whitman or Rimbaud, but Nietzsche, together with his daily work, had bred in him a disgusted contempt for what his poem 'The Doctor' calls 'the summit of creation, that swine Man', and as a result his often clinical free verse, written with a remarkable cliché-free forcefulness, hit Berlin like a smack in the face. Here for instance is the opening poem of *Morgue*, which is characteristic, though less famous than the longer 'Man and Woman go through the Cancer Hut'

> Ein ersoffner Bierfahrer wurde auf dem Tisch gestemmt.
> Irgendeiner hatte ihm eine dunkelhellila Aster
> zwischen die Zähne geklemmt.
> Als ich von der Brust aus
> unter der Haut
> mit einem langen Messer
> Zunge und Gaumen herausschnitt,
> muss ich sie angestossen haben, denn sie glitt
> in das nebenliegende Gehirn.
> Ich packte sie ihm in die Brusthöhle
> zwischen die Holzwolle
> als man zunähte
> Trinke dich satt in deiner Vase!
> Ruhe sanft,
> kleine Aster!

> (A drowned drayman is lifted on to the table.
> Someone had stuck a light-dark lilac aster
> between his teeth. As I
> took a long knife
> worked under the skin
> of his chest and
> slit out tongue and gums
> I must have dislodged it, for it slid
> into the brain alongside.
> I packed it into the hollow of his chest
> between the wadding
> and they stitched it up.
> Drink your fill from that vase!
> Sweet repose,
> little aster!)

Like others of Walden's circle, he was strongly impressed by the work and ideas of Marinetti, whose poems were published by A. R. Meyer in a German translation in 1912. The Futurists' chief literary follower in Berlin however was a senior postal official, August Stramm, who had hardly written in earnest before that year. When Marinetti's 'Technical Manifesto of Futurist Literature' (of May 1912) appeared in *Der Sturm,* followed by an influential lecture which he gave in Berlin early in 1913, Stramm destroyed all his previous writings and started to work along the principles laid down there; that is, reducing sentences to verbs and nouns, eliminating articles, adjectives and conjunctions, keeping the verbs in the infinitive, doing away with punctuation and introducing an element of noise. The result was the short, infinitive-riddled lines of poems like 'Weltwehe':

Nichts nichts nichts	(Nothing nothing nothing
Haucht	Breathes
Nichts	Nothing
Hauchen	To breathe
Nichts	Nothing
Hauch	Breath
Wägen	To weigh
Wägen wegen	To weigh away
Wegen regen	Away to sway
Stauen	To stow
Lauen ...	To low ...)

On Walden's advice he began to read the work of Arno Holz. He also wrote a number of short stage works, of which *Sancta Susanna* is the best known.

Some undefined barrier seems to have separated Benn, Stramm and the minor poets associated with Walden from the two principal theoreticians of literary Expressionism, Hiller and Pinthus, who paid them little or no attention in their essays or in the many anthologies for which they were between them responsible. The first of these was *Der Kondor,* edited by Hiller and published in Heidelberg in 1912 by Richard Weissbach, who also published Blass's first collection of poems *Die Strassen komme ich entlang geweht.* Primarily it displayed the work of the Berlin poets (less Van Hoddis, who had fallen out with the editor) broadened by the inclusion of some writers representative of slightly different directions. To Stadler, who wrote a generally favourable criticism of it, the poet who stuck out like a sore thumb was Elsa Lasker-Schüler, whose dreamy and emotional verses, among them the cutely poetic 'Ein alter Tibetteppich' which she had written for Karl Kraus 'the Lama's son', seemed to him to belong rather with Alfred Mombert and his generation. Lasker-Schüler, it is difficult not to feel, owes her place in the Expressionist movement more to her friendships (e.g. around this time with Benn and Franz Marc) and the verses arising out of them than to any specially Expressionist feature of her writing. But others of the outside contributors were to become important in the movement, particularly as the centre of its attention came to shift from the city setting to Humanity as a whole. They included Paul Zech, an idealistic and socially-conscious poet who in May 1913 started his own short-lived review *Das neue Pathos* – the title and introductory article came from Zweig's book on Verhaeren – with Meidner and Hans Ehrenbaum-Degele as co-editors; another 'committed' poet, Ludwig Rubiner; and René Schickele, who was then editing one of the more conservative Berlin magazines and was represented here notably by a poem addressed to 'The Pope', starting:

> Warum steht der Papst nicht auf
> Und spricht zur Menschheit in ihren Wehen ...
>
> (Why does the Pope not get up
> And speak to suffering humanity ...)

Finally there were the Prague writers Franz Werfel and Max Brod.

Werfel's first book of poems *Der Weltfreund* had appeared in Berlin in 1911; his second, *Wir Sind,* which Stadler saw as 'based on the new, intenser and more strenuous experience of the world first proclaimed by Whitman and Verhaeren', in Leipzig in 1913. It was he above all others who now began to apostrophise Man and Brotherhood, the great abstractions of the years to come, and it would be very easy to ridicule him. Thus his 'An den Leser' (which Hiller included in *Der Kondor* and which also introduces the last 'movement' of Pinthus's classic anthology *Menschheitsdämmerung* of 1920) opens

> Mein einziger Wunsch ist dir, o Mensch, verwandt zu sein!
> (My only wish is to be linked to thee, o Man!)

while his sonnet 'Der schöne strahlende Mensch', likewise from his first collection, ends

> O Erde, Abend, Glück, o auf der Welt sein
> (Oh world, night, bliss, oh to be on this earth!)

Similarly the 'dramatic poem' 'Das Opfer' by which he was represented in *Arkadia* (see opposite) is a curious mixture of *Faust II* and a sort of frivolous surrealism, almost with an element of self-parody.

Yet time and again the beauty of the language and the natural brilliance of his verse technique check the modern reader's temptation to titter, so that one begins to understand his publisher Kurt Wolff, who saw him as 'the quintessential poet'. Kafka, as so often, struck the right balance without wasting words when he wrote at the end of 1911:

All yesterday morning my head was as if filled with mist from Werfel's poems. For a moment I feared the enthusiasm would carry me on straight into nonsense.

This Kurt Wolff, the leading publisher of the Expressionist writers from 1913 onwards, was the well-to-do son of the professor of the History of Music at Bonn. In the winter of 1908-9, as a student at Leipzig University, he had met Ernst Rowohlt in that city, and became his partner in the new Rowohlt Verlag, which initially specialised in the work of Herbert Eulenberg, a now virtually forgotten dramatist, and one or two slightly older writers. Their *Cheflektor*, or chief editorial reader, was Kurt Pinthus. In 1911 the firm published Heym's first book *Der ewige Tag*, in 1912 Kafka's *Betrachtung*, which Brod was to review in the first of its almanacs (*Das bunte Buch*, 1914):

The immediacy with which Kafka substitutes his own formal language for reality brings him close to the Expressionist trend in modern painting.

It also recruited Werfel as a second *Lektor*, while the dramatist Walter Hasenclever, still at the university working on his thesis, was an intimate friend of the team. From February 1913 this became the Kurt Wolff Verlag, Rowohlt having been bought out. One of its first publications was the anthology *Arkadia*, edited by Brod, with contributions *inter alia* by himself, Werfel, Kafka (*Das Urteil*), another Prague author Hans Janowitz, and the Swiss Robert Walser; this was to some extent conceived as a counterweight to what Brod privately called 'a certain sterile radicalism emanating from Berlin cafés'. The same spring the firm launched its apocalyptically-named *Der jüngste Tag*, which quickly became the best known, most successful and (just about) cheapest series of Expressionist works and was to include such classics as Kafka's *Metamorphosis* (1916). Still in 1913, Wolff took on the publishing of Schickele's new journal *Die weissen Blätter*, previously edited by Blei and its owner Erich-Ernst Schwabach and generally regarded as the next most interesting review after Walden's and Pfemfert's. He also brought out Hasenclever's first volume of verse *Der Jüngling* and got in touch with two other poets whose contributions to magazines had interested him: Stadler, as translator of Francis Jammes, and Georg Trakl.

They were the last of the important early poets. Stadler had written little between 1905 and 1910, and his first poems had been quite un-Expressionist, in the backwash of George and Hofmannsthal. In 1911 however he began contributing to *Die Aktion* from Brussels, turning at times to themes akin to those of the Berlin poets (e.g. 'Madhouse' or 'Jewish Quarter in London') and often adopting an individual form of long irregular rhyming verse. One poem in particular, his 'Night Journey over the Rhine Bridge at Cologne' (1913) not only recalls Heym's and other verses about railway journeys, and Kirchner's painting of the same bridge, but ends by hacking its sentences apart with exclamation marks or full stops in a manner that again recalls Marinetti:

Und dann die langen Einsamkeiten. Nackte Ufer. Stille. Nacht. Besinnung. Einkehr. Kommunion. Und Glut und Drang.

Zum Letzten, Segnenden. Zum Zeugungsfest. Zur Wollust. Zum Gebet. Zum Meer. Zum Untergang.

(And then the lengthy solitudes. Naked banks. Silence. Night. Reflection. Inwardness. Communion. And ardour and thrust.

To the extreme, the consecration. To the feast of procreation. To luxury. To prayer. To sea. To go under.)

Trakl, a friend of Kokoschka and protégé of the editor Ludwig Ficker in Innsbruck, was influenced by Baudelaire and Rimbaud, perhaps also by Dostoevsky, and haunted by images of decay: dead orphans with worms dropping from their eyelids, women carrying home baskets of offal, a naked wounded nun praying, a sluice draining blood from the slaughterhouse. With him the colours pile up even more than in Heym; thus in the twenty-four lines of 'To one who

96

died young' there are twelve more or less arbitrary attributions of colour (blue smile, silver face, green decay). All this makes him now seem like a particularly morbid and tragic symbolist rather than a member of the movement with which he has often been counted.

In those days there was virtually no prose writing that could be termed Expressionist. Kafka was marginal to the movement and temperamentally very unlike the poets; Döblin, who had enthusiastically welcomed Futurism in art but rejected its literary manifesto, was publishing stories that had mostly been written a few years earlier in his pre-Expressionist vein. Arnold Zweig's *Novellen um Claudia* (1912) are conventionally, if sensually written, while neither of the other two most advanced stories was ever followed up by its author: *Tubütsch* (1911) by the Viennese Alfred Ehrenstein, which Kokoschka illustrated, and *Bebuquin* (1912) by Pfemfert's brother-in-law Carl Einstein, who is better known for his subsequent book on Negro sculpture. Accordingly the most influential novelists re-remained for the present Heinrich Mann and the stylistically expressive Carl Hauptmann, the elder brother of the playwright. Similarly in the theatre the older writers still held the stage, because although the early Expressionist playwrights were already writing there was as yet no director to stage their work in a suitable form and precious little chance of it getting put on at all. The apparatus still had to be won over; and convincing an editor (or a picture dealer for that matter) was a good deal simpler than convincing a state-, court- or municipally-appointed theatre *Intendant*. None the less 1912 did see the publication of the first true Expressionist drama, Reinhold Sorge's *Der Bettler*, which was selected by Richard Dehmel for the first award of the newly established Kleist Prize, as well as of Barlach's *Der tote Tag*. Georg Kaiser wrote his *Von Morgens bis Mitternachts* in the same year and published his pre-Expressionist *Die Bürger von Calais* inspired by Rodin. In 1914 Hasenclever published another influential but still unperformed play which was like a transition from Wedekind to Expressionism: *Der Sohn*. Furthermore, in the new medium of the cinema, the fantastic writer Hans Heinz Ewers was asked to write the script for *The Student of Prague* (1913), based on stories by Hoffmann and Chamisso, while in 1914 Pinthus edited a *Kinobuch* with proposed film treatments by some fifteen avant-garde authors. All this will be considered in the next two chapters, with the rise of the Expressionist theatre proper. For the moment we are still in the pre-1914 theatre, where 'experimental' methods are reserved for works by Strindberg or Maeterlinck, and German plays are expected to have a more conventional form.

In this context the playwright who now began to seem most revolutionary was Carl Sternheim, author of the cycle *Aus dem bürgerlichen Heldenleben,* with its eight satirical comedies, some of which Reinhardt staged in Berlin. The one new technical feature of his work, which was far more orthodox in structure than the plays just mentioned, was the compressed, oblique, so-called 'telegraphic' style of his dialogue: thus in *Bürger Schippel*, which is about the embarrassment of three solid citizens at having to recruit a social inferior as tenor for their prizewinning male voice quartet. Enter suddenly the local petty prince, who has had a motor accident:

Hicketier: Welcher Unfall ... Die Gnade, Durchlaucht.
Der Fürst: Wasser, Leinwand ... Ein Weib am besten.
Hicketier: Meine Frau flog davon.
Wolke *mit tiefer Verbeugung:* Wolke!
Der Fürst: Hörte schon. Was hat es für ein Bewandtnis? Nun, Herr Hicketier?
Hicketier: Zu dienen?
Der Fürst: Schinder. Blutige Schramme. Der Tag fing übel an. Lief ein altes Weib über den Weg, regnete langsam Tropfen, graue Wolke.

(Hicketier: What a smash ... Your grace, Highness.
The Prince: Water, linen ... Best, a woman.

Hicketier: My wife was scared.
Wolke *with a deep bow*: [he has already tried to introduce himself once] Wolke!
The Prince: Heard you the first time. What of it? Well, Mr Hicketier?
Hicketier: At your service?
The Prince: Butchers. Bloody scratches. The day started badly. Old woman ran across the road, slow rain dropping, grey cloud.)

This synthetic curtness, like some of the poetry of Blass and Lichtenstein, seems not so much Expressionist as an anticipation of the drily economical *Neue Sachlichkeit* of the mid-1920's. However, Sternheim's pointed criticisms of bourgeois society (even, in the slightly later *Tabula Rasa,* of the *embourgeoisement* of the Socialist working class) made his younger contemporaries see his writing as relevant to their movement. Though he has been compared with Molière, oddly enough nobody seems to have noticed his deep similarity to Labiche, the author of *An Italian Straw Hat,* who mocked the equally stodgy bourgeoisie of Napoleon III's empire in plays of comparable structure, tempo and wit. Sternheim, who lived in Brussels in a fairly lordly manner and considered himself a European, was well read in the French writers and certainly capable of learning from them how to write a skilfully-devised play.

Anatomies of Expressionism

With the end of the first period of German Expressionism it became possible for critics to start taking stock of the movement. Three of them now did so: Paul Fechter, (*Der Expressionismus,* 1914); Hermann Bahr, the rather older Austrian Naturalist writer cited in the previous chapter, whose *Expressionismus,* based on a series of lectures, was finished in 1914 though not published till 1916; and finally Walden, whose *Einblick in Kunst: Expressionismus, Futurismus, Kubismus* appeared in the same year but is considered here because it sums up *Der Sturm*'s early operations. This last is a document to be treated with care, since in it Walden is writing (and selecting his illustrations) clearly less as a critic than as an impresario, and more precisely as a dealer who has the sole management of a good proportion of the artists whom he cites.

If one conflates the views of these three very different observers one gets a picture of Expressionism as above all a reaction against Impressionism and the materialist nineteenth-century outlook from which it sprang. The acknowledged forerunners were Grünewald and El Greco in the past, and more recently Cézanne, in whom, says Fechter, all subsequent movements have their roots. The first signs of the new development were to be seen in Van Gogh, with his 'immense shortening of the distance between impression and expression', in Munch, and in Gauguin and the Pont-Aven school. Then comes the three-pronged movement – treated as one and the same by Bahr, and by Fechter as virtually so – of Expressionism, Cubism and Futurism. For Walden, however, this last is a stage between the Neo-Impressionists (who indeed did influence the Italian Futurists) and the Expressionists; he sees it as still based on the objective world, while Fechter too criticises its materialism and dependence on 'the rhythm of present-day existence'. Cubism is in Fechter's view a rather different 'variant of Expressionism': 'mysticism of the head' rather than 'mysticism of the heart', deriving not, like Expressionism proper, from Cézanne's metaphysics but only from his system of surfaces. Walden argues indicatively that 'the principal artists of this movement are: *Albert Gleizes* and *Jean Metzinger*', for both of whom his gallery was German agent, 'and not Pablo Picasso, as is mistakenly supposed'.

The chief Expressionist artists for Walden are Kandinsky, Chagall, Marc, Campendonk and Klee, with Kokoschka as a link between Expressionism and Impressionism. Their pictures are 'expressions of a vision', with the painting treated strictly as 'unity of a formally shaped surface'. The Brücke artists are not mentioned. Fechter on the other hand, who reproduces two Matisses and a Munch in this context, distinguishes between the transcendental Expressionism of Kandinsky and his Munich followers and the *extensiver Expressionismus* represented above all by Pechstein, with its intensified relationship to the world: that 'heightened will' which he attributes to Kirchner. Both he and Bahr regard it as an anti-rational movement, and also as a basically German one:

For the will ... is ultimately nothing new, but the same urge as has always been valid in the Germanic world. It is the old Gothic soul which ... despite all rationalism and materialism, again and again raises its head.

Thus Fechter, while Bahr, who stresses its wild and primitive aspects, sees Expressionism as 'the soul's struggle with the machine ...

Man is crying out for his soul, the whole period becomes a single urgent cry. And Art cries too, into the deep darkness, crying for help, crying for the spirit. That is Expressionism.

We have seen where this led Bahr. In much the same way Fechter too, arguing that the general movement is of more importance than the quality of any individual achievements, concludes with an appeal to a new religious sense. For that same general spirit, or *Gesamtgeist,* which he finds in the Expressionist artists, in Wedekind's plays, in the poems of Werfel and the young Berliners, is also, to his eye, visible in the spiritual experiments of, once again, Rudolf Steiner:

It is no coincidence that the writings of this prophet of a new spirituality should contain visions noted down prior to any cubist, futurist or expressionist picture, which seem like anticipations of modern art.

Critics of literature were, however, more reluctant to make such far-ranging generalisations. The few who tried to give any picture at all of the movement, like Hiller in his volume *Die Weisheit der Langenweile* which Wolff published in 1913, dealt with it only very partially, speaking of a group of young poets, or at best a 'new pathos', rather than of *Expressionismus.* About the first writer to refer to himself as an Expressionist was the young Alsatian Iwan Goll (Isaac Lang) who wrote a year later that although it was an accepted concept in painting:

It is a particular colouring of the soul which literary technicians have not so far found to be chemically analysable, and consequently it has had no name. Expressionism today is in the air ...

5 The pressure of events

The war

When the First World War broke over Europe no artistic or intellectual movement was so hit as the modern movement in the German-speaking countries. It was no longer a question of creaking timbers; the whole house seemed to be falling down: first the community of poets and artists, who were dispersed and within eight weeks had lost three of their best members; then the concept of socialist internationalism and brotherhood, which all but Karl Liebknecht and Rosa Luxemburg of the German Socialist leaders had promptly thrown aside; finally, to most people's great relief, the Hohenzollern and Habsburg empires, and with them the whole central structure of the prewar continent. Despite one or two prophetic poems by Heym or Stadler ('Der Aufbruch'), or Meidner's war premonitions of 1911-12, or the strange cannon-like objects in Kandinsky's 'Improvisation 30' of 1913, and despite the widespread sense of precariousness and fragmentation in pre-1914 art, the war came as a bolt from the blue, much as it did in placid Georgian England. It left the German intellectuals initially dazed, or momentarily enthusiastic. But in no western country did so powerful a revulsion against it develop, and because this was largely centred on the writers and artists it marked their movement for good.

At first there were some surprising instances of literary flag-wagging, as for that matter there were all through Europe; thus even Romain Rolland during the first month of the war could write to his friend Gillet of 'l'épopée française' and affirm his belief in a French victory, while the invasion of Belgium made Verhaeren drop his internationalism overnight and turn into a tedious Allied propagandist. 'The German people's hour of destiny', wrote the critic Julius Bab in the foreword to a new magazine called *Der Deutsche Krieg im Deutschen Gedicht,* 'has found, and is finding, a lyrical echo in thousands and thousands of poetically excited hearts'. The effect on the Whitmanesque poet Ernst Lissauer is notorious, for one of his poems gave the world the phrase 'Gott strafe England'. Richard Dehmel too, however, can be found in the same magazine

'The eve of the war', a pen drawing by Meidner, dated early August 1914, from the Recklinghausen Museum.

with verses like 'Der Feldsoldat' (printed in the Christmas 1914 issue, which was subtitled 'War on Earth') ending:

> Da alles ruht in Gottes Hand;
> wir bluten gern fürs Vaterland.
>
> (As all is safely in God's hand;
> we're glad to bleed for the fatherland.)

So can Rudolf Alexander Schroeder, Hofmannsthal and Gerhard Hauptmann, whose doggerel 'Reiterlied' is dedicated to 'Fritz von Unruh, Poet and Uhlan'. So, more surprisingly, can such Expressionists as Unruh himself, Schickele (whose 'August 1st 1914' ends 'Death or Victory!'), Rudolf Leonhard, Max Brod and Paul Zech. They were rapidly enough to change their minds.

What changed them, and changed the whole face of their movement, was a succession of losses which were only symptomatic of what the war was costing the country:

Alfred Lichtenstein	25 September 1914
Ernst Wilhelm Lotz	26 September 1914
August Macke	26 September 1914
Ernst Stadler	30 October 1914
Georg Trakl	3/4 November 1914
Hans Ehrenbaum-Degele	28 July 1915
August Stramm	1 September 1915
Franz Marc	4 March 1916
Reinhard Johannes Sorge	20 July 1916
Gustav Sack	5 December 1916
Wilhelm Morgner	August 1917
Robert Jentsch	21 March 1918
Gerritt Engelke	13 October 1918
Franz Nölken	4 November 1918

Pfemfert in *Die Aktion* was from the first tacitly opposed to the war, but for the less politically-minded the turning point seems to have come at the end of 1914, when a meeting was held at Weimar between Hasenclever, Pinthus, Zech, Leonhard, Ehrenstein, Martin

104

Buber and others to discuss their future attitude. Hasenclever then wrote to Schickele, whose *Die Weissen Blätter* had ceased publication with the outbreak of the war, begging him to carry the paper on as 'a power to *overcome* the national darkness', which is indeed what it now became. Other symptoms of the same change can be seen in Beckmann's *Briefe im Kriege,* where after a period of thoroughly enjoying the war he writes on 4 May 1915 from near Ypres, 'for the first time I've had enough', or in a small paper called *Zeit-Echo,* which was founded at the start of the war to be an 'Artists' War Diary', but opened its second volume that autumn with a lithograph by Picasso, a contemptuous review of the *War Songs of XV Corps* which Cassirer had published with drawings by Beckmann, and a leading article by its new editor Hans Siemsen saying that although the paper was supposed to mirror the 'war mood' (*Kriegsstimmung*) 'I'd say a year of Kriegsstimmung was enough'. The following issue accordingly contained an obituary by Franz Blei of Péguy, perhaps France's outstanding war loss, while in December *Die Aktion* published a special French number in memory of 'The writer Charles Péguy and the painter André Derain, victims of the war'. The report of Derain's death was of course apocryphal, but one of the war's less disagreeable legends was then circulating in Germany: that Péguy and his translator Stadler had recognised one another at the front and exchanged messages before both being killed.

The most famous of all early anti-war documents, Romain Rolland's *Au dessus de la mêlée,* appeared in the *Journal de Genève* on 15 September 1914, as an appeal to the 'European élite.' Except for Hermann Hesse, whose article 'O Freunde, nicht diese Töne!' was published in the *Neue Zürcher Zeitung* a month and a half later, the senior Austrian and German literary figures whom Rolland was hoping to turn against the war – Thomas Mann, Hauptmann, Hofmannsthal, Rilke – were unwilling to be associated with him, and in his own country he at first had scarcely a single supporter. In June 1915 he was joined in Geneva by Guilbeaux, who had been discharged from the French army, and shortly afterwards by René Arcos and Pierre-Jean Jouve, whose book of poems *Vous êtes des hommes* (1915) proclaimed 'Je veux être votre frère – famille – hommes, et peuples!'. Rolland's *Journal des Années de Guerre*, a neglected book, gives a picture of the novelist continually watching out for evidence of a saner attitude on either side of the front: the pacifism of his own translator Wilhelm Herzog's Munich review *Das Forum,* (suppressed in August 1915); the letters from Stefan

Die Aktion

WOCHENSCHRIFT FÜR POLITIK, LITERATUR, KUNST

IV. JAHR HERAUSGEGEBEN VON FRANZ PFEMFERT NR. 42/43

VERLAG / DIE AKTION / BERLIN-WILMERSDORF

HEFT 40 PFG.

A tribute from the German-speaking world to a fallen French poet. Egon Schiele's drawing of Charles Péguy, from the cover of Pfemfert's *Die Aktion* for 24 October 1914, which also included an obituary notice and a drawing by De La Fresnaye.

Zweig (then working with Rilke in the Austrian War Archives) and from Gorki; the anti-war activities of the Swiss-based Bolsheviks (Lenin, Lunacharsky, Sokolnikov, the later Commissar of Finance) with whom Guilbeaux was in touch and who organised the important congress of minority Socialist parties at Zimmerwald that September. Others also began to visit him: Einstein for instance, and Charles Baudouin of Geneva university. Schickele came for the first time on 29 October.

With the transfer of *Die Weissen Blätter* to Zürich early in 1916 Switzerland became a centre of the young German opposition to the war. The *Zeit-Echo,* now under Rubiner's editorship, followed in 1917. Iwan Goll was then studying law at Lausanne university; while Ernst Bloch, a thirty-year-old philosopher who had written for Blass's Heidelberg review *Die Argonauten* and arrived in Berne in 1915 (where Kessler was German cultural attaché), was writing his *Der Geist der Utopie*, published three years later. Arrivals in Zürich in 1916 included Ehrenstein, Hardekopf. Leonhard Frank, Richard Huelsenbeck and the Munich *dramaturg* Hugo Ball with his wife Emmy Hennings, of whom the last four, together with Goll, had been contributors to the short-lived Munich periodical *Revolution* in 1913. Wolfenstein too came from Munich to visit Rolland (24 May 1916), subsequently writing a sonnet to him. A year later Stefan Zweig arrived, ostensibly for the Zürich première of his pacifist play *Jeremias*. Though there was not much contact between these Zürich exiles and the group round Rolland, there was a growing mutual awareness of the work now being published and read in the two centres. On the one side this included the poems of Marcel Martinet, a schoolmaster friend of Guilbeaux's, which apostrophised 'Peuple', 'Homme', and 'Poètes d'Allemagne, O Frères inconnus' and had been banned in France. There were also Jouve's hospital stories *Hôtel-Dieu* (1918); and, from within France itself, Henri Barbusse's novel of life at the front *Le Feu*. On the other side were the first German war novel, Andreas Latzko's *Menschen im Krieg* (1917), Goll's *Requiem für die Gefallenen von Europa* (1918), Ehrenstein's *Den ermordeten Brüdern* and Leonhard Frank's idealist-

Below An illustration by Frans Masereel to Jouve's *Hôtel-Dieu*, Geneva 1918.
Right Max Beckmann's changed persona. 'Die Nacht', 1918-19, from the
Kunstsammlung Nordrhein-Westfalen, Düsseldorf.

socialist stories *Der Mensch ist gut* (1918), whose title was to become
almost a programmatic slogan. Illustrations for such works, of
which the German were mostly published by Rascher in Zürich and
the French by Arcos's Editions du Sablier in Geneva, were provided
irrespective of language by one of the great expressionist illustrators,
the Belgian Frans Masereel, who had been brought to Geneva in
1916 by Guilbeaux, his former editor, and from August 1917 drew a
daily cartoon for the Swiss anti-war paper *La Feuille*. In 1918 he
published the sequence of woodcuts called *25 Images de la Passion
d'un Homme,* the first of many albums which needed no translation
and made his name in several countries.

In Germany itself, the impact of the war in those years was a
double one. The individual writer or artist became aware that there
was an increasingly vocal alternative point of view to the official war

108

spirit. At the same time he was in many cases subjected to his own appalling war trauma. Admittedly there was a wide variation in luck (or influence), some people managing to get released from the army, as did Kurt Wolff, Barlach and Campendonk, while others had terrible experiences which changed their lives. A few of the painters, including Heckel, Otto Herbig and Max Kaus, joined a medical unit in Flanders under Walter Kaesbach, where they made contact with Ensor and other Belgian artists and were encouraged to carry on working, Heckel painting his 'Ostend Madonna' for Christmas 1915 on an army tent. Osthaus was put in charge of the Belgian monuments. But Kokoschka, after being wounded in the brain and lungs, went to convalesce at the Weisser Hirsch sanatorium near Dresden; Kirchner had a series of breakdowns during his army training, was discharged and became paralysed in the

The edge of breakdown. George Grosz's drawing 'Terror in the Street', 1916, from the Busch-Reisinger Museum, Harvard.

arms and legs; Beckmann, who had been in touch with Kaesbach's group, was discharged in 1915 after a nervous breakdown, then started working in isolation in the new expressive style of his unfinished 'Resurrection' of 1916. Of younger men, as yet barely on the fringes of the movement, George Grosz seems to have been driven by army discipline into some form of mental illness; Wieland Herzfelde, his editor and publisher, was called up, discharged in 1915, then called up again; while their friend Franz Jung, who had edited one issue of *Die Revolution*, deserted, was caught and imprisoned then discharged as manic-depressive. One of the Worpswede painters, Heinrich Vogeler, became an intelligence corporal, was converted by captured Bolshevik documents and goaled for protesting against the peace of Brest-Litovsk. The poet Ernst Toller enthusiastically volunteered at the beginning of the war at the age of twenty, was found to be unfit after a year's service, then called up again in 1918, to be sent successively to prison, hospital and a psychiatric clinic. A military doctor who caught him reading a poem by Werfel told him, 'Nobody who reads trash like that ought to be surprised if he lands up in gaol'.

The establishment of Expressionist poetry

It was the war which turned the young poetic movement of 1910-14 into what became known as the Expressionist school. Superficially this recalls what had happened earlier to Die Brücke, whose first four years were like an unselfconscious preparation of Expressionism and who notably changed once the larger movement was under way. With the poets however the reasons were very different. The deaths of Heym, Trakl, Stadler and Lichtenstein, together with the illness of van Hoddis, not only halved the young movement's potential; it also wiped the smile off its face. Nobody now could go on writing ironically; Blass was the one survivor of the lighter poets, and he had started writing obscure, somewhat classical 'Gedichte vom Krieg' which led him right out of the movement. Those poems of decay, moreover, which before the war had seemed a little strained, now in the everyday light of the battlefields looked almost realistic: Trakl's last poem 'Grodek', for example, describes the place in south Poland where the medical unit in which he served had to function without doctors and without bandages:

111

Am Abend tönen die herbstlichen Wälder
Von tödlichen Waffen, die goldenen Ebenen
Und blauen Seen, darüber die Sonne
Düster hinrollt; umfängt die Nacht
Sterbende Krieger, die wilde Klage
Ihrer zerbrochenen Münder ...

(The evening hears the autumnal woods speaking
Of deadly weapons, the golden plains
And blue lakes, above them the sun
Rolls murkily down; the night surrounds
Dying warriors, the wild complaint
Of their broken mouths ...)

And yet war poetry of this kind, which was to become so important in the English literature of the same years, is startlingly rare in the work of the German Expressionists. What now became predominant was rather the high rhapsodic style of Werfel, with its vast generalities and its avoidance of specific detail. Precarious enough in his marvellously skilled hands, it was a cracked vessel in any others, so that today much of this wartime Expressionism is hard to read.

'Lachen Atmen Schreiten', the poem which Toller was caught studying, appeared in the Kurt Wolff almanac *Vom Jüngsten Tag* in 1916, and is a hymn to Man, in whom, according to Werfel, all concepts of light, freedom, the Godhead and the world itself are rooted. In this representative anthology of the poetry of the time Hasenclever also appears with two political poems on the death and resurrection of the murdered French Socialist leader Jaurès, appealing to the

Soldaten Europas, Bürger Europas!
Hört die Stimme, die Euch Bruder heisst.

(Soldiers of Europe! Citizens of Europe!
Hear the voice that calls you Brother.)

– and ending 'Aufwärts, Freunde, Menschen!' ('Upwards, friends, Men!'). Ehrenstein contributes a poem in memory of Trakl, Rudolf Leonhard one in memory of Stadler. Wolfenstein's long poem 'Licht' describes, in jingly couplets, an idyllic life in a countryside illuminated

In einem Schein des Friedens, leicht und dunkel
– Und plötzlich bebt sie hier und wird noch dunkler –
Steht auf mit tierischem Gefunkel – Hände
Voll Waffen drücken sich in unsre Hände
Dass wir sie nehmen, aber drücken Wunden
In uns!

(By a glow of peace, airy and dark
– And suddenly it starts to heave and grows yet darker –
Stands up with bestial sparkle – hands
Full of weapons press into our hands,
For us to take them, but press wounds
Into us!)

Then in the darkness, as light is murdered, the poet finds his hands touching the enemy opposite:

O F r e u n d! Kaserne steht um unser Haupt,
Um Schönheit, die sich plözlich gleicht und glaubt!

(O *friend*! Barracks plead about our heads
For beauty, suddenly similar and confident!)

But all such works were, as Pinthus put it in his long editorial essay 'On the newest writing', 'drowned by the sound of the enormous outbursts of Becher's wildly exuberant talent …' There were five of these outbursts in the book, varying from the short 'Since the war started', with its personal pain, to 'Verbrüderung' (brotherhood or fraternisation), the title poem of a collection which Becher published that year: an immense appeal, in telegraphic phrases spattered with invocations and exclamations that brightness should be brought to bear on 'the desolate battlefield of the cities'. It ends:

Tretet an den Marsch! Freiheit auf die Fahnen!!
Dich antike Welt zertrümmere solcher Schwung!
Ein Gestirn enttaucht, kreuzt ob unserem Plan:
Himmel der Verbrüderung.

(Join in the march! Write Freedom on our banners!!
Our rhythm smash thee, ancient world, for good!
A star looms up. Mark above our plan:
Paradise of Brotherhood.)

Johannes R. Becher, son of a district judge in Munich, was twenty-three when the war broke out. Influenced above all by Kleist,

Baudelaire and Rimbaud, he was, like his friends Frank, Hennings and the anarchist poet Erich Mühsam, one of the main writers of *Die Revolution*. As a schoolboy he had shot a girl and tried to commit suicide; he also, like Lasker-Schüler, took morphine. At the age of eighteen he had written to Dehmel for advice about his writing:

I love you, life! Aims! Aims! Clarity! The words erupt from my lips like a stammer. Redemption! Redemption!

– to which the older man replied that he had better learn to write a good essay; at the moment there was more smoke than fire. Whatever it was, there was plenty of it, and from 1914 onwards it came pouring out in great billowing clouds, sometimes full of sparks but sometimes not.

> Der Dichter meidet strahlende Akkorde,
> Er stösst durch Tuben, peitscht die Trommel schrill.
> Er reisst das Volk auf mit gehackten Sätzen.
>
> (The poet avoids shining harmonies
> He blows through tubas, shrilly whips the drum.
> He tears the People open with chopped up phrases.)

– so runs the start of one of his most quoted verses, first published in 1916. But in many of these high-pitched poems of peace, brotherhood and socialism – and it was amazing that so many of them got through the censorship – tubas, trombones and thickly chorded harmonies are more in evidence than the telegraphic style. Whitman once again seems to inspire so much of the verse of this time. Thus in Herzfelde's *Neue Jugend,* one of the very few new periodicals, Gustav Landauer translated and interpreted Whitman; Becher's poem 'To Peace' introduced the opening issue of July 1916; while its 1917 almanac (another important anthology, with essays by Buber and the pacifist F. W. Foerster as well as Däubler's 'Hymn to Friedrich Nietzsche' and drawings by Meidner, Kokoschka and Grosz) was prefaced by the conclusion of Whitman's 'Poets to come': 'Expecting the main things from you'. . .

As the tide of war turned in 1917 further trombones joined the band, till it grew positively Wagnerian; the *Posaune* becomes one of the props of the Expressionist vocabulary. For instance in Hasenclever's '1917':

> Tritt mit der Posaune des jüngsten Gerichts
> Hervor, o Mensch, aus tobendem Nichts!

> (Step forth with the trombone of the Last Judgment
> O Man, from raging nothingness!)

The forest of exclamation marks thickens. And undoubtedly this helps to give the school as a whole a utopian-rhetorical character recalling Beethoven's Choral Symphony and the spirit in which Rolland had played it thirty years earlier. Indeed on 18 October 1918 Gustav Landauer wrote an appeal (later published in the anthology *Die Erhebung*) comparing the writer with the soloist in the last movement of that work. The focus is now on Man, 'der Mensch', and the poets on the other side of the front who seemed to share it are (as named by Pinthus, who for some reason omits Romains's poem 'Europe') Duhamel, Péguy, Vildrac, Guilbeaux, Rolland and Jouve – whose free verse poem in this vein 'Les Voix d'Europe' was printed in French in the same *Almanach der Neuen Jugend*. Karl Otten writes a set of poems 'To Martinet', answering his appeal; Mühsam addresses a poem 'An die Dichter' appealing to poets to abandon trivialities; Rubiner publishes *Das himmlische Licht*, which Pinthus calls 'the first great lyrical-political poetry'; Hasenclever his book *Tod und Auferstehung,* containing the well-known poem 'Der politische Dichter'. Not only does this swamping of the movement with new interests (and a not-so-new style) rather drown out a number of the less obtrusive poets such as Wilhelm Klemm, Max Herrmann-Neisse, Klabund (Alfred Henschke) and, in his posthumously published verses, E. W. Lotz, but it also makes it difficult for the critics to reconcile the latest developments with what had been written before the war. In 'On the newest writing' Pinthus does his best to tie it together thus:

The latest generation, developing since 1900, found themselves without protection in the midst of the shimmering magic of travel and adventure, of free sexuality, of streets, landscapes, cafés and amusement palaces fizzing with a mixture of secret sounds, colours and figures, of mysterious factories, machines and forms of motion ... and wrote intoxication, tension and hangover. Till suddenly the realisation came on them, heard softly in the bliss of being, then with a blare of trombones: ... We are! And are Men!

There were also two other developments that should be noted. First of all the poetry of August Stramm, one of the victims of the war, became from 1915 on the main literary model for the rather undistinguished writers of the *Sturm* group. Walden, according to his wife's memoir, was insistent that 'art and politics have nothing in common', and since she (like that other non-German Paul Klee) believed that Germany was fighting a just war, they would no doubt have parted company from the Expressionists even if their paper had not now been reduced to appearing every two months. In their readings and performances (from 1916 on) they particularly cultivated Stramm's work, which takes the telegraphic style close to the limits of intelligibility, to the borders of sheer sound poetry. The best known of his immediate followers was Kurt Heynicke, whose 'Attack' published in 1918 has the same characteristic one-word lines: ('Blood/Mud/Death/Brown flood again/Back/Past') and so on.

The second new factor was the publication of a few works of more or less Expressionist prose, such as Kasimir Edschmid's *Die sechs Mündungen* and Döblin's novel *Die drei Sprünge des Wang-Lun*, both of which appeared in 1915. Edschmid, a prolific Darmstadt author whose real name was Eduard Schmid, owes his prominence in the history of the movement perhaps less to his somewhat exotic novels and stories than to the lecture which he gave in 1917 'Uber den dichterischen Expressionismus': on Expressionism in imaginative writing. According to this the Expressionist writer deals with much the same outward subject-matter as his Naturalist predecessors, but

he does not see, he looks. He does not depict, he lives. He does not reproduce, he creates. He does not select, he searches. Today we no longer have a chain of data: factories, buildings, illness, whores, outcry and hunger. We have them in visionary form.

Expressionism accordingly is unlike Futurism, which deals with surface appearances rather than with essential truths. None the less Edschmid put forward very similar verbal techniques as a way of penetrating to the latter, and preached a new grammar and syntax which would not be descriptive but concise, abrupt, dynamic. Something of this is perhaps visible in Benn's 'Rönne' stories, with their exceptional economy and force: e.g., in 'Die Reise':

He stepped out of doors. Bright avenues, light full of withdrawal, daphnes in bloom. It was in the outskirts: wretched things from basements, cripples and graves, such a lot unlaughed. But Rönne thought, each person I pass is still lucky enough to be a tempest. Nowhere my heavy, oppressive disorientation.

Based on his service as an army medical officer, however, and detachedly introspective, these stories seem not so much contorted or emotive as just extraordinarily modern. And none of these three authors, let alone the stylistically traditional Leonhard Frank, has quite the same twisted, hectic quality as the prose writings of the painter Meidner (*Septemberschrei* and *Im Nacken das Sternenmeer*), who was then in the thick of the movement and drew many portraits of its members.

Expressionism in the theatre

In a 'Speech addressed to young writers', published in 1918, Pinthus asked if they yet realised:

that the drama is going to be the most passionate and effective form for your writing? ... Possibly more than anything else that we have termed Expressionist. There Man explodes in front of Man.

In the second half of the war such dramas at last began to reach the stage, starting with Hasenclever's *Der Sohn* in Dresden in 1916. Some of these plays, notably those of Georg Kaiser, had been waiting up to seven or eight years for a performance. Now a few outstanding provincial theatres summoned up enough courage to put them on, above all in Frankfurt, where Arthur Hellmer ran the private Neues Theater and Carl Zeiss from Dresden came to manage the city theatre; at the Düsseldorf Schauspielhaus under Gustav Lindemann; and at the Munich Kammerspiele, which was taken over in 1916 by Otto Falkenberg, with Otto Zoff as *dramaturg*. There Falkenberg began a series of performances under the title *Das jüngste Deutschland* (the latest, or youngest, or last Germany, an untranslatable triple meaning) and in the 1917-18 season Reinhardt followed suit, introducing the new playwrights at last to Berlin in a series similarly called *Das junge Deutschland*. This consisted of afternoon performances at the Deutsches Theater: *Der Bettler* in 1917, Kaiser's *Der Koralle* and Reinhold Goering's *Seeschlacht* the same winter, followed by *Der Sohn*, the Kokoschka plays, Unruh's *Ein Geschlecht* and Lasker-Schüler's *Die Wupper* in the next season. Though all but the first were given some months after the provincial première, they represented a marked change in Reinhardt's attitude to the new German drama, which he now provided with stunning casts, producing *Seeschlacht* himself for instance with Conrad Veidt, Emil Jannings, Werner Krauss and Paul Wegener, the powerful actor who figures in some of Nolde's pre-war drawings. Such

Productions of the Expressionist theatre before 1919

1916

20 September	Hasenclever *Der Sohn*	Deutsches Landes-Theater, Prague
*8 October	Hasenclever *Der Sohn*	Albert-Theater, Dresden

1917

29 January	Kaiser *Die Bürger von Calais*	Neues Theater, Frankfurt
28 April	Kaiser *Von Morgens bis Mitternachts*	Kammerspiele, Munich
3 June	Kokoschka *Mörder, Hoffnung der Frauen, Hiob* and *Der brennende Dornbusch*	Albert-Theater, Dresden
27 October	Kaiser *Die Koralle*	Neues Theater, Frankfurt Kammerspiele, Munich
2 November	Johst *Der Einsame*	Schauspielhaus, Düsseldorf
8 December	Kornfeld *Die Verführung*	Schauspielhaus, Frankfurt
15 December	Hasenclever *Antigone*	Stadttheater, Leipzig
*23 December	Sorge *Der Bettler*	Deutsches Theater, Berlin

1918

*10 February	Goering *Seeschlacht*	Königliches Schauspielhaus, Dresden
*16 June	Unruh *Ein Geschlecht*	Schauspielhaus, Frankfurt
*October	Stramm *Sancta Susanna*	Sturmbünne, Berlin
28 November	Kaiser *Gas*	Neues Theater, Frankfurt Schauspielhaus, Düsseldorf

* club or otherwise restricted performance

performances were not open to the general public: a rule which also applied to *Der Sohn* in Dresden and to the premières of *Seeschlacht* and *Ein Geschlecht,* plays thought likely to be too disturbing by the censor. Hasenclever's *Antigone,* too, was banned after its first production, while Sternheim's *1913* and *Tabula Rasa* were held up throughout the war, only reaching the stage in 1919.

Some of these plays certainly owed their impact to the war, and now seem a good deal less powerful. *Seeschlacht,* which Goering wrote in a sanatorium in Davos after being invalided out of the army, is a disillusioned picture of the battle of Jutland as experienced by the sailors in a single gun-turret, who fight blindly in their armoured box, have memories and visions and – something inexcusably concealed in the modern reprints of the play – speak in verse. At the end, for instance, when the three survivors are all dying, the fifth and most rebellious sailor says:

> Die Schlacht geht weiter, hörst du?
> Mach deine Augen noch nicht zu.
> Ich habe gut geschossen, wie?
> Ich hätte auch gut gemeuteret! Wie?
> Aber schiessen lag uns wohl näher? Wie?
> Muss uns wohl näher gelegen haben?
>
> (The battle's going on, do you hear?
> It is too soon to close your eyes.
> I am a good shot, don't you think?
> I'd have made a good mutineer! Don't you think?
> But I suppose shooting came easier to us? Don't you think?
> It must have come easier to us?)

Ein Geschlecht, meaning 'a lineage' or almost 'stock', was written by Unruh at the front and dedicated to his dead brother; it was produced by Gustav Hartung. It is set in a cemetery on a mountain peak and shows a mother who has lost one son in the war and now confronts two others, the one found guilty by the army of cowardice, the second of looting or rape. This second son, in fury at his mother's family pride (they are all noble), tries to strangle her and ravish his sister. Though the incidents are explosive enough and the motivation abrupt, everybody speaks old-fashioned 'poetic' blank verse; thus the mother:

> Ich heb mich auf! Wo bist Du, Henker, Richter?
> Und klängen deine Schwerter wie Posaunen

> um das Gericht, das Euch verdamm zu sterben,
> erst treffen sie die Brust, die Euch gesäugt.

> (I raise myself! Where art thou, judge, thou hangman?
> Now if thy swords be resonant as trombones
> Around the court that utters your death sentence,
> First they shall strike the breast that suckled you.)

When the second son kills himself the mother at last revolts, and is slain by the soldiers, who then follow the fourth son down into the valley. *Antigone* likewise is a verse play conceived as a comment on the war, with 'the People' playing a major part and Creon apologetically abdicating after the burning of Thebes (something that is not in Sophocles).

> Einst aber, wenn die Toten erwachen,
> Wenn die Unsterblichen
> Wandeln in ihr Reich,
> Kehre ich wieder zu meinen Sternen,
> Ich
> Der Vieles wusste und viel getan hat,
> Im Guten und Bösen: ein Mensch!

> (But one day, when the dead awaken,
> When the immortals
> Move to their kingdom
> I shall return to my stars,
> I –
> Who knew much and did many things
> In good and evil: a Man!)

The Mob (no longer the People) storms the palace, but is halted by a sound of thunder and a Voice from the Grave, telling them that God has judged and they should fall on their knees. This they do as the curtain comes down.

Other plays express the clash of the generations, with passionate and talkative young heroes standing more or less openly for the author. Thus in *Der Sohn* The Son breaks away to experience life, harangues a Wedekindish secret society of pleasure-loving young

people whom he turns against their parents, then comes home with a revolver to threaten his severe father, who has a fatal stroke; at one point the Choral Symphony is played as music off. In Johst's *Der junge Mensch,* subtitled 'an ecstatic Scenario', another play often reminiscent of Wedekind, the youth sets out in the same spirit and from an equally intolerable professional-class background, but lands in more absurd situations, is less indulgently handled by the author, and finishes by leaping out of his coffin and deciding to grow up. In *Der Bettler*, subtitled 'a dramatic Mission', The Son poisons his mad father (at the latter's request) and his mother (by accident), ending with ecstatic visions both of his future as a writer:

> *Jäh empor, mit Händen aufwärts*
> O Trost des Blitzes … Erleuchtung …
> Schmerztrost des Blitzes …
> SYMBOLE DER EWIGKEIT …
> Ende! Ende! Ziel und Ende!

> (*Leaping up, raising his hands*
> O consolation of lightening … Illumination …
> The lightning's consolation of pain …
> SYMBOLS OF ETERNITY …
> End! End! Aim and end!)

– and of life with The Girl; the reminiscences here are above all of *Faust Part II.* In *Die Verführung* by the Prague writer Paul Kornfeld, who had settled in Frankfurt and become acquainted with a group including Zeiss, Hartung (who produced the play) and the Mannheim producer Richard Weichert, the young hero wages frantic war against all around him, starting with the gratuitous murder of a stranger and ending up poisoned and abusing God. This play again, over two hundred pages long and written in elevated prose, was felt at the time to have Faustian echoes.

Such 'I – dramas', as the critics termed them, made sense in those days as symbols of the struggle between the younger generation, or even the 'new man' proclaimed by certain Expressionists, and the Hohenzollern father-figure, backed by the whole pre-war German way of life. They were written, as Günther Rühle has pointed out, during the years of Strindberg's domination of the repertoire (a thousand performances in Germany between 1913-16), which no doubt explains their often anonymous characters – of whom only the 'I' normally comes to life – and their sometimes episodic 'Stations of the Cross' form. Similar features can be found in the works by Goering and Unruh, of which the latter is a mixture of war drama and generation conflict: the figures are meant only as vehicles for the author's ideas. And in a sense the same thing applies also to the plays by Georg Kaiser, who from now on was to be one of the two most widely successful dramatists of the movement. For it is only in *Die Bürger von Calais* that his characters have names, while *Von Morgens bis Mitternachts* is in its comic-grotesque way a series of 'stations', ending up with its runaway cashier whispering 'Ecce homo' as he shoots himself against a Salvation Army Cross.

Kaiser, however, was basically unlike any other of these playwrights except perhaps Sternheim. To begin with, he wrote many different types of play, and even those which are commonly regarded as Expressionist vary from the modernistic symmetry of *Die Koralle* and *Gas*, set in a new mythical world of enormously powerful technologists and managers, to the angular distortions of *Von Morgens bis Mitternachts*. The author is never himself profoundly involved in the arguments of his characters, which is no doubt why he was considered a cerebral dramatist, sometimes even to be compared with Shaw. Also – a not unimportant distinction – he does not seem ambitious beyond his talents, so that, unlike some of his contemporaries, he seldom strikes the modern reader as ridiculous. None the less his dialogue, with its percussive punctuation by exclamation marks and chains of dashes, its staccato phrases and (in *Von Morgens bis Mitternachts*) its telescoped sentences, is much less traditional than that of the other playwrights, and closer to the 'chopped up' style recommended by Becher. It has been argued that Kaiser only used such mannerisms for their theatrical effect, and indeed he may not have had his heart in it; he may not have had a heart at all. But the theme of *Gas* is one of the central Expressionist concerns:

Tell me: where is Man? When will he appear – and call himself by his own name: – Man? When will he grasp himself – and shake his knowledge from the branches? When will he overcome the curse – and achieve the new Creation, which he spoilt: – Man?!

And his plays remain something more than period pieces.

Elsewhere, as Pinthus puts it, 'the cry of desperation and ecstasy blooms sharply upwards'. Kornfeld, for instance, at the beginning of 1918 edited the first two issues of a magazine called *Das Junge Deutschland,* which the Deutsches Theater published for three years to accompany its afternoon productions. In it he printed his own essay 'Der beseelte und der psychologische Mensch', calling on the theatre to abandon not merely naturalism but all psychology too, on the grounds that it was 'soul' that mattered and not 'character'. This may well have furthered the emergence of an intense, angular, exclamatory Expressionist style of acting; at any rate it was in these years that the (subsequently) most famous of the Expressionist actors staked their claims to such parts: Ernst Deutsch with his performance in the Dresden *Der Sohn,* Heinrich George in the Dresden *Seeschlacht,* Krauss in Reinhardt's, Gerda Müller as the daughter in *Ein Geschlecht* in Frankfurt. On the other hand the corresponding style of production was established only later. Reinhardt staged *Seeschlacht* quite naturalistically, and if his use of spotlights in *Der Bettler* seemed more expressive this was only as prescribed in the author's stage directions. Generally the producer's contribution as yet tended to be less powerful than the effect of the plays themselves, only Weichert's work at Mannheim, with Ludwig Sievert as his designer, constituting an exception.

In short, the breakthrough of Expressionism to the stage was not yet complete. None the less, the movement which before 1914 was only understood to apply to painting was now seen to embrace poetry and the theatre, and to a lesser extent prose writing and architecture too. The exact relations between these different aspects was still somewhat unclear; the Berlin theatre critics for instance seem to have fought shy of the term Expressionism until *Gas* was produced there in 1919. A lot of people, however, must have shared the experience of Robert Musil, who returned from army service at the end of the war to sum up the whole change of scene in a few graphic words:

Before I joined up we had an explosive, intellectual poetry of ideas, a poetry of intellectual intuition, blown-off bits of philosophical thinking festooned with scraps of emotional flesh that had been torn away with them. When I came back we had Expressionism.

The German Revolution and the Arts

The revolution of November 1918, which finally overthrew the Hohenzollerns and brought the troops home, at first affected architects and artists more profoundly than writers. This, after all, was what so many of the latter had been writing about, and when it came its immediate effect was to explain the new movement rather than to change it. In the visual arts, on the other hand, nothing much

124

new had happened since 1914, apart from the obvious cutting-off of relations with France, something that was symbolised by the impounding of Matisse's pictures at the Gurlitt gallery after his second Berlin show. Pechstein and Nolde had had a certain amount of difficulty in getting back from the South Seas, Nolde's paintings being confiscated by the British in the Suez Canal, to turn up in a Plymouth warehouse some three years after the Armistice. Kandinsky and Chagall had gone back to Russia, leaving a number of canvases with Walden, whose subsequent failure to make what they considered adequate payment ended their relations with him and put a permanent stop to Chagall's German career. Kirchner went into a Davos sanatorium in May 1917; though he was able to paint before the end of that year he never lived in Germany again. Carl Hofer, who had had one show at Cassirer's in 1914, came back from French internment to paint in a new, mildly Expressionist manner, while in 1917 and 1918 respectively Barlach and Meidner had their first big one-man exhibitions at the same gallery: a reflection, perhaps, of the change in collectors' tastes. Feininger too at last broke through to public recognition with an exhibition at the Sturm gallery in 1917. The younger artists, unlike the younger poets, were not yet known.

With the revolution, there was a further upheaval, this time of a social-aesthetic rather than a 'purely' artistic kind. 'I had no hesitation' wrote Pechstein later, 'in putting myself at the disposal of the Social-Democratic government'. Two new groups were organised whose concern was primarily with relations between the arts and society, and both were so bound up with Expressionism – personally, ideologically and in the design of their publications – as to mark a new stage in the development of the movement. First, in November an *Arbeitsrat für Kunst* was formed in Berlin, a 'working council for art' paralleling the 'soldiers' and workers' councils' being set up in many parts of the country in imitation of the Russian Soviets of the year before. Its presidents were Walter Gropius, Cesar Klein and the architectural critic Adolf Behne, whose book *Wiederkehr der Kunst,* written in August 1918, is an appeal for a reconciliation of the new art with the masses, characteristically dedicated 'To the dead combatants in sorrow./ To all brothers of the planet Earth/In love'. The committee members included Pechstein, Schmidt-Rottluff, Heckel, Meidner, Feininger and the architects Bruno Taut, Max Taut and Otto Bartning. Then, partly overlapping with this body, there was a *Novembergruppe* of artists,

125

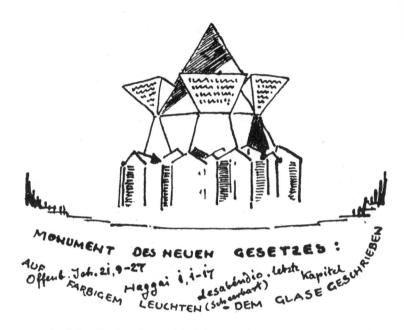

MONUMENT DES NEUEN GESETZES :
AUF Offenb. Joh. 2i, 9-27 Haggai i, i-i7
FARBIGEM LEUCHTEN (Scheerbart) (Lesabéndio) letzte Kapitel
DEM GLASE GESCHRIEBEN

organised by Pechstein and Klein (with Georg Tappert, Moriz Melzer and Hermann Richter), which held its first meeting in Berlin on 8 December, attended among others by Otto Mueller, Campendonk, Purrmann and the sculptor Rudolf Belling. In 1919 some of its members issued a flaming appeal 'to all artists', *An alle Künstler*, which embraced poems by Becher, Hasenclever and Zech, illustrations by Pechstein, Klein and Feininger, Socialist articles by Pechstein and Meidner, a speech by the Bavarian premier Kurt Eisner and a statement by the Prussian Minister of Education. Both organisations seem to have sprouted branches in the provinces, including an *Arbeitsrat* at Darmstadt and a *Novembergruppe* in Dresden. The last had three interesting young artists among its members: Lasar Segall, Conrad Felixmüller and Otto Dix, all then working in an Expressionist style.

A programme was issued by the Berlin *Arbeitsrat* calling for the dissolution of existing academic bodies, reform of the art and architectural schools, establishment of Palaces of the People and democratisation of the museums; also for the demolition of ugly buildings and monuments and the institution of 'a comprehensive utopian building programme including pictorial and sculptural

Left Utopian Expressionist architectural fantasy. Bruno Taut's project for a 'Monument of the New Law: inscribed on coloured, shining glass'.
Below Max Pechstein's cover for the revolutionary pamphlet *To all artists*, 1919.

designs'. It published a booklet of comments by its members, which included a plan for an ideal city by Klein and Schmidt-Rottluff, and in 1919-20 held a series of exhibitions in the Lehrter Station. Such utopian schemes were traceable above all to Bruno Taut, who together with Gropius and Behne organised an exhibition of 'Unknown Architects' at J. B. Neumann's gallery in April 1919 and published four books of architectural fantasy, such as *Die Auflösung der Städte* (1920) in which his extraordinary, clumsy drawings of 'the great star-temple' ('no hotels, you put up tents') or the ruby-red glass temple called 'sanctity of all who glow' are bolstered by long quotations from Landauer, Kropotkin, Nietzsche, Paul Scheerbart, the German Romantics and Whitman's *Pioneers*. Taut had an evident influence on Gropius, whose conception of a 'cathedral of the future' was outlined in a pamphlet issued for the exhibition, and the architects whom he showed in it or recruited into a 'Glass Chain' of like-minded utopians produced a number of exceedingly original, more or less unrealisable and (in terms of the social needs of the time) incongruous schemes of which those of Hermann Finsterlin in particular still seem entirely amazing. Beside Gropius and Finsterlin this group included Hans Scharoun and the Luckhardt brothers. Erich Mendelsohn and Hans Poelzig, who were to build the actual buildings most often termed Expressionist, were not of the party.

Even in so heady an atmosphere not all the avant-garde ranged itself on the Left. Dehmel's Christmas declaration of 1918, proclaiming (in thirty newspapers) that it was a crime for England to 'enrich herself with our colonies' and accusing Germany's southern and eastern neighbours of acting as 'jackals' by annexing districts which 'for centuries had been respected as bastions of German culture', was signed not only by such older writers as Eulenberg, Holz, Mombert and Thomas Mann but also by certain of those now counted as Expressionists, notably Heynicke, Johst and the playwright Julius Maria Becker (author of *Das letzte Gericht,* 'a passion in fourteen stations'). But the overwhelming mood of the movement was Socialist, and several of its members were even more to the left: thus Becher had joined the USPD (or Independent Socialists) when that party was formed in 1917, as did Pfemfert and Hasenclever, then went over to the Spartacists, though he was unwilling to join in their Berlin revolt of January 1919. Rubiner, who now propagated the ideas of the Proletkult, was certainly pro-Bolshevik, as was Otten. The nearest realisation of such people's idea of the revolution occurred in Bavaria, where there was a USPD premier, Kurt Eisner, who not only was prepared to take an interest in the arts (and had himself written a play) but invited the twenty-four year old poet Ernst Toller to be his secretary. Toller almost immediately became vice-chairman of the central council of workers', peasants' and soldiers' councils, then, after Eisner's assassination in Munich by a young aristocrat in February 1919, chairman of the party in that city. In April the Bavarian *Räterepublik*, or Republic of Councils, was set up with Landauer and Mühsam among the People's Representatives as well as some genuine madmen, one of whom became Commissar for Foreign Affairs. According to Count Kessler's diary Mühsam asked Becher to come and take part too, but he refused on the grounds of political inexperience.

After a week General von Epp's right-wing private army began advancing, and the new Communist party took control of the flimsily-based republic. 'I most bitterly regret' wrote Landauer to its 'action committee' on 16 April, 'that my work, the work of warmth and revival, culture and renewal, is not what is now primarily being promoted.' Toller became military commander defending the northern suburbs, towards Dachau, but by his own account refused either to shell that town as ordered by the Communists or to shoot five White officers who were made prisoner when he none the less took it. After some ten days he resigned. This did not stop him from being arrested once Epp's troops had entered Munich, and sentenced to five years' imprisonment for high treason. Mühsam was given fifteen years for the same offence. Landauer, so an eyewitness told Toller, was captured and knocked about, beaten to the ground with a whip by a Major von Gagern, then shot two or three times by a lance-sergeant, who finally trampled him to death. Utopia had been put down.

Bayerisches Polizeiblatt.

Herausgegeben von der Polizeidirektion München.

3040

10000 Mark Belohnung.

Wegen Hochverrats

nach § 81 Ziff. 2 des RStGB. ist Haftbefehl erlassen gegen den hier abgebildeten Studenten der Rechte und der Philosophie

Ernst Toller.

Er ist geboren am 1. Dezember 1893 in Samotschin in Posen, Reg.-Bez. Bromberg, Kreis Kolmar, Amtsger. Margonin, als Sohn der Kaufmannseheleute Max u. Ida Toller, geb. Kohn.

Toller ist von schmächtiger Statur und lungenkrank; er ist etwa 1,65—1,68 m groß, hat mageres, blasses Gesicht, trägt keinen Bart, hat große braune Augen, scharfen Blick, schließt beim Nachdenken die Augen, hat dunkle, beinahe schwarze wellige Haare, spricht schriftdeutsch.

Für seine Ergreifung und für Mitteilungen, die zu seiner Ergreifung führen, ist eine Belohnung von

zehntausend Mark

ausgesetzt.

Solche Mitteilungen können an die Staatsanwaltschaft, die Polizeidirektion München oder an die Stadtkommandantur München — Fahndungsabteilung gerichtet werden.

Um eifrigste Fahndung, Drahtnachricht bei Festnahme und weitmöglichste Verbreitung dieses Ausschreibens wird ersucht.

Bei Aufgreifung im Auslande wird Auslieferungsantrag gestellt.

München, den 13. Mai 1919.

Der Staatsanwalt bei dem standrechtlichen Gerichte für München.

6 Establishment and inflation

Expressionism and the Weimar Republic

By the summer of 1919 the shape of the new Germany had more or less been decided. The Treaty of Versailles was ratified, the new Weimar constitution approved, the threat of Communist revolution eliminated, the concept of a planned economy abandoned. For those who had hoped for a state based on the ideals of the war – on revolutionary ethics, spiritual renewal, a pulsating collective feeling and the emergence of the 'new man' – the disillusionment was absolute, and since it was primarily the writers to whom this applied it is not surprising that the number of Expressionist magazines published should decline after the end of that year. In one respect at least the party was over: anybody seeking the hopes and tensions which he had found in wartime Expressionism would henceforward have to look somewhere else.

And yet it was not over, because great cultural movements just do not work in so simple a way. To begin with there is a natural time-lag before even the leaders can accept what is happening, then another between setting down their reactions and seeing these in print. There is also a momentum which keeps the original influences still fanning outwards to more distant centres, to new young writers and artists who have not come across them before, or into areas of the arts which have so far been immune. 'Heckel and Kirchner are established classics', wrote Hans von Wedderkop in a report on three west German exhibitions for the 1920 *Jahrbuch der Jungen Kunst*. 'For a time they were regarded as finished, but now there's heckling and kirchnery from every wall.' Not only did a great number of minor Expressionist artists and playwrights, many of them of some merit, spring up after the poetic movement had more or less fizzled out, but the main assault on the apparatus of the German theatre was only just beginning. For the more complicated the machinery of communication, and the less subject to the will of the individual writer and artist, the longer it takes for a given movement to get hold of it. Thus although in painting or in poetry readings, where the artist himself can deliver the finished article, the process

131

is a quick one, the printed word takes longer, the theatre longer still. The cinema only began to become Expressionist in the period which we are dealing with, and the same is true of opera. Architecture, Expressionist enough on paper in 1919, failed to translate such ideas into buildings even in modified, practical form until Mendelsohn's Einstein Tower at Potsdam in 1920-1 and Rudolf Steiner's second Goetheanum at Dornach in Switzerland some five years later.

The running down of a movement like Expressionism would anyway be a staggered and contradictory business, even apart from the question of its survival within the movements now getting ready to succeed it – Dada, the Bauhaus, 'Neue Sachlichkeit' – something which we will leave to be examined in the next chapter. But there was also a special factor in post-revolutionary Germany which had an obvious influence on the further spreading of Expressionist ideas and techniques. The new state, and the new provincial and city governments, which were for the moment predominantly under majority socialist (SPD) control, saw the leading Expressionists as representative of the changes in German society brought by the revolution, with whose aims the movement had associated itself. It was only natural for the authorities to support them with official jobs and official purchases, and this in turn left a lasting mark on the galleries, art teaching and publicly managed theatres of the Weimar Republic long after the movement was supposedly dead. It was not unlike the situation which was developing almost at the same time in the new Soviet Union, where avant-garde artists, writers and theatre people who had associated themselves with the revolution were briefly put in a position to propagate their own revolution in the arts: a parallel which may explain why there were so many cultural exchanges between the two countries in the early 1920s, notably the big Soviet art exhibition at Van Diemen's gallery in Berlin in the winter of 1922. The difference in Russia was that 'advanced' art was less well rooted, so that when the reaction against it came it was a reaction against advanced art as such.

A *Reichskunstwart* or State Art Supervisor was now appointed, Erwin Redslob, whose function was to ensure a worthy standard of

Rise and fall of the Expressionist magazine.
Number of different German-language Expressionist
periodicals being published

Year	At beginning	At end
1917	7	10
1918	15	23
1919	35	44
1920	36	22
1921	?	15
1922	?	8

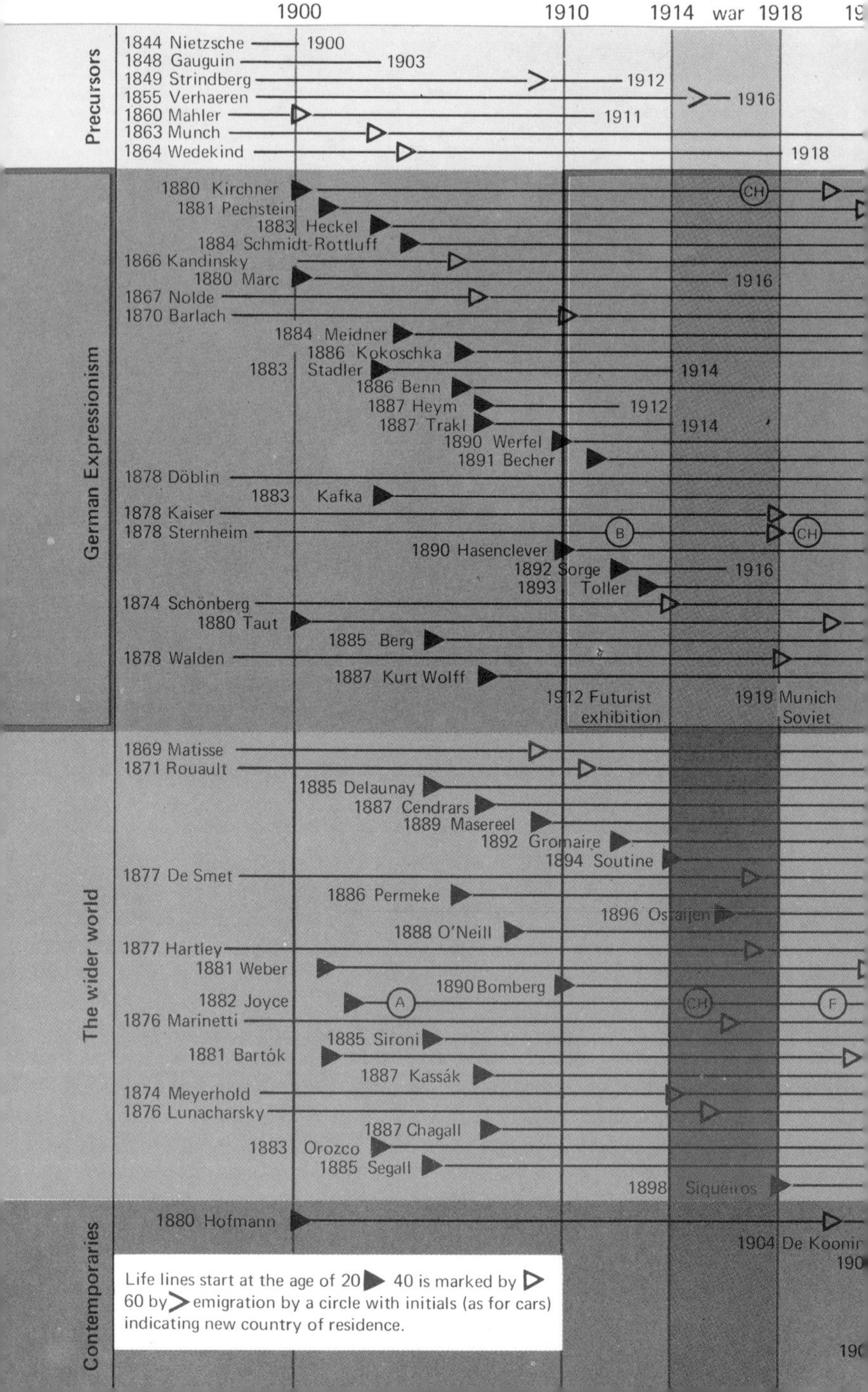
1900
1910
1914
war
1918
Precursors
1844 Nietzsche 1900
1848 Gauguin 1903
1849 Strindberg 1912
1855 Verhaeren 1916
1860 Mahler 1911
1863 Munch
1864 Wedekind 1918
German Expressionism
1880 Kirchner
CH
1881 Pechstein
1883 Heckel
1884 Schmidt-Rottluff
1866 Kandinsky
1880 Marc 1916
1867 Nolde
1870 Barlach
1884 Meidner
1886 Kokoschka
1883 Stadler 1914
1886 Benn
1887 Heym 1912
1887 Trakl 1914
1890 Werfel
1891 Becher
1878 Döblin
1883 Kafka
1878 Kaiser
1878 Sternheim
B
CH
1890 Hasenclever
1892 Sorge 1916
1893 Toller
1874 Schönberg
1880 Taut
1885 Berg
1878 Walden
1887 Kurt Wolff
1912 Futurist exhibition
1919 Munich Soviet
The wider world
1869 Matisse
1871 Rouault
1885 Delaunay
1887 Cendrars
1889 Masereel
1892 Gromaire
1894 Soutine
1877 De Smet
1886 Permeke
1896 Ostaijen
1888 O'Neill
1877 Hartley
1881 Weber
1890 Bomberg
1882 Joyce
A
CH
F
1876 Marinetti
1885 Sironi
1881 Bartók
1887 Kassák
1874 Meyerhold
1876 Lunacharsky
1887 Chagall
1883 Orozco
1885 Segall
1898 Siqueiros
Contemporaries
1880 Hofmann
1904 De Koonin

Life lines start at the age of 20 ▶ 40 is marked by ▷ 60 by > emigration by a circle with initials (as for cars) indicating new country of residence.

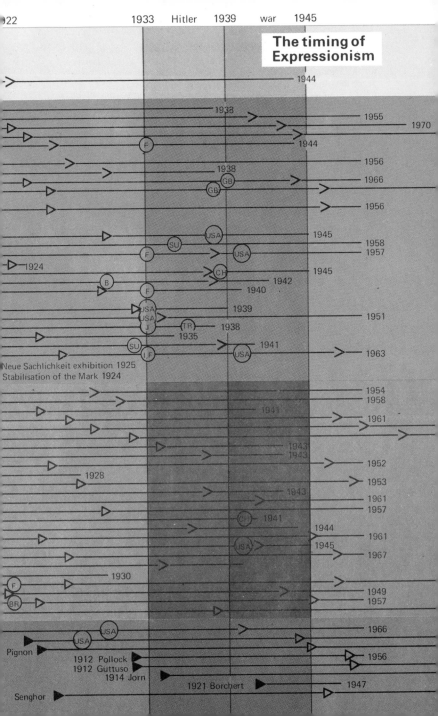

The timing of
Expressionism

922   1933   Hitler   1939   war   1945

1944

1938   1955
                              1970
                    1944

1938   1956
                    GB   1966
    GB
                              1956

            USA   1945
    SU   1958
    F   USA   1957
1924
                CH   1945
    B   1942
    F   1940
    USA   1939
    USA
    J
        TR   1938
1935
    SU I.F   1941
                    1963

Neue Sachlichkeit exhibition 1925
Stabilisation of the Mark 1924

                    1954
                    1958
        1941
                    1961

        1943
        1943
                    1952

1928
                    1953

            1943
                    1961
                    1957

        CH 1941
            1944
                    1961
        USA 1945
                    1967

1930
F   1949
BR   1957

USA
USA   1966

Pignon   1956
1912 Pollock
1912 Guttuso
1914 Jorn
            1921 Borchert
Senghor   1947

The association of Expressionism with the German revolution, in its phase of consolidation and establishment. From left to right: Poster for the Weimar National Assembly, 1919, by Cesar Klein of the Neue Sezession, an artist best known for his stage and film work. New republican German eagle by Karl Schmidt-Rottluff of the Brücke (from Hellmut Lehmann-Haupt's *Art under Dictatorship*). Lyonel Feininger's

design in all government publications, coins, stamps and other national emblems. Symbolically, Schmidt-Rottluff designed a new, republican German eagle. Among those given professorships in the art schools under its wing were Kokoschka (Dresden, 1919), Klein and Hofer (Berlin Kunstakademie, 1919), Otto Mueller and Oskar Moll (Breslau, 1919), Nauen (Düsseldorf, 1920), Campendonk (Essen, 1922), and in due course Beckmann (Frankfurt, 1925). In 1919 again Gropius took over the former Grand-ducal art and applied art schools in Weimar and was authorised by the USPD-led provincial government to rename the combined establishment 'State *Bauhaus*', issuing the first manifesto very much on *Arbeitsrat* lines that spring. The cover of this document bore a woodcut called 'Cathedral of Socialism' by Feininger, who was one of Gropius's first two appointments to the staff. A comparable process took place rather more slowly in the Prussian Academy of Arts, the nearest German equivalent to an Académie Française.

136

woodcut 'Cathedral of Socialism' for the Bauhaus manifesto of April 1919 (a print that is now generally reproduced without mention of its hopeful political title).

Liebermann, then aged 73, became the president in 1920, and new members included Barlach (1919), Rohlfs (1920) and Pechstein (1922); though the major transformation did not occur till 1931, under the Socialist education minister Adolf Grimme, when Nolde, Schmidt-Rottluff, Kirchner and Erich Mendelsohn were among those elected and Heinrich Mann was made president of the writers' section formed four years before. In the theatre the most important appointment was that of the Socialist Königsberg *Intendant* Leopold Jessner in the summer of 1919 to direct the newly-named Staatstheater in Berlin, the former Prussian Royal Theatre. A year later Weichert was appointed to Frankfurt, Gustav Hartung to Darmstadt and Carl Zeiss to the theatres in Munich.

In the museums there was a marked change of policy, summed up in the government's decision during the spring of 1919 that the National-Galerie in Berlin should be allowed to buy modern pictures. Accordingly a separate offshoot of the gallery was opened that

137

A new public gallery for modern art: the Kronprinzenpalais in Berlin. *Above* Kokoschka's 'The Friends', 1917-18, a Dresden group including Hasenclever, centre, which was sold after 1937 and is now in the Neue Galerie der Stadt Linz. *Below* View of the gallery around 1925, showing Marc's 'Tower of Blue Horses', right, subsequently destroyed, and Heckel's 'Ostend Madonna', far left through door.

August, the Kronprinzen-Palais under Kaesbach, who had become a member of the Arbeitsrat. Among the first works which he acquired were Marc's 'The Tower of Blue Horses' two Feiningers, Kokoschka's 'The Friends' (a group painted in Dresden in 1917-18), a Pechstein, two Schmidt-Rottluffs, the 'Ostend Madonna' and three other Heckels, Kirchner's 'Kölner Rheinbrücke' and 'The Street' (now in the Museum of Modern Art, New York), and a still-life by Nauen. Ludwig Justi, the director, himself introduced these pictures in the official guide book, speaking of Expressionism's distortions as 'a sharp, conscious renunciation of accuracy', and the actual term as being 'commonly used for present-day forms which in certain respects differ widely from one another, the definition varying with the agency or group of artists making it'. In Dresden, where Paul Ferdinand Schmidt became director of the municipal gallery in 1919, the main (State) gallery bought a Hofer in 1918 and works by Kokoschka, Pascin and Beckmann in 1920, while Schmidt bought the local artist Lasar Segall's 'Die ewigen Wanderer', Kokoschka's 'Die Heiden' and works by Dix, Grosz and Schwitters in his first two years of office. One provincial gallery after another shows a similar pattern: nothing, or at best the odd water-colour, bought from the Expressionists before about 1920, then a succession of purchases from the more representational (or Brücke-influenced wing), often followed by exhibitions mainly of the Brücke artists. At the same time important private collectors were also picking on these painters; thus an exhibition of Berlin private collections at the Kronprinzenpalais in 1928 showed the pictures bought by Bernhard Koehler (who had died the year before), the banker and former USPD Finance Minister Hugo Simon (early Kirchners, Kokoschka, Marc, Feininger etc.), Walter Heymann (sixty-five Pechsteins) and a number of others including Fritz Schön, Hugo Benario, Julius Freudenberg, Robert Graetz and Erich Mendelsohn. In Frankfurt one substantial collection of Kirchner's work (now in the Städelsches Institut there) was made by the industrialist Carl Hagemann; another by Rosi and Ludwig Fischer. Kaesbach was appointed to the Erfurt museum, and in 1922 commissioned Heckel to paint

138

Private patrons. *Below* Pechstein's woodcut of Alfred Hess, the Erfurt industrialist. *Right* Kirchners hanging in the Frankfurt flat of Ludwig and Rosi Fischer, around 1920.

murals there; he gave his own Expressionist collection (primarily Heckel, Nauen and Rohlfs) to his home town of Mönchen-Gladbach. The Erfurt industrialist Alfred Hess bought Pechstein and Feininger, Rohlfs, Schmidt-Rottluff and much else; his close relations with the artists can be judged from the drawings and remarks in his visitors' book, published by his son under the title *Dank in Farben*.

All this made a market not only for Expressionist paintings – it has been reckoned that Brücke prices had already gone up ten times by 1919 – but for portfolios of prints and illustrated books, which dealers or publishers now hastened to provide. These and the many art books now appearing (such as Klinckhardt and Biermann's sixty or so *Junge Kunst* monographs on the new painters, starting with Georg Biermann's own study of Pechstein in 1919), got around Germany far faster than the pictures themselves could do. They included such sequences of prints as those by Beckmann (*Die Hölle* 1919, *Stadtnacht* 1920, *Der Jahrmarkt* 1921, *Berliner Reise* 1922) and Otto Dix (six portfolios in 1921–22 and the fifty horrifying

140

etchings of *Der Krieg* in 1924). Kurt Wolff published Masereel's masterpiece *Mein Stundenbuch* in 1921, following it with both limited and cheap editions of his other woodcut series, and commissioning him to illustrate four novels by Charles-Louis Philippe which appeared between 1920-2. Also in 1922 Hans Mardersteig, Wolff's adviser in these matters (who figures with Carl Georg Heise, the subsequent director of the Lübeck Museum, in a splendid double portrait of 1919 by Kokoschka now in the Boymans Museum), arranged for Kirchner to make one of the finest of all such books, the illustrated reprint of Heym's *Umbra Vitae* which appeared in 1924. For five or six years there was what G. F. Hartlaub has called 'an avalanche-like increase in production', promoted above all by the inflation of the Mark; too much quick profit chasing too few stable investments. It was to shut off like a tap once the currency had been got under control at the end of 1923, Dix's *Der Krieg* for instance, finding only a single subscriber.

The history of Expressionism's conquest of the provinces has yet to be written. In Dresden, where the movement now got a second wind, a number of young artists including Segall and Dix formed a 'Gruppe 1919' in the local Sezession, while new periodicals such as the characteristically-named *Menschen* (1918-21), the *Neue Blätter für Kunst und Dichtung* (1918-21) and *Die neue Schaubühne* (1919-22) mixed local with nationally known contributors. A report published in the art review *Ararat* in 1920 found that the Dresden critics were only too anxious to keep up with the latest developments, and that both city and provincial authorities were supporting the purchase of modern pictures for the galleries; lectures were being given on Expressionism and there was no sign of opposition. A comparable situation existed in Hanover, where the formation of a Sezession in 1917 had been followed by the arrival of the painters Max Burchartz, a characteristic minor Expressionist (e.g. his *Raskolnikoff* portfolio of lithographs published by Flechtheim's gallery in Düsseldorf), and Otto Gleichmann. Kurt Schwitters too was then painting in a sombrely Expressionist style, while the reviews *Das hohe Ufer* and *Der Zweemann* (both 1919-20) together with Paul Steegemann's publication of the 'Silbergäule' series of booklets (from 1919 on) helped create a genuine local movement. In Darmstadt, the home of Count Keyserling's mystical-philosophical 'School of Wisdom', there were Hartung's stage productions and a new periodical *Das Tribunal* (1919-21) modelled on *Die Aktion,* which emerged from a wartime writers' group called 'Die Dachstube' and was edited by the subsequent SPD deputy Carlo Mierendorff with Edschmid's support. In Hamburg there was the magazine *Die rote Erde* (1919-23) directed by Karl Lorenz, whose opening editorial was in the high utopian vein:

Man, we say! Only Man! Earth, we say! Only Earth! All must become, will become! So we hammer, we glow and send out sparks, we wield paintbrush and charcoal, we manipulate the pen! ..

In Düsseldorf in 1920, where Alfred Flechtheim had just started dealing seriously in the modern French and Germans, a group of artists including Max Ernst and Otto Pankok formed 'Das junge Rheinland', a society which lasted till 1926 and was supported by another local dealer, Johanna Ey. This was already moving away from Expressionism, but even leaving aside the old centres like Vienna, Zürich, Munich and Leipzig, with their internationally important galleries and publishers, there were nodules of Expressionist activity in Mannheim, Kiel, Königsberg, Brno and many other places.

Spreading the Expressionist gospel. Cover of the first of Klinckhardt
and Biermann's *Junge Kunst* booklets. 1919.

15. Januar 1918 – Nr. 1

Copyright by Felix Stiemer Verlag 1918

Wundern Sie sich Ausrufungszeichen Es gibt Menschen Punkt Wundern Sie sich, daß es Menschen gibt Fragezeichen Ja, es gibt Menschen Punkt Punkt Punkt – es gibt Menschen.

Der Blitz dieser Entscheidung treffe Sie, das Feuer dieser Erkenntnis zerschlage Sie so tief – bis .... Wie, Sie sitzen noch immer regungslos vor mir, Sie beten noch immer die lange steife Linie an, statt einmal, ein einziges Mal den Sprung ins Chaos zu wagen, den Sturz, dessen Wirbel allein die Flamme, die heilige Flamme der Menschlichkeit aufschließt bis in die tiefste Höhe der absoluten Bewußt= heit. Aber – träg und schwer liegt die Erde, der Rest von Glut=Geist in den Händen der Erniedrigten und Beleidigten, die ihren Herz= körper zuckend aufrissen, Mensch um Mensch zu rühren, bereit den wahren Blutbund der Menschen zu formen. O, um dieser neuen Form willen – Menschen auf Erden – wurden Milliarden und Milliarden anderer verschwendet, das wache Leben zu töten. Aber – und verpufften sie alles für den Tod des Geistes, – das absolute Bewußtsein wäre stärker, schüfe sich einen letzten Träger. Ihr Menschen vor mir, gedankt sei dem Leben, noch ist diese letzte Zeit nicht da, aber – Minuten zählen – sie kommt, wenn Ihr Euch nicht schleunigst besinnt und jubelnd – denn es muß jubelnd geschehen – den Sprung ins Erleben wagt. Sekunde zählt! Wagt den Sprung in das Leben, das heilig tiefe Leben; erst, wenn Ihr Euch in Menschlichkeit aufge= löst, werden gerührt und überinnig aus Eurer Mitte Zerstehen der Zeit Not, der Unendlich= keit Träger,

Menschen!

Bess Brenck Kalischer

FELIX STIEMER
VERLAG DRESDEN

Left The cover of the characteristically-named Dresden magazine *Menschen*, with woodcut by Conrad Felixmüller. *Right* Lettering on the cover of Alfred Wolfenstein's *Die Erhebung*, vol. 2.

The poetic climax

Like Reinhardt and Cassirer before November 1918, so now Samuel Fischer, the Insel-Verlag and other orthodox publishers saw that the Expressionists were not to be laughed off any longer. One result was Fischer's publication in 1919-20 of a new big two-volume Expressionist anthology called *Die Erhebung* edited by Alfred Wolfenstein; then Wolff's old partner Rowohlt followed suit at the end of 1919 with *Menschheitsdämmerung*, the most famous of all collections of Expressionist poetry, and a prose counterpart called *Die Entfaltung* a year later, with Pinthus and Max Krell respectively as editors. Though there were other anthologies published in the same years, and some even later, it was these that most came to represent Expressionism in the public mind. *Die Erhebung I* immediately reprinted, to total 7000 copies in 1919, while *Menschheitsdämmerung* had reached 20,000 by 1922. The 1959 paperback edition has sold even better.

Both collections were evidently planned at the climax of the literary movement, as Pinthus's foreword shows clearly enough, with its concept of a 'symphony of the newest poetry' (this being

145

his collection's sub-title) in four movements – 'Collapse and Cry', 'Awakening of the Heart', 'Exhortation and Anger' and 'Love of Man' – and its reference once more to Beethoven's Ninth. Wolfenstein, who had discussed the plan of his two volumes with Landauer before his murder, spoke of the masses as feeling

with confident joy the self-abandonment of their oceanic movement, the gradual fusion of the individual in an increasingly jubilant Humanity

– a sensation which he felt his contributors would voice for them. Pinthus, who must have concluded his essay a little later, appeals to 'Future Humanity'

not to condemn this procession of those condemned to their aspirations, with nothing left but their hope in Man and their belief in Utopia.

Thus the interest of the four volumes is a double one. They are at once a last parade of the writers before disillusionment broke them up, and a first effort to relate the movement's multiple aspects. *Die Erhebung* in particular includes not only prose and dramatic works alongside the poetry but interesting studies of the other arts.

Any curious member of the public around 1920 who picked up these books to see what Expressionism was about must have concluded that its essence was high social-humanitarian generalisation of the kind described in the preceding chapter. For in *Menschheitsdämmerung,* whose very title 'Dawn' (or twilight) 'of Humanity' is hardly suggestive of small-scale private poetry, the dominant voices are those of Becher, Werfel, Ehrenstein, Däubler, Rudolf Leonhard, Heynicke and Wolfenstein (all of whom are represented in *Die Erhebung* too) together with Hasenclever, Rubiner, Otten and Zech (who are not). Pinthus's aim was to blend these with the more ironic, imaginative or symbolist verse written before 1914 – e.g. by Heym, Van Hoddis, Lichtenstein, Trakl and Lotz – though another school of thought argued that two such distinct groups would not mix. The inevitable Else Lasker-Schüler is also there, and so, on sheer merit no doubt, is Benn. Werfel, with twenty-seven poems, is quite rightly the star of the show; for he was not only the apparent originator of much that came to be thought characteristic of the movement but also responsible for some of its (alas rather infrequent) work of real quality. In *Die Erhebung,* for instance, there is an outstanding childhood story of his, actually no more Expressionist than his fine neglected novel of adolescence *Der Abituriententag* (1928), and a reflective, intuitive 'Song of a Woman' which seems

far above the ordinary level of the times: for instance the first
section –

> Warum warum diese neue Angst? Die Welt ist schon so oft.
> Und Oft ein Wort, das fort und fort ins Ohr tropft unverhofft,
> Ein rundes Wort, ein runder Laut, der endet und beschliesst.
> Mir graut vor meinem Haar,
> Es war so oft, mein Hand war oft, mein Mund war oft, war, war!
> Meine Zunge war oft, meine Brust und was er geniesst.
> Mir graut, es graut auch meinem Haar.
> Oft ist unfassliche Gefahr.
>
> (Why, why this latest terror? The world's often like that.
> And 'often' is a word you've heard and heard, yet still baulk at,
> A rounded word, a rounded sound to shut things off.
> I'm frightened by my hair,
> It was so often, hand was often, mouth so often was, was there!
> My tongue was often, my breast and all I love.
> I'm grey with fright, as grey as is my hair.
> 'Often's' a threat of which you're unaware.)

Apart from Heynicke, who sometimes combined the worst
features of Stramm and of Becher (there is an unbelievable poem of
his called 'Volk', which starts 'My People/Bloom for ever, People...'),
the one notable new recruit to both anthologies was Wilhelm
Klemm, a thirty-eight year old army doctor whose poems had been
published by *Die Aktion*. His condensed style and sometimes
artificial word order, together with his images of 'staggerings and
confusions', link him with the movement, even though a good deal
of his work seems to reflect earlier influences: e.g. the poem 'Moon-
light', with its 'sea-blue harps' and 'The moon's silver dolphins'.
Another good poet printed by Pinthus was Iwan Goll, whose long
poem of 1912 on the digging of the Panama Canal put modern
technology in the utopian, brotherly light which it was to lose with
his development away from the movement. In Wolfenstein's
selection, which includes none of the pre-war poets, there is a much
better representation of quite new or unknown writers. Among them
are notably his wife Henriette Hardenberg, whose 'Southern
Heart' has authentic Expressionist features:

> Blüte sitzt tief,
> Bergspitzen biegen sich hin,
> Wind ausgeruht liegt
> Der Baum steht starr.

> (Blossom sits deep,
> Mountain peaks bend over,
> Wind rested lies,
> The tree stands stiff.

Da plözlich erblüht	Then suddenly there blooms
Mitten ins Herz hinein	Straight into the heart's centre
Brennend sitzt du in mir Baum.	Burning you sit in me, tree.
Nirgend ist Ruhe in mir,	Nowhere is rest in me,
In Flammen schreie ich auf,	In flames I cry aloud,
Ein Meer in allem bewegt.	A sea set moving.
Da zucken auch sie	Then they too twitch,
Blüte und Baum	Blossom and tree,
Schon rot von ihrer Süsse.	Now red from their sweetness.)

and Georg Kulka, an Austrian who was to die in 1929 in his early thirties: part of his 'The Voice' goes:

Aufgeschleuderte Gassen hangen fest mit geborstnem Gewimmel.
Menschen, an Gletschern gespiesst und geklammert an Kluft.
Rauchend Signal ist als Nordschein droben am Himmel.
Lange Aschenwolken der Städte dunsten pfeilschnell durch die Luft.

Strasse gellt schweifend. Und wie
Gewölbt wir auch weinen,
Stäubt recht indiskutabel
Ein Oh
Zentimeterhoch auf.

(Upslung streets hang on by their teeth with bristling crowds.
People pierced by glaciers or wedged in crevasses.
A smoke signal stands like northern lights in the clouds.
Long sooty fog from the cities exhales as it rapidly passes.

Street resounds slanting. And however
Arched our weeping,
Incontrovertibly like dust will rise
An Oh
Some inches high.)

Not all the contributors to *Die Erhebung* can be called Expressionist; Rilke is there for instance, also Oskar Loerke, who had by then started his long stint as a *Lektor* for Fischer: and of course no editor, offered a good poem, is going to be all that rigid about its affiliations. Perhaps the most interesting instance in this book is Max Herrmann-Neisse, a long-standing contributor to *Die Aktion* and other Expressionist journals, whose poems 'Busse' and 'Der zuletzt Verlorene' have just that combination of formal smoothness and resigned pessimism which was the opposite of the utopian Expressionist formula and soon became characteristic of Neue Sachlichkeit.

Ideally the Expressionist poets should be taken singly. For such great group demonstrations only show up the weaknesses of the movement. These are not so much formal – though aside from Stramm it is striking how very few formal innovations there were – as a monotony of theme, tone and vocabulary which becomes all the more trying for the reader because the poet's idea of his role is so inflatedly public-spirited. The reiterated emphasis on Man ('Ever unites us the word: MAN' writes Heynicke, all too truly), on Brotherhood, on *Volk* ('*Mein Volk! Mein Volk!*' shouts Becher, while the same term occurs nine times as single lines in Heynicke's short 'Sturmgesang'), on Ecstasy, and on the *Schrei* (shout, or cry) very soon seems bombastic and unconvincing. The favourite verbs grow too forcedly dramatic (*schwanken, wanken, stürzen, zacken, beben*) or portentous (*jubeln, jauchzen, tönen, glühen*) in both sound and meaning; there are too many exclamations, too many crystal cathedrals of the future, shapeless jellies like Taut's architectural projects or the mystical erections of anthroposophy. The 'existential' thinking is often hollow, especially with Werfel, who makes the 'life-affirming' discovery that 'We are!' serve not only as the punch line of more than one poem but also as the title of a book of verse, reminding us embarrassingly of P. G. Wodehouse's poet Rockmettler Todd who wrote such lines as 'Be!/Be with every drop of your red blood!' and never got up until lunchtime. Nor would it be easy anywhere to find a poem quite to match Becher's 'Hymn to Rosa Luxemburg', with its lines

> Notschrei Jeremias
> Ekstatischer Auftakt
> Gewitter-Sätze versammelt in dir.
> Blanke unschuldvolle
> Reine jungfrauweisse
> Taube Glaubens-Saft*
> Ob Tribünen-Altar schwebend Hostie hoch.

---

*Unhappily suggestive of *Traubensaft*, or grape-juice, as used for non-alcoholic communion wine. Becher had no sense of the ridiculous.

> (Alarm-cry Jeremiah
> Ecstatic upbeat.
> Thunder-phrases collected in you.
> Shining innocent
> Pure virgin-white
> Dove love-juice
> Over rostrum-altar hovering Host high.)

and its ending:

> Den geschundenen Leib
> Abnehmend vom Kreuz,
> In weicheste Linnen ihn hüllend
> Triumph dir durch die Welten blase ich:
> Dir, Einzige!! Dir, Heilige!! O Weib!!!
>
> (Taking the flayed body
> Down from the cross,
> Wrapping it in softest linen
> Through the worlds I blow you triumph:
> You, peerless one!! You, holy one!! O woman!!!)

It is still exceptional to come across writing that can properly be called Expressionist prose, not just imaginative fantasy, or Old Testament legend, or poetic fine writing, or quite orthodoxly-expressed humanitarianism, or work by authors known as Expressionists primarily for their work in other media. One instance is Hans Fallada's (pseudonym for Rudolf Ditzen) first 'novel of adolescence', *Der junge Goedeschal*, published by Rowohlt in 1920, which includes such characteristic imagery as:

He staggered. Garishly lit houses loomed up out of the dark as if seen from a speeding train, then removed themselves from sight with a sombre, arbitrary gesture. No resting place! Stumbling, falling forward, he began to run, brushed past walls whose pores seemed to exude a sweaty slime ...

Of the writers represented in *Die Erhebung* and *Die Entfaltung,* for instance, starting with Sternheim, Buber, Heinrich Mann and Annette Kolb, only Edschmid and Gustav Sack (yet another victim of the war), and perhaps Döblin, wrote truly Expressionist stories, to be identified by their hacked-up sentences, jerky continuity and emotive use of visual distortion. Even they did not always do so, and not in the examples selected by Krell. Against that, *Die Erhebung* did include important plays by Kornfeld and Arnolt Bronnen and

150

above all part of *Die Wandlung* by Toller, who by that time was famous as a revolutionary leader but still scarcely known as a writer. And at least Wolfenstein as editor attempted to draw the various threads of the movement together, getting Bruno Taut to present his concept of architecture as 'crystallisation of the sense of community', with illustrations by himself and several of his utopian colleagues, while Hermann Scherchen wrote on 'The new leadership in music'.

Music, theatre and film

This essay of Scherchen's is interesting, because it apparently did not occur to him to class Schönberg and his followers with the Expressionists. Of the three great personalities whom he put forward as 'leaders' it was Mahler, he felt, whose creative springs lay in his 'very deep love of all human Brotherhood and his belief in the equal power of all hearts', while Schönberg, as a pioneer whose work could in those days only be grasped by initiates, was 'far from our time'. It is true that the visionary element in this composer had been appreciated by Kandinsky, who also wrote the chapter on his paintings for a pre-war Schönberg symposium by Alban Berg and others; but Schönberg himself had no use for the typical Expressionist characteristics of exaggeration and chaos, since he felt that he was above all searching for order. If the term 'Expressionism' has any meaning at all in connection with the music of this period it is rather in relation to the stage. Here the works of Bartók, such as his opera *King Bluebeard's Castle* to a text by Béla Balász, which was produced in Budapest and at Frankfurt in May 1922, were perhaps more relevant than those of the Viennese school, since Bartók's combination of elemental dynamism with primitive influences (folksong) and distorted harmonies can at least be said to have some analogies with Expressionist painting. Admittedly, with the development of Expressionist methods in the theatre the German opera houses became inclined to apply them to any more or less contemporary work. But no composer of consequence seems to have worked on actual Expressionist libretti till the young Paul Hindemith made operas of Kokoschka's *Mörder Hoffnung der Frauen* (first performed at Stuttgart on 4 June 1921) and Stramm's *Sancta Susanna*. The outstanding opera of this period, Berg's *Wozzeck,* based on the unfinished Büchner play which itself was one of the forefathers of theatrical Expressionism, was not staged till 1925

151

(Berlin State Opera). Kurt Weill made operas of Kaiser's short plays *Der Protagonist* and *Der Zar lässt sich photographieren* (1926 and 1928) but both text and music were already in the style and spirit of Neue Sachlichkeit. Berg's other opera *Lulu* was far closer to the Expressionist tradition, but was only performed after his death in 1935.

In the theatre proper the great Expressionist boom began in Berlin in 1919. The three immediate landmarks here were Jessner's own first production at the reorganised Staatstheater; the opening of Reinhardt's Grosses Schauspielhaus, designed by Hans Poelzig (an architect whose massive and arbitrarily-formed buildings are sometimes termed Expressionist) and seating five thousand; and the production of Toller's first play *Die Wandlung* at a tiny short-lived left-wing theatre called Die Tribüne. In a sense they were complementary events. Jessner's success meant not only the establishment of a new style of production, based on the use of great flights of steps (clearly derived from Appia and Craig) and of sculptural and

atmospheric spotlighting, but above all the emergence of a theatre
to set against Reinhardt's, and one in which experimental ideas
would not be ruled out. Reinhardt's own concern with the mass
audience, though it did not last long, was partly a development of
his previous interest in open-air or circus productions – the Grosses
Schauspielhaus itself was the former Zirkus Schumann – but also a
product of the revolutionary, democratic climate, which was to
some extent reflected in the plays which he chose to present there:
not only *Hamlet* and the *Oresteia* but Rolland's *Danton,* Hasenclever's *Antigone* (April 1920) and Toller's *The Machine Wreckers*
(June 1922). Finally, the impact of *Die Wandlung* was a multiple
one, simultaneously making the reputations of the theatre's two
founders, the producer Karlheinz Martin (who went to the Grosses
Schauspielhaus) and the actor Fritz Kortner (who went to the
Staatstheater), establishing a new form of setting (by Robert
Neppach) which was expressive but economical, and introducing
the second generation of Expressionist playwrights.

Until 1923, when the Berlin theatre fell into a strange crisis of
uncertainty, there was throughout Germany a brief golden age for
the Expressionist drama, accompanied by such secondary symptoms as passionately involved audiences and a quite outstanding
group of critics. The theatres were now open to the Expressionist
playwright – to an extent that is almost unbelievable when one reads
some of the scripts – while powerful actors like Kortner, George,
Deutsch, Krauss, Agnes Straub and Gerda Müller were prepared to
identify themselves with Expressionist productions. As a result the
earlier group of playwrights, apart from Goering, who abandoned
writing for ten years after his *Der Erste* had fallen flat in 1918, now
found itself on the crest of a wave. Unruh's *Platz,* an immensely
long sequel to *Ein Geschlecht* with interminable blank-verse
monologues and a Parsifal-like hero, was produced by Hartung at
Frankfurt in June 1920. Other new plays given that year included
Hasenclever's *Menschen* and *Jenseits* (respectively cinematic and
mystical, but both pretty hollow), Johst's *Der König* (on the quite
common Expressionist theme of the ideal autocrat, whether monar-

153

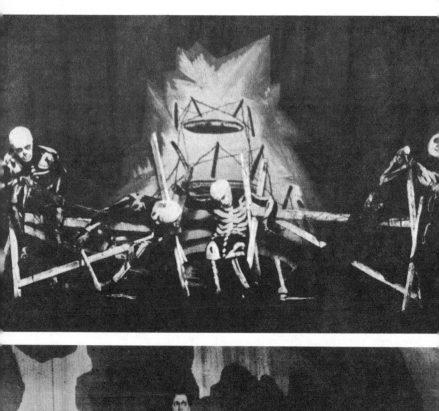

chical, dictatorial or, as in *Gas,* industrial), and Kornfeld's confused, abrupt, declamatory *Himmel und Hölle.*

Kaiser remained extremely productive, and as variable as ever in his approach. *Europa,* written five years earlier and staged by Martin in the Grosses Schauspielhaus in November 1920, is a totally un-Expressionist piece of light classical pastiche, with a good deal of dancing. *Gas II,* staged at Brno the previous month, is a Wellsian fantasy, ending up with total destruction as the new hero, the Millionaire-Worker, reluctantly lets off the lethal gas bomb which his *Grossingenieur* or super-engineer has devised. *Hölle Weg Erde,* first produced by Hellmer in Frankfurt in December 1919, then immediately after at the Lessing Theatre in Berlin with sets by Cesar Klein, is a much more Expressionist play, combining the desperate 'station-drama' restlessness of *Von Morgens bis Mitternachts* with Kaiser's particular balance and symmetry. It deals with an artist called (no doubt symbolically) Spazierer, or Walker, who tries to raise money to save a friend from suicide and ends up leading a mixed mob of the prisoners, warders, lawyer, hotel-keeper, society girls among whom his 'stations' have taken him, to build a whole new world. The dialogue here is perhaps the most stylised and compressed of any Kaiser play: for instance the Escaped Convict's Joycean exclamations 'I broke out – wallover – jumpdeep –' or the formal exchanges which occur twice at the start and once at the end of the first prison scene, so as to frame it in:

Haftsoldat:	Der Häftling.
Hafthausleutnant:	Person nach dem Rotzettel?
Häftling:	Ich bin – nicht schuldig!
Hafthausleutnant:	Die Frage gilt nur: die Person nach diesem Rotzettel?
Häftling:	Ich bin – so nicht schuldig!
Hafthausleutnant:	Die Frage dreimal: die Person nach diesem Rotzettel Sie?
Häftling:	Niemand ist so schuldig –: nier losgerissen von Menschen!
Hafthausleutnant:	Person ist Häftling.

(Warder:	The prisoner.
Lieutenant:	Individual on this warrant?

Prisoner:	I am – not guilty!
Lieutenant:	The question is simply: the individual on this warrant?
Prisoner:	I am – not guilty like that!
Lieutenant:	For the third time, same question: the individual on this warrant you?
Prisoner:	Nobody is guilty like that – : here torn away from people!
Lieutenant:	Individual is prisoner.)

(The stage directions are here omitted.) *Kanzlist Krehler*, another play which seems to echo *Von Morgens bis Mitternachts,* was written in 1922.

Some of the most famous of the Expressionist playwrights only emerged now. The chief of these was Toller, whose passionate play *Die Wandlung,* subtitled 'A Man's Wrestling' had enough genuine feeling and personal experience behind its six 'stations' to come as a breath of fresh air. This was still a wholly Expressionist play, from its prefatory verses (with the phrase 'There cried a Man'), through its almost entirely anonymous characters, its initial bow in the direction of Strindberg, its assumption that the ego-hero is called on to be a *Führer,* and the imagery of his utopian visions:

> Nun öffnet sich, aus Weltenschoss geboren
> Das hochgewölbte Tor der Menschheitskathedrale.
> Die Jugend aller Völker schreitet flammend
> Zum nachtgeahnten Schrein aus leuchtendem Kristall.

> (Now open themselves, born of the world's womb
> The high arched doors of Humanity's cathedral.
> The youth of every people strides flaming
> To the glowing crystal shrine they sensed in the night.)

right up to the ending, where he leads the People to win over the rich by peaceful persuasion, then to storm the 'false strongholds' shouting 'Revolution! Revolution!' So is the much inferior *Masse-Mensch* ('Masses and Man'), a wholly verse play, again with dream interludes, where the opposition of the heroic woman revolutionary and the Nameless One incorporating the Masses seems to represent a conflict in the author's thinking between utopianism (*Mensch*) and the only slightly less abstract Communist concept of *Masse* or the working class. It was staged first in Nuremberg in November 1920, but because the police insisted on an invited audience and a maximum of two performances the general public could not see it till it was produced at the Berlin Volksbühne in September 1921. *Die Maschinenstürmer* the following year was however a fairly straight-

156

forward historical play, with named characters and nothing very Expressionist about it, and the same is even more true of *Hinkemann* ('Brokenbrow') (Leipzig, 19 September 1923), a savage tear-jerker about the strong man who comes back from the war emasculated, with characters (named) and relationships that are sometimes reminiscent of Büchner's *Woyzeck*. Toller's weakness in all these plays was his dialogue, which lacks tension; but the fact that they were written in prison clearly added to the impact which they made. His release in 1924 found him embarrassingly famous, but at the same time somewhat isolated from the changes in his country's climate, which he was never entirely to catch up with. According to his friend Oskar Maria Graf he spoke of those prison years as the happiest time of his life.

There were other new writers, some of them only briefly Expressionist, like Friedrich Wolf (who had taken part with the painter Vogeler in a short-lived utopian community) and Carl Zuckmayer, while Werfel, whose earlier adaption of Euripides's *The Trojan Women* had borne little relation to the movement, now between 1920 and 1922 published three plays of which the ambitious 'magic trilogy' *Spiegelmensch*, dedicated to Alma Mahler, represents a mystical-Faustian development that seems to have made little or no impression on the stage. Leaving aside Arnolt Bronnen, whose best play *Vatermord* combines typically Expressionist themes (parricide and incest) with a new ear for dialogue:

> Fessel: Giftiges Vieh hh du hh
> Frau Fessel: Walter ch Walter ch lass ihn doch zu mir
>
> (Fessel: Poisonous beast hh you hh
> Mrs. Fessel: Walter ch Walter ch leave him to me.)

or again:

> Fessel: Red hh red nicht hh schweig
> Walter: Du
> Fessel: Schweig
> Walter: Du
> Fessel: Schweig
> Walter: Du
> Fessel: Schweig
>
> (Fessel: Don't hh don't hh speak hh quiet
> Walter: You

Still a symbol of Expressionism for non-Germans: Robert Wiene's film *The Cabinet of Dr Caligari*, 1920. Delaunay saw his own influence in the sets, which also relate to the angular, splintery Brücke style illustrated on pages 78 and 84.

> Fessel: Quiet
> Walter: You
> Fessel: Quiet
> Walter: You
> Fessel: Quiet)

– but who was already seen as part of the reaction against the movement, the other outstanding figure is Ernst Barlach, whose *Der arme Vetter* and *Der tote Tag* had been staged in the provinces (Hamburg and Leipzig respectively, in March and November) in 1919 and who first reached Berlin with Jessner's production of *Die echten Sedemunds* in April 1921. It may have been Jessner's fault – for Barlach went home and noted:

I saw a play by Herr Jessner, not by me … Film tempo and expressiveness, not the kind of thing I want to have anything to do with … shouting and monumentality.

– but it was another two years before he really broke through with Fehling's production of *Der arme Vetter* at the Staatstheater. It is surprising that Barlach's quality as a dramatist should not have been seen at once. For *Der tote Tag*, which had been begun as long ago as 1908, is remarkable above all for the absolute consistency of the extraordinary timeless, isolated world of its sharply individualised yet half-mythical characters, while *Der arme Vetter,* which followed, is about a succession of odd, ambiguous, more or less tragic, sometimes riotously funny incidents one Easter by the Elbe. This is a wholly original work written with complete mastery and many individual twists.

It was the theatre, far more than the writers or the artists, that brought Expressionism to the attention of foreign critics, not least through its stage settings, which were often in the distorted architectural style of Delaunay's Saint-Séverin. Perhaps this was even more true of the cinema, above all of one film: Robert Wiene's *The Cabinet of Dr Caligari*. The script of this fantasy about the diabolical director of a mental hospital was written in 1918-19 by Carl Mayer, till then the *Dramaturg* of the Berlin Residenz-Theater, together

158

with the Prague writer Hans Janowitz, a contributor to several Expressionist publications. Though it was not overtly set in Prague, the atmosphere of that city, with its medieval streets and old Jewish legends, certainly entered into the film, as it had into its principal forerunners – Stellan Rye's *The Student of Prague* (1912) and *The Golem* (1914), both with Paul Wegener as the chief actor – and into Gustav Meyrink's best-selling novel *The Golem* (1916) which had helped make the fortunes of the Kurt Wolff Verlag. Janowitz later said that he specified in the script that 'the sets ought to be realised in the style of Kubin's paintings', meaning presumably Alfred Kubin's drawings, and that the artist was offered the job and refused. There is no reference to this, however, in the account given by the art director Hermann Warm, who claimed that he and his two colleagues Walter Röhrig and Walter Reimann read the script and decided that it demanded the Expressionist style in which Reimann was then painting. Their painted sets, deliberately stagey in order to save money, were later more often identified with the style of Feininger than with that of Kubin, and they seem to have forced an angular, Expressionist style on the actors: at least on the two principals, Werner Krauss and Conrad Veidt. The only real compromise with the box office lay in the beginning and ending of the film, which took much of the menace out of the story by presenting it as a fantasy on the part of one of the hospital inmates. It is not clear who was responsible for this, but the script writers were very upset.

The première of *Caligari* was in February 1920, and although it was taken off after only two showings a concentrated publicity campaign turned it into a success and in due course into a classic. Other more or less Expressionist films followed. Karlheinz Martin's *Von Morgens bis Mitternachts* (1920), which was turned down by the exhibitors, had sets by Neppach and Ernst Deutsch in the leading part; though without dialogue, it is even eerier than Kaiser's original play. Mayer's second script *Genuine* was shot in 1920, again under Wiene's direction, with sets by Cesar Klein, but the film reputedly lacked the Expressionist quality. In 1922 Jessner made a film of Wedekind's *Erdgeist,* once again scripted by Mayer, with Asta Nielsen, Alexander Granach and Rudolf Forster; in 1923 Wiene made *Raskolnikoff* with Expressionist sets by Andreiev. By then Expressionism was already becoming a bit of a joke; thus Fritz Lang, in his fantastic *Dr Mabuse the Gambler* of that year, makes one of the characters say 'What do you think of Expressionism?' as a piece of party conversation; there are also, so far as one can see, Expressionist paintings on the walls of the relevant set. *Menschen hinter Gittern* ('The Big House'), which MGM made in 1931 on a script by Toller and Hasenclever, with Heinrich George in a leading part, is no longer counted as an Expressionist film. Yet there is still something Expressionist about the strong fantastic and sinister element in the whole Weimar cinema – what Lotte Eisner calls 'l'écran démoniaque' – right up to Lang's *Das Testament des Doktor Mabuse* in 1933. Perhaps nothing was more influential in bringing the movement to the notice of the outside world, or deciding how we now use the term.

7 The wider world of the 1920s

Western Europe

From 1914 on the close links between the modern movement in France and the development of Expressionism in Germany were broken. This was most obviously because of the war, but also because anti-war sentiment and revolutionary optimism were so much less strongly felt by French writers and artists than by German. Though we shall find everywhere that the actual recording of war experiences often called for expressionist methods – as in France in the case of the painter Luc-Albert Moreau – the hatreds or the hopes that welded German Expressionism into a movement are very rare. Even the school of French writing that had contributed most to this process appeared to disperse or to drop out of fashion: thus Verhaeren has been largely forgotten ever since the day when he fell under a train in Rouen station in 1916, while the Unanimists and Abbaye poets are now best known for the novels which they wrote after the war. Of the group around Rolland in Geneva, Jouve (like Werfel, whose work he introduced to France), turned towards religious mysticism; Martinet (like Becher) became one of his country's leading Communist writers. Admittedly Barbusse tried to preserve the links between that group and the German pacifists by the international 'Clarté' movement which he founded in 1919 (with Latzko, Schickele and Stefan Zweig among its committee members), but within two or three years this had become a too obviously Communist body and was already breaking up. Outside all such groups Apollinaire, whose 'Zone' is one of the French poems nearest the German movement (and incidentally brings in Prague), had died in 1918, while Cendrars too wrote little poetry of significance after that date, devoting much of the 1920s to travel and the cinema.

In French painting after the war there were three distinct threads. First and foremost there was Rouault, who had begun applying his highly original and expressive art to religious themes shortly before 1914, but from about 1917 to 1927 painted little and concentrated on producing the great series of aquatints *Miserere et Guerre*, which were intended to accompany a text by Suarès and were not in fact

A French reaction to the war. Georges Rouault's *Miserere et Guerre* (not published till 1948), plate XXXVI 'Ce sera la dernière, petit père'.

to be published for another twenty years. With him may be associated the religious painter Georges Desvallières, who founded the Ateliers d'Art Sacré with Maurice Denis in 1919, while Amédée de La Patellière was another heavily expressive artist devoted mainly to more realist themes. Secondly, there was the group of largely east European artists who became known as the Ecole de Paris, of whom Soutine, a product of the same Vilna art school as Mané-Katz and the slightly older Lasar Segall, was an expressionist in a style comparable to that of late Van Gogh or the much more self-aware Meidner; he too was influenced by El Greco and concerned to convey passion and force. Though it is not known how far he or his fellow-Lithuanians Krémegne and Kikoïne were directly aware of any contemporary German work, he did know Chagall, Pascin, Cendrars and the Czech Otakar Coubine, all of whom were in some measure acquainted with what had been going on. Soutine was also close to Modigliani, who twice painted his portrait. By temperament, however, he was a solitary, obsessive and uncommunicative artist, who belonged to no groups, sold only to a few devoted collectors, neither drew nor wrote, and remained constant in style from 1922 (the end of his so-called Céret period of extreme violent distortion) till his death in 1943.

If these (mostly Jewish) artists of the Ecole de Paris were the likeliest to know about German Expressionism – a possibility which still needs investigation – there was also a third, more indigenous thread, which partly derives from Le Fauconnier and relates to the Abbaye-Clarté tradition in literature. After the war the poet Joseph Billiet started a Paris gallery (later taken over by his friend Pierre Vorms) which not only became the main showroom for Le Fauconnier and Masereel after their return to France in 1921 and 1922 respectively but also introduced the work of Grosz (November 1924), Albert Servaes (February 1929) and other Belgian, Dutch, Russian and German expressionists. Le Fauconnier himself from 1925 on became increasingly academic; even his portraits of the writers Duhamel, Romains, Billiet and Chennevière (published in Antwerp under the title *Figures contemporaines* in 1922) were far from expressionist. But his pre-war pupil at the Académie de la Palette, Marcel Gromaire, a teacher's son from near the Belgian frontier, now became one of the outstanding French painters in that vein. Gromaire himself disliked being called an expressionist, claiming (in the 1950s) that he was against distortion: 'à la déformation j'oppose l'affirmation de l'objet'. And indeed his pictures, if

From northern France. Marcel Gromaire's 'Les buveurs de bière', 1924.
(Musée d'Art Moderne de la Ville de Paris.)

far from naturalistic, are calm and always strictly organised, with a monumental geometry not unlike that of Léger (or Schlemmer or William Roberts). All the same, in theme, in colour, and in a certain exaggerated lumpiness they are much like those of the modern Belgians, so that it is not surprising that his first show abroad should have been in Brussels or that a monograph on him should have been published by *Sélection* in Antwerp in 1929.

This Belgian movement had, as we saw, its own native roots in the work of Ensor and Laermans and the first Laethem Saint-Martin group, of whom Servaes formed the main link with their successors. There was also Jakob Smits, a fine artist working in an individual peasant-symbolist-religious style in the countryside near the Dutch frontier. Building on such foundations as these, a second group of artists had come together at Laethem-Saint-Martin around 1909: Frits van den Berghe, Gustav de Smet (and his brother Léon), Constant Permeke and the critic P. G. van der Hecke. They were the men who were to make Belgian Expressionism, even though nothing resembling expressionist painting was seen from any of the group until well into the war. Permeke then painted his 'L'Etranger' while convalescing from wounds in England in 1916; De Smet and Frits van den Berghe moved into neutral Holland and established what seems to have been a decisive contact with Le Fauconnier and the short-lived Dutch expressionist tendency known as the *Nieuwe Beweging*. Unlike the Belgians, the Dutch artists concerned, notably Leo Gestel, Jan Sluyters and Lodowijk Schelfhout, had worked in Paris and been directly influenced by both Cubism and Futurism. Schelfhout (the one Dutchman to figure in the German *Junge Kunst* series after the war) had got to know the Germans at the Dôme; Sluyters had seen Uhde's and Kahnweiler's collections, Gestel the Futurist exhibition at the Hague in 1912. In 1910 Sluyters, with Mondrian and Toorop, had formed the Moderne Kunstkring, which from 1911 to 1913 held important international autumn exhibitions at the Stedelijk Museum in Amsterdam, showing 38 Cézannes at the first; 33 Le Fauconniers and 23 Gauguins at the second; and Le Fauconnier again, with 14 Kandinskys and 17 Marcs, at the third. In 1914 Le Fauconnier came to stay the summer, got caught by the outbreak of war and remained based on Amsterdam till 1921. Other artists spending the war in Holland included Campendonk, the Czech Emil Filla (then in his cubist period) and the Hungarian Bela Czóbel.

In Holland, as in Le Fauconnier's own painting, the expressionist

tendency hardly outlasted the war. In Belgium however it developed into a movement which spread to embrace such artists as Floris Jespers, Henri-François Raemaker (or 'Ramah') and the more light-hearted Edgard Tytgat as well as others like the excellent Jean Brusselmans who are only marginally expressionists. Indeed it was the dominant tendency in Belgian, and more specifically in Flemish painting right up to 1939. This contrast within so geographically compact and linguistically unified an area is undoubtedly attributable to the special need of the Belgian Flemish to assert their cultural independence of the French. Thus from 1920 to 1930 Van der Hecke and André de Ridder (author of a monograph on Le Fauconnier as well as of a polemical attack on French cultural chauvinism entitled *Le Génie du Nord*), supported the movement in their French-language Antwerp review *Sélection*, which printed contributions from Germany as well as France. For a short time there was also a Flemish review called *Ruimte* (1920-21), which was published in the

Flemish Expressionism. *Left* Albert Servaes's 'L'Enterrement' from the Musée Royale des Beaux-Arts, Antwerp. *Below* Constant Permeke's 'Les Fiancés', 1923, from the Brussels museum.

An Italian expressionist of the 1920s: one of Mario Sironi's 'Urban Landscapes' (Collection E. Estorick, London).

same city and seems to have been more concerned with German Expressionism than any other non-German organ in western Europe. It was primarily a literary magazine, printing the more or less expressionist poems of such writers as Paul Ostaijen, whose volume *Het Sienjaal* of 1918 seems to reflect his reading of Whitman, Werfel and Lasker-Schüler, and Wies Moens, another admirer of these poets and also of Tagore. Though such influences had already been felt in Belgium before the war, when the Antwerp library first started subscribing to *Die Weissen Blätter,* they were certainly helped on by the wartime occupation and by the German administration's policy of turning Ghent into a strictly non-French university (it was in its library that Moens came across the German poets). *Ruimte* not only printed translations of poems by Däubler and Rubiner, and for that matter Herbert Read, but reported on Expressionist productions in Cologne, including *Ein Geschlecht,* and reviewed *Menschheitsdämmerung.* Thus Belgian Expressionism, alone in western Europe, set out from an awareness of the German movement and owed its impetus to more than purely artistic reasons.

In Sweden too there was to some extent a common heritage. This lay on the artistic side in the teaching of Matisse, from which much of modern Swedish painting derived, and on the literary side in the influence of Strindberg. Right into the 1930s many of the painters indulged in a certain mildly expressive distortion, though the French influence, whether Fauve as with Isaac Grunewald and Sigrid Hjerten or derived from Le Fauconnier as with Vera Nilsson, seems to have prevented it from being anything like as passionate, 'Nordic' or intense as that of Munch in Norway. On the other hand the author Pär Lagerqvist, who came to Berlin in 1915 with Grunewald when the latter showed at Walden's gallery, wrote a number of genuinely expressionist plays, starting with the apocalyptic *Sista mänskan* ('The Last Man') of 1917. Two men in particular constituted a link between the German and Swedish theatre of that period: Per Lindberg, who worked with Reinhardt, and Knud Strom of the Düsseldorf Schauspielhaus, who staged Lagerqvist's one-acter *The Tunnel* there in 1918, then joined the writer Hjalmar

168

Bergman in managing a theatre at Göteborg (till 1923). Bergman's own play of 1923 *Spelhuset* ('The Gambling House') likewise has some expressionist features.

Finally in Italy the Futurist movement in one sense died with the war. For Boccioni and Sant'Elia were killed (as members of the cycle corps which several of the movement joined), while Severini settled in Paris and Balla and Russolo returned to representational painting. In another sense it got a new lease of life after Mussolini's March on Rome in 1922, since Marinetti had allied himself with the Fascists and spoken on the same platform as Mussolini as early as 1919. 'Fascist art = Futurism', he told one of the party journals, and he was made a Senator and elevated to the new Fascist Italian Academy in 1929. Admittedly the art of the post-war recruits, apart from Prampolini, who had some ties with the Dadaists, made little impression outside Italy. But there was one artist of the earlier movement who turned to painting in a sporadically expressionist style and became one of the chief Italian painters of the Fascist period. This was Mario Sironi, who had worked in Balla's studio and fought in the cycle corps, then in 1923 formed the Novecento group

169

with Tosi, Marussig, Campigli and Funi and the support of the critic Margherita Sarfatti, a friend of Mussolini's who seems to have been responsible also for getting the German Expressionists shown at the 1928 Venice Biennale. Many of Sironi's pictures of the 1920s, notably some of the *paesaggi urbani,* have the mournful city themes, the exaggerated melancholy and sombre colours associated with Expressionism; and indeed he had visited Erfurt before 1914 and is thought to have had some knowledge of contemporary German painting. Later, like so many Italian artists, he was tempted into classical pastiche, painting some deplorable official murals for the Fifth Milan Triennale and the Studium Urbis in Rome in the mid-1930s.

Britain and the Americas

Though Britain had become something of a backwater so far as the modern movement was concerned, the group around Wyndham Lewis and Ezra Pound on the eve of the war contained the same seeds which elsewhere gave root to expressionism. That is to say that they too were in revolt against the impressionists (and against the gospel of Cézanne as preached by Clive Bell and Fry); they had picked up certain ideas from Cubism and from Marinetti, who came to London following the Futurist exhibition there and issued an English manifesto with the painter C. R. W. Nevinson in June 1914; and in the first number of *Blast* in the same month they appealed in true Nietzschean style to primitivism, the unconscious, the 'crude energy' of the world and the 'mysticism, madness and delicacy peculiar to the North'. They also printed an excerpt from Kandinsky's *On the Spiritual in Art* (though Lewis found that artist's work too 'cloud-like'), while paintings by Nolde, Marc and Pechstein were included in a 'Post-Impressionist' show organised by the critic Frank Rutter in London in the autumn of 1913 and Walden sent a show over in the following February. Once again, however, the energies which might have turned such elements into a movement seem to have been drained off by the war, which killed two of the

170

group's chief members, the philosopher T. E. Hulme and the sculptor Henri Gaudier-Brzeska (a Frenchman who had worked in Nuremberg and Munich in 1909), and canalised the painting talents of Lewis and Nevinson into some fine pictures of the Western Front. After the armistice the group was dispersed. Nevinson went academic, the sculptor Jacob Epstein lumpy or (in his bronzes) sentimental, while others tended to surrealism (Paul Nash), 'Magic Realism' (Edward Wadsworth) or a stylised monumentality (William Roberts). Lewis himself continued to fight a one-man battle as a painter-writer-poet detached from all the -Isms. Only the artist David Bomberg remained as something of an expressionist, and he spent most of the 1920s outside England, either in Palestine (1923-7) or in Spain.

Among the avant-garde writers of the early 1920s there were at least some points of similarity with the early German Expressionists. In the case of T. S. Eliot, who had been strongly influenced by Laforgue and studied at Marburg in 1914, this can be seen in poems like 'Prelude' and 'Rhapsody on a Windy Night', or in the highly stylised dramatic fragment *Sweeney Agonistes,* all of which would certainly have counted as Expressionist if written by a German. The closest English (or more strictly Irish) parallel is however to be found in the 'Nighttown' sequence of *Ulysses* which Joyce was writing in Zürich during the war. Much of this, with its succession of

171

nameless figures, would translate as a characteristic piece of Expressionist theatre: such stage directions, for instance, as

A deafmute idiot with goggle eyes, his shapeless mouth dribbling, jerks past, shaken in Saint Vitus's dance. A chain of children's hands imprisons him.

– or examples of chopped-up dialogue like Bloom's 'Wait. Stop. Gulls. Good heart. I saw', and so on. How far its affinities were in any way attributable to the gathering of German writers in that city is impossible to say, but Joyce did meet Schickele (who wanted him to translate his play *Hans im Schnakenloch*) and Goll, corresponded with Zweig and showed a certain interest in Wedekind's plays. Another element of liaison immediately before and after the war was provided by Ashley Dukes the playwright, who after studying in Munich in 1907-8 and being swept off his feet by Nietzsche became the theatre critic of A.R.Orage's paper *The New Age*, sharing a flat in Mortimer Street in London with Hulme in 1912 and eating with a group that included Nevinson, Gaudier and Epstein. At the end of the fighting Dukes found himself in the Rhineland, where he saw *Der Bettler* and *Von Morgens bis Mitternachts* at Cologne and determined to devote himself to 'the task of furnishing new material for our stage'. His translation of Kaiser's play was performed by the Stage Society in London, where it was the first post-war German play to be seen, then in May 1922 by the Theatre Guild in New York. That summer Dukes saw *Die Maschinenstürmer* in Germany and visited Toller in prison to discuss its translation, which was performed by the Stage Society (with Herbert Marshall as Jimmy Cobbett) in the following spring. Dukes wrote in his auto-biography:

I could not be interested in his politics, which were of the sentimental left-wing rather than the communist order, or in his *Weltschmerz*. But for a while he wrote marvellous things, and he touched expressionism with poetry.

A number of other plays by the German Expressionists were performed during the 1920s in London and New York – notably *Gas*, *Masse-Mensch* (with Sibyl Thorndike) and *Hinkemann* in the former and three of the Werfel plays in the latter – but only Toller, with Edward Crankshaw succeeding Dukes as his translator, seems to have found a regular platform in the Gate Theatre under Peter Godfrey, while among a number of amateur productions of his work was one of *Masse-Mensch* at Liverpool directed by David L.Webster. What really saved Expressionism from being written

172

off, in the English critic St John Ervine's words, as merely 'the despair and neurosis of a defeated people' was its triumphant application by the American playwright Eugene O'Neill, followed by such writers as the Americans Elmer Rice and (in his play *The Moon is a Gong*) John dos Passos, and the Irishman Denis Johnston. O'Neill indeed was the one great expressionist dramatist in any country, and he managed to assimilate the ancestry, the attitude and to some extent the conventions of German Expressionism and reproduce them absolutely naturally in English, by absorption rather than imitation. The ancestors in question were Nietzsche and Strindberg, who seem continually to have been in his mind; the attitude was above all that of concentrating on a single character, as in *The Emperor Jones* and *The Hairy Ape,* and taking him through a succession of 'stations' (eight in each of these plays); while the conventions can be seen in the nameless subsidiary characters and expressive settings of his early plays. Thus the opening stage direction of *The Hairy Ape* for instance runs:

The treatment of this scene, or of any other scene in the play, should by no means be naturalistic ... The lines of bunks, the uprights supporting them cross each other like the steel framework of a cage. The ceiling crushes down upon the men's heads.

Writing both this and *The Emperor Jones* before any German Expressionist work had been seen in New York, O'Neill told Kenneth Macgowan of the Provincetown Players that he would 'run the whole gamut from extreme naturalism to extreme expressionism, with more of the latter than the former'.

Just how far O'Neill was familiar with the contemporary Germans is not known, but he claimed to have learned the language to read Wedekind and recommended that the Provincetown Players should perform Wedekind and Hasenclever in their 1923-4 season, as well as Strindberg's *Ghost Sonata.* (In the event they skipped Wedekind altogether and did *Jenseits,* or 'Beyond', in January 1925). Elmer Rice on the other hand, while acknowledging that his *The Adding Machine* of March 1923 was 'written in the stylized, intensified form loosely known as expressionism', said that the term was then almost unknown to him. With its seven 'stations', its schematic characters and its bookkeeping protagonist, this immensely successful play was far too reminiscent of *Von Morgens bis Mitternachts,* staged only a few months earlier by the same company, to be regarded now as more than a clever exercise in a new and exciting convention. Another American expressionist flash in the pan, *Beggar on Horseback* (February 1924), was an adaptation by George Kaufman and Marc Connelly of a comedy called *Hans Sonnenstossers Höllenfahrt* by the now forgotten Paul Apel. With its use of caricature, quick scene-shifts and the telegraphic style it was one of the models for the Irishman Denis Johnston's first play *The Old Lady Says 'No!'*, which was written in 1926 and first performed by the Gate Theatre Studio in Dublin in July 1929. Though Johnston himself termed this work 'an expressionist gesture of dissent', his second and best-known work *The Moon in the Yellow River* (staged at the Abbey Theatre in April 1931) is scarcely in any sense expressionist, despite having a German engineer as its hero and a power house as its principal symbol; it is too full of talk and conscious eccentricity. Johnston later collaborated with Toller on a play *Blind Man's Buff* derived from the latter's *Die Blinde Göttin,* but this was long after Toller's Expressionist days, and he is quite right in refusing to be classed as one of Toller's disciples.

There were also one or two North American painters of the 1920s who were in some measure expressionist. The chief was the Russian-born Max Weber, who was twenty-eight when he returned from Paris to New York in 1909; he described his *The Geranium* of 1911 as showing:

Two crouching figures of women dwelling and brooding in a nether or un-worldly realm. The conception and treatment spring from a search of form in the crystal.

Even when he was most under the influence of cubism, between 1912 and 1919, there was a latent expressiveness in his work: e.g. in another medium, these lines from his *Cubist Poems* of 1914:

Again the groan, the moan, the howl, the rage, the frozen passion,
Destruction, quake, crash, blast, forewarns,
And fright and fear prophetic soothes
And all the senses wait.
Tormented, turbulent space a moment breathless hangs.

Max Weber: 'The Geranium', 1911, in the Museum of Modern Art, New York (who bought it in 1944 from the Lillie P. Bliss Bequest).

In 1913 he painted New York with the broken angularity of his friend Delaunay, much as John Marin was then doing; then in 1919 he painted such expressionist works as 'The Visit' and the Nolde-like 'Invocation', before going into a neo-classical phase. Besides him there was the slightly older Marsden Hartley, who worked in Berlin and Munich before the war, coming under Kandinsky's influence around 1913, then again in Berlin in 1914-15 and after the war in 1922-3; he showed his abstract-symbolic pictures in the Deutsche Herbstsalon of 1913. Hans Hofmann was in Munich in the 1920s, running an obscure private art school and painting little; he only came to teach for the first time at Berkeley in 1930. Albert Bloch however, who had been in touch with the Blaue Reiter and shown at the Sturm gallery in 1912, returned to the United States in 1922 and subsequently became Professor of Art at Kansas. Yet with all these contacts very little of the work of the German painters was seen in America, thanks in part to the war and in part, perhaps, to their almost complete absence from the 1913 Armory Show, where they were represented only by Kirchner's 'Wirtsgarten in Steglitz' (Kirchner Estate), Kandinsky's 'Improvisation 27' (which Alfred Stieglitz bought) and some prints by Munch. Things began to improve in the second half of the 1920s, when some of their graphic work was reproduced in *Vanity Fair* (whose editor Frank Crownin-shield owned at least two of Masereel's paintings) and J. B. Neumann's gallery moved to New York. There were exhibitions of Beckmann's work there in 1926-7, and of Klee, Kandinsky, Feininger and Jawlensky on the West Coast a year later. But no major show of modern German art was seen in America till that at the Museum of Modern Art in March-April 1931.

In Brazil there was one outstanding Expressionist artist: Segall, who emigrated there from Dresden in 1923. To judge from the reproductions of his work he found no difficulty in adapting his style to Brazilian themes, though a certain simplicity and calmness came over it towards 1930, bringing him at times close to the Belgians. In Mexico however there was a genuine indigenous movement, linked once again, as in Germany and Belgium, with the country's political development. It began when José Vasconcelos became Secretary of Education in the Obregon Government in 1921, and at the end of that year commissioned Diego Rivera to paint a mural in the National Preparatory School in Mexico City. A year later Rivera was joined by David Siqueiros, who had gone to Europe after fighting in Obregon's revolutionary forces and in May

177

The Mexican mural school.
Left David Siqueiros's woodcut
of a kneeling worker, flagellated,
from *El Machette*, 1924.
Right Jose Orozco's 'Prometheus' fresco
from Pomona College, California.

1921 issued a form of manifesto emphasising the need to learn from pre-colombian art, the importance of subject matter and the claim to expression of 'our marvellous dynamic age'. Until the middle of 1924 these two, together with the caricaturist Orozco, who likewise announced that 'My one theme is Humanity; my one tendency is EMOTION TO A MAXIMUM', laid the foundation of the Mexican mural style, which was largely expressionistic. It was also more or less Communist, and the paper *El Machete* which began as the organ of the new Syndicate of Revolutionary Painters, Sculptors and Engravers under Rivera and Siqueiros became the party organ after the artists had split and Vasconcelos resigned, leaving Rivera alone to continue working under the new Calles regime. Siqueiros spent a year in gaol in 1930, then lived in the United States from 1932 to 1934; Orozco was in that country from 1927-34; while Rivera followed suit in 1930. Thus they not only evolved a style of revolutionary symbolist painting which, while taking account of some of the lessons of Cubism, became a model for Latin American painters

178

throughout the sub-continent (as did the not dissimilar pictorial language used by Segall farther south), but also took their methods to the United States, where further murals such as Orozco's at Pomona College, Los Angeles (1930) and Dartmouth College (1932-4), and Rivera's in the Detroit Institute of Arts and the Rockefeller Center had a certain influence in the period of the New Deal.

Points East

Expressionism during the 1920s also got a certain footing in what is now the Communist world. Because the axis of the pre-war movement had lain along the line Vienna-Prague-Dresden-Berlin – in other words very much that of the subsequent Iron Curtain – it naturally spilled over into the new states set up by the Versailles Treaty, notably Czechoslovakia, Hungary and Poland. In Budapest, where Iván Irta Hevesy and F. Lehel published books on the subject between 1920 and 1922, the chief channel of activity was the poet-

179

painter Lajos Kassák's magazine *Ma*, which was modelled on *Der Sturm,* and to a lesser extent the same editor's *Tett* ('Action'). Kassák himself for a time wrote expressionist verse (even with the odd invocation of 'O Man!') before coming under the influence of the Constructivists around 1921-2, while the Activists included the painter Béla Uitz, a frequent contributor to early issues of *Ma* who was active in the Hungarian Soviet of 1919 and emigrated to Russia the next year. Besides the Matisse pupil Czóbel, who was in Berlin between 1919 and 1925, there was the gifted but short-lived painter Jószef Nemes Lamperth (1891-1924) and the expressive sculptress Erzsébet Forgács Hann. Other Hungarian painters like Béla Kadar were among the Sturm artists of the middle and late 1920s, when Walden was showing mainly rather second-grade abstract works, many of them by non-Germans.

The Czechs began with a triple basis for a possible expressionist movement: the Whitmanesque verse of Otakar Březina, the work of the *Osma* group and the particular German-Jewish Prague climate which produced Kafka and Werfel and (indirectly) *The Cabinet of Dr Caligari.* After independence, however, the German element was regarded as very subordinate – indeed even Kafka was badly

Central Europe.
Left Bela Uitz's drawing of
a landscape, 1916 (Hungarian
National Gallery).
Right Linocut by Josef Čapek,
1918, to illustrate
Apollinaire's poem 'Zone'.

neglected in Czechoslovakia till the 1960s – while the artists of the *Skupina* can no longer be seen as Expressionist after their whole-hearted conversion to cubism during 1912. Within two years the Czech and German movements had divided, partly no doubt because of the war; thus Filla took refuge in Holland, Coubine and Gutfreund in Paris, while Kubišta died of influenza in 1918. Generally the Czech artists and poets now looked to Paris, so that the dominant school of the 1920s in Prague was surrealism, with Russian-Hungarian constructivism as the alternative attraction. If some vestiges of Expressionism lingered on it was mainly in the decorative arts, e.g. in Jiri Kroha's Montmartre Club in Prague or the odd set by Vlastislav Hofmann, who became the National Theatre's principal scene designer. Other instances are Langer's play *Periferie* (1921), which has echoes of Dostoevsky and was successfully staged by Reinhardt in Berlin, and Karel Capek's *R.U.R.,* with its analogies with Kaiser's *Gas* cycle. First staged in Prague in 1921, this work was performed effectively in translation in England and America, and also (in an adaptation by Alexei Tolstoy) in the USSR. It incidentally introduced the word 'robot' into the English language.

181

Expressionism in the Soviet theatre. *Above* A scene from *200,000* after Sholem-Aleichem at the State Jewish Theatre, Moscow. *Below* Toller's Hinkemann, staged by Sergei E. Radlov at the Michailovsky Theatre, Leningrad, in 1923. Setting by V.V. Dmitriev.

The new Soviet Russia was at first very open to expressionist ideas. Kandinsky and Chagall both held important official posts under the Commissariat of Education; Blok's poem *The Twelve* expressed much the same utopian-symbolist spirit as the Germans with their crystal cathedrals and other semi-religious images; in the theatre the way had been paved by Meyerhold's writings about the grotesque (1908) and by his experimental laboratory in St Petersburg (1913–17); while presiding over all cultural developments was Lunacharsky, a utopian writer who had been in touch with such movements as Cubism in Paris before the war. Of the painters who had previously shown expressionist symptoms only such Jewish artists as Altman and Falk (and, briefly, Chagall himself) seem to have carried them further, with Pavel Filinov as an influential newcomer. Others such as Goncharova and Larionov had left the country before the Revolution; David Burliuk emigrated to the United States in 1918; Kandinsky and Chagall left in 1922, the year when the experimental period in Russian art came to an end. None the less the Museum of Modern Western Art in Moscow under Boris Ternovetz continued buying modern German art throughout the 1920s, while Lunacharsky sponsored exhibitions of Masereel's woodcuts there in 1926 and again in 1930. In the theatre too the expressionist trend continued. Though Meyerhold himself soon turned away from expressionist stage methods a number of Expressionist or related plays from western Europe were seen at his Revolutionary Theatre, sometimes in constructivist sets: Toller's *Die Maschinenstürmer* (November 1922), *Masse-Mensch* (January 1923) and *Hoppla* (December 1928), Verhaeren's *Les Aubes,* Martinet's *La Nuit* (first published by *Clarté* in 1922) and Crommelynck's *Le Cocu magnifique*. In Leningrad his pupil Sergei Varnov staged works by Toller, Werfel and Sternheim in the mid-1920s, while the theatre director Alexei Gribich's persistence with Expressionist works was reputedly encouraged by Lunacharsky.

As for Expressionist production methods and settings, they could be seen above all in the two Jewish theatres: the Habima, which became attached to the Moscow Art Theatre in 1918 and emigrated

182

'Woosh! The turbid waters engulf a miserable soul.' Chinese woodcut illustration by Li Hua, (1930s).

樸通⋯⋯汚濁的水淹沒了一個
受了傷的靈魂。

en bloc ten years later, and the State Jewish Theatre under Alexander Granovsky, who had worked with Reinhardt. Evgenyi Vakhtangov directed *The Dybbuk* in grotesquely distorted sets by Altman for the Habima (1918), while the chief achievements of the State Jewish Theatre, apart from Chagall's subsequently destroyed murals in the theatre itself, were *200,000* after Sholem-Aleichem, *The Sorceress* by Goldfaden (1922) and *A Night in the Old Market Place* by Peretz (1923) in a set by Falk. 'Unforgettable evenings', wrote Toller of the last two, and Granovsky in turn came to Berlin to stage the unsuccessful Toller-Hasenclever comedy *Bourgeois bleibt Bourgeois* in 1929. During the 1920s Toller in fact was something of a favourite in the USSR, where nine of his books were published and his plays performed also in Kiev, Tiflis, Odessa and by the Siberian State Theatre. Yet even Lunacharsky, who wrote the foreword to a translation of his prison poems in 1925, was by no means

184

uncritical either of Toller or of Expressionism in general, which he saw as subjective and quasi-religious rather than Marxist. It is not surprising that after Lunacharsky's departure from the Commissariat of Education in 1929 the movement lost support.

Even China assimilated certain Expressionist influences in the early 1930s, when the great novelist Lu Hsün introduced the work of Masereel and Käthe Kollwitz, thus paving the way for a new, westernised and politically progressive Chinese graphic school. One of its best-known members (at least to the Anglo-Saxon countries) was Jack Chen; others included the wood-engravers Hsin Po, Li Hua and Liu Lun, and the cartoonist Yen Chen-yu. A selection sent anonymously by Lu Hsün himself was shown by Billiet in Paris in 1934.

The German disenchantment

The curious thing about this extension of expressionist influence elsewhere was that it coincided with the decline of the movement inside Germany. We have already noted the first symptoms in the disillusionment felt by the poets, who found out very soon that the new republic was less nervous of compromise on the right than of the risk of further revolution on the left. The implications of this were seen long before the rot had spread to other areas of the arts; thus G. F. Hartlaub, director of the Mannheim Kunsthalle, was writing in an article of 1920 that Expressionism was bankrupt, while Iwan Goll's often-cited article 'Expressionism is Dying' appeared in 1921 in the Belgrade review *Zenit*. More subtly, perhaps, the weaknesses of the Expressionist style of writing were already being publicly ridiculed. Thus an early story called *Auf die Strasse* (1920) by Theodor Tagger satirised the Becher type of poet, who read his ecstatic verses to provincial culture-lovers all over Germany. Karl Kraus thought that the movement (particularly its Prague branch) was a mutual admiration society, and attacked it for debasing the language with its syntactic distortions and overworked vocatives. In 1921 he even parted company with his publisher Wolff, whom he regarded as still committed to Werfel, Ehrenstein and other writers of whom he now disapproved. In fact, however, Wolff himself had already begun to lose interest in German avant-garde literature, turning his attention more to illustration and art books. He told Werfel in August 1921 that he could see no authors of the younger generation to compare with those already emerging

Below 'Disillusioned'. Beckmann's lithograph 'Die Enttäuschten II' from the series *Berliner Reise*, 1922, showing boredom emanating from the works of Marx, Liebknecht and Rosa Luxemburg. *Right* 'Paysage de Céret', 1921, by the Russian-French artist Chaim Soutine, from the Collection Galerie Kruger et Cie., Geneva. (See page 163).

in France. 'German writing today', he felt, 'has achieved a standard of indescribable sterility'.

With varying delays the other arts too now moved away from Expressionism, so that by 1924 the whole movement really was over. Kokoschka's 'The Painter and his Model II' of that year symbolises the distance travelled; it is painted in the flat, brilliant, relatively calm style of his Dresden period, but includes the passionate self-portrait which he had made before 1912; moreover he was just about to abandon Germany and his role as an avant-garde figure in favour of the modified impressionism of his middle age. Most of the angularity left the Brücke artists' work, so that Heckel became gently academic, while Kirchner within two or three years had adopted the curvilinear style of middle-period Picasso. Kandinsky, who joined the Bauhaus staff soon after his return from Russia, grew rapidly less explosive and more geometrical, no doubt reflecting the influence of constructivism and the later Malevitch, though without losing his underlying mysticism. As for the Sturm, Lissitzky in

The new objectivity. Otto Dix's portrait of his parents, 1921, until 1937
in the Wallraf-Richart Museum, Cologne, and now in the Basel Museum.

1922 found that 'this ocean giant has turned into a dingy little ship'.
Walden was already becoming more interested in politics (in 1924
his wife left him partly for this reason) and was made chairman of
the Friends of the Soviet Union, closing his gallery for good in
1929. In architecture too there was the startling evolution of Bruno
Taut, who, after a brief spell from 1921-3 as City Architect of
Magdeburg, became architect to the GEHAG housing society, a
socialist-sponsored body which was responsible for much of the
ultra-functionalist Berlin working-class housing of the later 1920s.

In the theatre the crucial year was 1923, when the audiences
began to fall off and the critics were already on the lookout for
signs of the next trend. Three playwrights seemed to herald a change,
though only the first was a newcomer: Bertolt Brecht, whom
Herbert Ihering had singled out the previous autumn for the Kleist
Prize on the strength of the Munich performance of his *Trommeln in
der Nacht*, a play whose language and characterisation seemed quite
un-Expressionist despite the Expressionist style of its production.
Next, Barlach at last established himself, with *Der arme Vetter* in
Fehling's production, immediately followed by the Volksbühne
production of *Der tote Tag*; to Julius Bab he was 'the true nemesis of
Expressionism in German drama'. The third was the prolific
Kaiser, who now scored a great success in Berlin with his 'Volksstück
1923' *Nebeneinander*: a neat interweaving of characteristic social
milieux, which combined realistic observation with Expressionist
economy of dialogue. Within a few months it became clear that
styles of production too were changing: Erich Engel and Erwin
Piscator, the new producers at the Deutsches Theater and Volksbühne respectively, no longer strove for emotional effects but for
strength, clarity and (in Piscator's case) the display of modern
technologies. Finally in 1925 Zuckmayer's undemanding *Der
fröhliche Weinberg* began a two-and-a-half year run in Berlin.
'Wonder of wonders! ...' wrote the critic Bernhard Diebold: 'An
author who from the outset abandons all claim to be the Messiah',
and Alfred Kerr: 'sic transit gloria expressionismi'.

There was a new spirit in the arts which seemed to reflect the

stabilisation of the Mark at the end of 1923. Inflation and Expressionism had been apt companions, so long as the note circulation kept spiralling giddily upwards, but with the sobriety and realism of Stresemann's premiership a more unpretentious approach was needed. During 1925 Hartlaub at Mannheim organised a large exhibition which he called 'Neue Sachlichkeit' – new objectivity, or new matter-of-factness – a phrase which admirably conveys the climate of the time. For this was the age of jazz, of sport, of the silent cinema and of a new cult of everything Anglo-Saxon, from Bernard Shaw to Edgar Wallace; it also saw the establishment of functionalism in architecture and the modernisation of whole districts of such cities as Frankfurt and Berlin. A common attitude seemed to link such things as the war books of Renn and Remarque,

189

the drily contrapuntal music of Hindemith, the cynical comedies of Brecht's Berlin period, the social novels of Fallada, the ironic light verse of Kurt Tucholsky and the young Erich Kästner, and the Bauhaus's new slogan of 1923 'Art and Technology – a New Unity' which marked the arrival of the Hungarian constructivist Moholy-Nagy. Formally, such artists and writers followed widely differing principles, so that some of them are now thought of as having contributed to the further development of the modern movement while others are dismissed as conventional. But the mentality applying those forms was a consistent one: a non-utopian, even rather prosaic concern with clarity, accuracy and economy of means, biassed towards the collective rather than the personal, and informed by a realistic social analysis. It is very much what was to be found in the best of the painters exhibited at Mannheim – in Beckmann, Grosz, Dix and Rudolf Schlichter – and it was in almost every way the opposite of the impulses that had moved the Expressionists.

This development had its political side, to which the polarisation of political life in Germany before 1924 and again after 1928 gave a certain prominence. With Becher and Friedrich Wolf the sobering-up process was a consequence of their joining the Communist Party; thus Becher later claimed to have learnt 'severity and matter-of-factness' in his Berlin party cell in 1923, though in fact his *Hymnen* of the following year were still in the high rhapsodic vein, complete with further cries of 'O Man!' In other cases there was a dual revulsion against Expressionism and against bourgeois society; thus within the Novembergruppe a left-wing opposition had crystallised by 1921, including Dix, Grosz, and Schlichter as well as the Dadaists Raoul Hausmann and Hannah Höch; this being before Dix and Grosz had moved away from Dadaism. After the middle of the 1920s 'Neue Sachlichkeit' itself developed a Communist wing, with Piscator's theatre (set up as an independent entity in 1927) and the formation of two new groups in 1928, a League of Proletarian-Revolutionary Writers and an Association of Revolutionary Artists. In the first the new writers like Renn and Egon Erwin Kisch joined with such converts from Expressionism as Becher to form the most important Communist writers' organisation outside Russia, with Georg Lukács as its chief theoretician. In the second the new socially-conscious objectivity, which Dix and Grosz had applied to working-class themes, was taken up by minor Communist artists like Otto Nagel (a former Soldatenrat and self-taught painter), Hans Grundig, Max Lingner and Hans Baluschek. Käthe Kollwitz

The Communist wing.
Otto Nagel's 'Wochenmarkt',
1926, in the possession of
the artist's widow, East Berlin.

showed with some of its members, as also did the young Werner Scholz, then a melodramatically expressive painter in the Nolde tradition.

It is common today to draw a line under the Expressionist movement somewhere between 1920 and 1925, treating 'Neue Sachlichkeit' as if it had been the death of the modern movement in Germany and a foretaste of the reactionary art which was to dominate central and eastern Europe after the end of the 1920s. True enough, there was a general turning point in the arts throughout Europe around 1922. Russian constructivism and German Dadaism came to a stop; neo-classicism began to interest such men as Picasso, Stravinsky and Cocteau; Chagall became prettily poetic, while the *Valori Plastici* group in Italy introduced a semi-academic form of mildly 'metaphysical' art which is typically embodied in the work of Casorati and is very like that of the Munich (or 'Magic Realist') artists in the 'Neue Sachlichkeit' show. But the very fact that the

191

spread of Expressionism in other countries was part of this process – that similar formal conventions, in other words, could appear intensely modern in one context and relatively 'reactionary' in another – shows how misleading it is to treat artistic tendencies in such a clear-cut way. This is something that is realised more easily outside Germany, and away from the narrow concentration on Expressionism which has inspired so much of the relevant research. For elsewhere it seems self-evident that 'Neue Sachlichkeit' was to a great extent an offshoot of German Expressionism as well as a reaction against it; in other words that what had changed was not so much the principles and formal innovations arrived at from 1910 onwards as the spirit in which they were applied. The movement as such had run down; the ideological pressures driving it had fallen with the establishment of the Weimar Republic; its financial stimulus went with the end of the inflation. Yet it had left far too deep a mark on the country's cultural life to be considered in any way dead: influencing not only the whole structure of the arts (museums, teaching, the theatrical repertoire and all the backlog of experience) but also countless individual writers, actors and artists.

Even the very first counter-movement, that of the Dadaists, began within Expressionism; thus Ball, Hennings and Arp had all come from it, while the Rumanian Marcel Jancu at first shared some of its conventions and Berlin Dada developed out of Herzfelde's utopian-Expressionist *Neue Jugend.* Kurt Schwitters too, whose one-man *Merz* movement in Hanover from 1923 on is nowadays related to Dada and to non-figurative art, painted Expressionistically between 1917 and 1919, in which year he became one of Walden's artists at the Sturm gallery. He also contributed one or two conventionally Expressionist poems to *Der Sturm* – for instance, 'Erhabenheit', which has the words *Mensch, Glut* and *Zacken* all in the first five lines – before turning to a form of sound poetry clearly derived from Stramm; his biographer Werner Schmalenbach calls him 'a late Expressionist in Dadaist clothing'. Another illuminating evolution can be seen in the case of Goll, whose conscious adherence to Expressionism, with such poems as 'The Panama Canal', was followed by flippant surreal farces like *Methusalem der ewige Bürger* (1922, staged in Berlin by William Dieterle in 1924) or the 'filmpoem' *Die Chaplinade* (1920, with drawings by Léger). 'Der neue Orpheus', a poem which he dates 1923 and which Kurt Weill set to music, has exactly the new matter-of-factness:

192

Orpheus: wer kennt ihn nicht:	(Orpheus: why, everybody knows him:
1 m 78 gross	I metre 78 tall
68 Kilo	68 kilos
Augen braun	Eyes brown
Stirn schmal	Forehead narrow
Stiefer Hut	Bowler hat
Geburtsschein in der Rocktasche	Birth certificate in his pocket
Katholisch	Catholic
Sentimental	Sentimental
Für die Demokratie	In favour of democracy
Und von Beruf ein Musikant ...	And by profession a musician ...)

Yet Goll himself called this an Expressionist poem, and with some justification. For much of the early Expressionist verse of men like Van Hoddis, Blass, Lichtenstein and Herrmann-Neisse was far closer to that of Tucholsky and Kästner in the later 1920s than to the more symbolist or declamatory poets of the movement's climax.

The Expressionist background is also present in the work of such apparently new writers as Brecht, Zuckmayer, Wolf and (as we have seen already) Fallada, though in Brecht's case many of the clues were rubbed out during the continual revisions of his early plays. The Bauhaus too, as we saw, began life under utopian-Expressionist auspices. Indeed to Lothar Schreyer, an early member of the staff who (like Georg Muche) had been a collaborator of Walden's, it was 'a stronghold of Expressionism' devoted to 'the teaching of the STURM, Herwarth Walden's teaching': a judgment that was all the more understandable in view of the dominant early role of Johannes Itten, who felt that art teaching should be directed to making a 'new man', and accordingly inflicted the school with a Steinerish cult called Mazdaism, propagated from Switzerland by Dr Zaradusch (?Zarathustra) Hanisch. This nonsense was only knocked out of the school by the combined efforts of Van Doesburg outside and Moholy-Nagy in, together with the departure of Itten. Even then Kandinsky, and to some extent Klee, Feininger and Oskar Schlemmer, remained as a check on the new utilitarian course, particularly after the move from Weimar to Dessau.

As for the painters who gave the whole 'Neue Sachlichkeit' trend its name, they were really soberer and more disillusioned Expressionists. Dix set out from his Expressionist beginnings (as seen in the war drawings), went through a Dadaist phase, then painted portraits and socially critical works with a highly sadistic element of distortion dominating their apparent literalism; only to turn truly academic with his appointment to a professorship at Dresden in 1927. Grosz's evolution was very similar; his literalistic paintings of the middle 1920s (of which the best known was probably his portrait of Herrmann-Neisse, which remained in Mannheim), did not stop him from continuing to produce savage satirical drawings and watercolours right up to his departure for America in 1932; he was always a very hard man. Beckmann admittedly had at first painted very differently, but he too turned to a form of Expressionism in the war, whose results are particularly evident in his graphic work – thus Paul Ferdinand Schmidt in 1920 called his etchings *Die Hölle* 'a terrifyingly vivid parallel to the writings of Fritz von Unruh, Toller and R. Becher' – and persist beneath the sometimes heavily symbolic literalness of his paintings. Perhaps the most characteristic artist of those years, at least for middle-brows, was the undemanding Carl Hofer, whose first real success in Germany came with his one-man show at Flechtheim's new Berlin gallery in 1924. His mixture of a modified Expressionist distortion with a largely Parisian technique and sense of volume, and a Mediterranean nostalgia that recalls Marées, seemed a welcome relief after the hectic art of the previous fifteen years. So experienced a judge as Meier-Graefe ranked him with Beckmann as the most worthwhile of the postwar German painters, and in 1928 both men were given large retrospectives at Mannheim.

It was all something a good deal more complicated than a mere return to nineteenth-century realism; for even the extreme political wing of 'Neue Sachlichkeit', despite its concern with working-class artists and audiences, accepted many Expressionist conventions and saw no necessity to condemn the modern movement as such. Admittedly there was at the same time a much more radical form of reaction, which was racially and politically motivated and directed more or less blindly against the whole modern movement, including 'Neue Sachlichkeit' itself. This began as a campaign against 'racially impure' art, sponsored by a body called the Deutsche Kunstgesellschaft which had been founded in 1920 by an otherwise obscure painter called Bettina Feistel-Rohmeder. It was not at first associated with any particular artistic movement, but in 1923 it got an ally of some slight distinction in Anton Faistauer, the painter of the Salzburg Festspielhaus murals, who wrote that 'the so-called Expressionist movement' founded by Kandinsky, is an Eastern affair ... The Jews, particularly those from the East, seem to be the leaders of Expressionism, and have also been the chief participants in the social revolution. Against that, the countries which put up the greatest resistance to this movement are those which have preserved some degree of social order. Its expression is a purely proletarian one.

– though in fact the only important Jewish Expressionist painters inside Germany were Meidner and (for a few years) Segall.

In 1926 the prolific racial theorist Hans Günther brought out his *Rasse und Stil,* arguing that even Impressionism had been un-Nordic 'because it treated ugliness as the sole truth'. Two years later the architect Paul Schultze-Naumburg, soon to become director of the Weimar Kunsthochschule (where he had Schlemmer's Bauhaus murals obliterated), published his *Kunst und Rasse,* with its shocking juxtapositions of deformed human bodies and artistic distortions, its chapter on The Nordic Bosom and its complaints that 'foreign, exotic features now predominate in the representation of human beings'. In 1929 a Kampfbund für Deutsche Kultur (or Militant League for German Culture) was founded by the National-Socialist ideologist Alfred Rosenberg to turn such arguments into an organised campaign. That year Barlach, who had perhaps rashly accepted commissions for a number of war memorials, found himself increasingly attacked by the nationalists, even by such petty means as anonymous letters and messages pinned to his door. Two of his commissions (at Malchin and Stralsund) were cancelled, while those at Kiel and his own town of Güstrow ran into controversy. Such backward steps were not, alas, the work of a 'lunatic fringe', but the start of something that was to mean a good deal more than the natural succession of one artistic tendency by another.

8 1933 to 1945

The Nazis

If it was the shock of the First World War which largely brought German Expressionism into being it was Adolf Hitler's accession to power which really finished it off. 1933, not 1923, was the death of the movement, and just as in the case of Trakl and Stadler and Marc much of this death was literal, whether in freedom or in a camp, by the man's own hand or by that of an unknown SS guard:

Erich Mühsam	10/11 July	1934
Reinhold Goering	7 November	1936
Ernst Ludwig Kirchner	15 June	1938
Ernst Toller	22 May	1939
Carl Einstein	5 July	1940
Walter Hasenclever	15 August	1940
Paul Kornfeld	January	1942
Stefan Zweig	22/3 February	1942
Jakob van Hoddis	after 30 April	1942
Rudolf Levy		1943
Alfred Wolfenstein	22 June	1945

So many of those whose names make up the history of the movement as we have seen it now left the country, whether to save their lives or because they found Hitler and all his works intolerable, that there is no point in listing them. We can take it that they just dropped out of the cultural life of the country, later in some cases to play an influential part in that of others. It is simpler to mention the exceptions who are known to have stayed: the dozen or so artists, writers and theatre people whose particular situation as supporters of the new regime or victims of its repressions will emerge below. During

Adolf Hitler opening the House of German Art in Munich in 1937. (This photo from the Ullstein archives proves to have been faked: Hitler was originally standing beside the rostrum, and a completely new photograph of him has been gummed in above the rostrum to raise him higher than the others; the gentleman on the left has also been gummed in on top of the original print.)

two or three years after the initial purge it did look as if certain aspects of the Expressionist movement might be tolerated under National Socialist cultural policy, together with a minority of the more sympathetically Nordic writers and artists. The ambiguities and misunderstandings to which this led were to be of some import-ance in determining the subsequent evolution of the arts not only in Germany but in Europe as a whole.

The basis of the Nazi reaction against Expressionism and all its works was threefold. First and foremost, Nazism was a racialist movement, relying on 'thinking with one's blood' rather than with the (always suspect) intellect, so that not only were a good propor-tion of Expressionist writers and theatre people liable to internment (and eventual murder) as Jews if they remained in the country but Expressionism itself could be regarded as racially impure on the lines argued by Günther and Schultze-Naumburg. Besides this there was the concept, first outlined in Max Nordau's *Entartung* at the turn of the century, of modern art as somehow pathologically 'decadent' and symptomatic of the decline of western civilisation: a notion which it was not difficult to link to the racial one. Finally there was the close association of Expressionism and its spiritual heirs both with the peace campaign in the First World War and with the subsequent establishment of the Weimar Republic. For an aggresive nationalist political movement dedicated to avenging the 'stab in the back' of 1918, overthrowing the Treaty of Versailles and setting up the new glorious Third Empire of which Moeller van den Bruck had dreamed, the demolition of the whole republican cultural apparatus was an automatic step.

The Reichstag Fire which marks the beginning of Hitler's full authoritarian rule took place on 27 February. Mühsam, who had already spent six years in goal after the Munich Soviet, was arrested the next night, his beard pulled out and a swastika cut in his hair; he was tortured and murdered in Oranienburg concentration camp. Hiller was likewise arrested within a few days but released a year later, soon afterwards fleeing the country. On 10 May uniformed Nazi students from Berlin University, led by Alfred Bäumler, their

Deutſche Studenten marſchieren
wider den
undeutſchen Geiſt

12238

new 'Professor of Political Pedagogy' and accompanied by SA and
SS military bands, burnt some 20,000 books on the Opernplatz,
singling out for formally chanted denunciation, among others,
those of Heinrich Mann, Freud and F. W. Foerster. During the same
month Barlach was forced to leave the new house which he had built
himself in Güstrow, the Magdeburg city council having already
had his war memorial taken down from the cathedral, to be stored
in the cellar of the National-Galerie (whence friends later recovered
and preserved it). The purging of the former Expressionists from
official positions was in full swing. In September a law was passed
setting up the new *Kulturkammer* system, in which all those profes-
sionally engaged in the arts now had to be grouped in six subsidiary
chambers under the direction of Goebbels's Propaganda Ministry.
At the party rally in Nuremberg that month Hitler proclaimed his
confidence in the works of art that would result simply from
'consciously emphasising the racial substance which bears our
people'. He denounced any artistic distortion as not only technically
inept but morally deficient, and laid down that:

In all cultural matters too the National-Socialist movement and state leadership cannot allow such incompetents and charlatans suddenly to change their allegiance and move into the new State as if nothing had happened, with a view to once again having a big say in its art and cultural policy.

In October he addressed the first *Tag der Deutschen Kunst* in Munich and laid the foundation stone of a *Haus der Deutschen Kunst* designed by Paul Ludwig Troost, whom he held to be the greatest German architect since Schinkel.

The main work of the first year of National Socialism was to undo that establishment of the modern movement described in chapter 6. Thus Hofer, Moll (who had shifted to Düsseldorf in 1932), Campendonk and Beckmann all lost their professorships, Otto Mueller having died in 1930. Dix was sacked in April 1933 on the grounds that

among his pictures are some which are most deeply wounding to the moral feelings of the German people, while others are calculated to sap the people's will for defence.

Nauen and Klein managed to hold out until the second wave of purges in 1936-7. The Bauhaus had already been the target of many attacks, having to leave first Weimar in 1924 then Dessau in 1932 because the provincial government in the one case and the city council in the other refused to go on supporting it. Now in a much reduced form in Berlin it was closed provisionally on 10 April and finally in August. In February Kollwitz and Heinrich Mann had resigned from the Prussian Academy, which shortly afterwards expelled Döblin, Kaiser, Leonhard Frank, Schickele and Werfel. On 7 May Liebermann, who had been made its honorary president in 1928 at the age of eighty, resigned with a public statement that 'it is my conviction that art has nothing to do either with politics or genealogy'; when he died in 1935 the only painters who chose to attend his funeral were Kollwitz and Purrmann. A week later Max von Schillings, Liebermann's successor as active President, asked a number of the other 1931 appointees to resign: Schmidt-Rottluff and Dix did so, while Erich Mendelsohn, Kirchner and Nolde were among those who refused. Jessner, who had already resigned from the Staatstheater in 1930, emigrated. Franz Ulbrich from the National Theatre at Weimar now became *Intendant* of the Staatstheater, with Johst as his *Chefdramaturg*. Hartung left Darmstadt (for the second time), Carl Zeiss at Munich having died in 1924.

At the National-Galerie Justi and his assistant Ludwig Thormaelen were dismissed in July; Kaesbach, who had been made director of the Düsseldorf Academy, likewise lost his job. So did Paul Ferdinand Schmidt at Dresden, Heise at Lübeck, Gustav Pauli at Hamburg, Lili Fischel at Karlsruhe, Ludwig Grote at Dessau, Hartlaub at Mannheim, Osthaus's successor Gosebruch at the Folkwang Museum (which had moved to Essen after its founder's death), and Tschudi's successor Friedrich Dörnhöffer in Munich. In some cases this was specifically on account of their support for modern and/or foreign art. Justi was succeeded first by the more nationalist Alois Schardt from Halle, an admirer of Nolde and Marc, who was almost immediately dismissed too, and emigrated; then in the same year by Eberhard Hanfstaengl, a cousin of Hitler's former ADC. Gosebruch at Essen was succeeded by the SS officer Count Klaus Baudissin, who considered that the pictures in his gallery gave 'the image of a collapsing world'. Redslob's post of *Reichskunstwart* was abolished. Of the private dealers concerned with modern art, who were mainly Jewish, very few remained in operation; Buchholz and Nierendorf still held out in Berlin, and Günther Franke in Munich, but those artists who had contracts with Cassirer or Flechtheim now had to look elsewhere. For the same reason they also had in many cases to find new patrons, so that one way and another the market for their work was disappearing.

Nordic or decadent?

From the outset the question was whether the Nazi cultural purge, having gone so far, was going to stop, or to go on and enforce the conservative standards preached by Rosenberg, Schultze-Naumburg and the other experts associated with the *Kampfbund für deutsche Kultur*. In the middle of 1933 the uncertainty on this point within the party hierarchy came to something of a climax, with Goebbels on the one side and Rosenberg on the other. The occasion was an exhibition which the Nazi students of Berlin university mounted under the title 'German Art', consisting of work by Barlach, Nolde, Schmidt-Rottluff and Goebbels's own ministry official Hans Weidemann, who was alleged to be an Expressionist painter. When Goebbels was seen to have won this battle and the Kampfbund itself became ignominiously absorbed in the *Kraft durch Freude* organisation it looked as if Expressionism, at least in the visual arts, might survive under the wing of the new ideology. Gottfried Benn, at this stage an enthusiastic supporter of the new regime, which he foretold in his *Kunst und Macht* (1934) would 'pour the floodwaters of its vitality, heavy with ancestry, across Europe's jaded surfaces' praising it for its 'enormous biological instinct for racial perfection', clearly thought that a similar position might be won for Expressionist literature. As one of its few representatives left inside Germany, he wrote a 'Bekenntnis zum Expressionismus' which appeared in November and was included in his book *Kunst und Macht* the following year. Among the grounds for optimism was the fact that Goebbels himself had not only been a student of Friedrich Gundolf's at Heidelberg but in 1929 had published a novel called *Michael* which contained the passage:

We are all Expressionists today: people who want to shape the outside world from within themselves. Expressionism is building a new world inside itself. Its power and its secret lie in its passion.

Now he borrowed flower paintings by Nolde from the National-Galerie to hang in his own office. Moreover where Goering in February 1933 had criticised Munch's pictures there and refused to accept the assurance of the experts that they were profoundly nordic, in December Goebbels sent a message to the Norwegian paper *Tidens Tegn* for the artist's seventieth birthday, praising him as 'springing from nordic-germanic stock' and working in a style entirely free of naturalism.

From the outset of the movement Expressionism had been interpreted by some critics as essentially German and Nordic, while there were other obvious arguments which might have been expected to tell in its favour once its pacifist, Jewish and left-wing associations has been expunged. For, as Benn pointed out, it developed in the first place as a reaction against materialism and a return to the primitive, or *Ur-*; it lost some of its best people in the war; it spoke in the name of Youth; it found its precedents in such approved German sources as Meister Eckehart, *Faust II* and Nietzsche; and it was closely linked with Italian Futurism, which was one of the constituent elements of Mussolini's Fascism. Indeed when Marinetti was entertained by the Union of National Writers in Berlin on 29 March 1934 it was Benn who welcomed him at once as a modernist pioneer and as the man responsible for giving Fascism its hymn 'Giovinezza' and its symbolic black shirt – 'the colour of terror and death'. Nor was Benn the only Expressionist writer who had moved into a position of supporting National Socialism. Johst, most conspicuously, wrote the first officially acknowledged Nazi play, *Schlageter* – a rather conventional drama about a young *Freikorps* member who was shot by the French for sabotage during the Ruhr Occupation in 1923, containing one famous, always misquoted and usually misattributed line: 'When I hear culture I take the safety-catch off my Browning' – which opened the reorganised Staats-theater on 20 April 1933. He became the chairman of the writers' section of the Prussian Academy in June and first president of the *Schrifttumskammer,* the writers' chamber. Heynicke too, the *Volk* enthusiast, wrote two of the type of open-air mass plays known as 'Thingspiele': *Neurode* (1934), about a labour camp, and *Der Weg ins Reich* (1935). Bronnen was no longer writing, but he had moved over to the Nazis in the second half of the 1920s, when he wrote his nationalist novel *O.S.*

At the least it looked as if Barlach and Nolde would now flourish. They were both north Germans, little involved in the actual politics of Expressionism, Nolde having even been an early member of the Schleswig-Holstein Nazi party. Accordingly a number of other modern artists evidently decided that there was a good chance, if they played their cards right, of continuing to work in their own way without further difficulties. Thus the 1933 Sezession showed work by Hofer, Purrmann, Pechstein, Schmidt-Rottluff and Belling, while Hofer wrote an article in the *Deutsche Allgemeine Zeitung* on 13 July arguing that their work was quite free from Jewish influence. Beckmann moved to Berlin, where he painted the first of his big symbolic triptychs; Feininger had a joint exhibition with Muche in the Nierendorf Gallery in Berlin in 1934, and one-man shows there and at the Galerie Ferdinand Möller in the two succeeding years. Even Gropius made an attempt early in 1934 to persuade the presi-dent of the Kunstkammer that modern architecture was very Germanic. Apart from Kirchner, whose last visit to Germany was in 1932, the Brücke painters continued to work there, though not very productively; Heckel for instance averaged eight pictures a year between 1934-9, his only exhibition during the Nazi period being that organised by the Kestner-Gesellschaft in 1935. Their effort to maintain what was left of their position led them into some not wholly worthy arguments. Kirchner could tell the Prussian Acadamy that 'I am neither a Jew nor a Social-Democrat; nor have I been politically active apart from that. In other respects too I have a clear conscience', while Nolde pointed to his party membership and his roots in German territory lost under the Treaty of Versailles, and Pechstein claimed credit for having painted pictures of a former German colony.

As early as 1934 there were already signs that all this was a rearguard action, Dix for instance being forbidden to exhibit, while the Schrifttumskammer refused to let Barlach carry out his project for the grave of Theodor Däubler, who died that year. In Munich in 1935 the Bavarian Minister of the Interior, Adolf Wagner, ordered 26 works to be removed from a show in the Neue Pinakothek called 'Contemporary Art from Berlin', among them pictures by Nolde, Beckmann, Heckel, Purrmann and Feininger; the local Neue Sezession too was dissolved and its president Max Unold interviewed by the Gestapo. Just why Goebbels now reversed his policy is not clear even today, though it is true that Hitler's *Parteitag* speeches in these years complained that 'the artistic cultural stuttering of cubists, Futurists and Dadaists' was still going on, and warned his listeners to 'be increasingly sharp in rejecting it'. Whatever the reason, a second, quite unmistakeable offensive against the modern movement began in 1936, when the abstract gallery designed by Lissitzky for the Hanover Landesmuseum was destroyed, a Rohlfs retrospective at Barmen closed, work by Kollwitz, Barlach and Lehmbruck removed from the Prussian Academy's jubilee exhibition, a book of Barlach drawings suppressed before publication, Schmidt-Rottluff forbidden to exhibit and the Kronprinzenpalais in Berlin shut down. In May of the same year an attack was launched on Benn and his 'swinish' writings by the SS paper *Das schwarze Korps*.

At the end of 1936 a Munich academic painter called Adolf Ziegler, who had painted a portrait of Hitler's niece after her suicide in the Brown House in 1931, was appointed president of the Fine Art chamber of the Kulturkammer. He was already the party's art adviser in Munich, and seems also to have cultivated Darré, the Minister of Agriculture who originated the classic phrase 'Blood and Soil'. Now it became plain to even the most optimistic that no breakaway from strict naturalism would be tolerated, however Germanic its ancestry. The Prussian Academy was finally purged of Kirchner, Pechstein and Barlach; Rohlfs was expelled the next year at the age of 89, and within a few months had died in his studio at Hagen; Nolde managed to hang on till 1941. Barlach's *Geisteskämpfer* in Kiel university church was taken down on 20 April

204

1937, (Hitler's forty-eighth birthday) and subsequently smashed up, though a cast was saved; the flying angel which he had given to Güstrow cathedral was removed in August and melted for scrap in the war. In the same year the Buchholz Gallery in Berlin had three exhibitions shut down: Corinth's, Barlach's and a retrospective for Kollwitz's seventieth birthday. In Munich, which was now seen as the centre of the new movement in the arts, a vast *Haus der deutschen Kunst* – itself a copybook example of the Nazi monumental architectural style – was opened by Hitler on 18 July, together with a large, exceedingly solemn exhibition of bad modern academic art and party propaganda paintings, no fewer than eighty works having been thrown out at the last moment by Hitler himself. 'From now on', he told his guests, 'we are going to wage a relentless cleaning-up campaign against the last subversive elements in our culture'. Almost simultaneously a book by a mediocre racially-conscious artist called Wolfgang Willrich, a protégé of Darré's, appeared under the pleasant title *Säuberung des Kunsttempels,* or 'Cleaning up the Temple of Art'. A day later the greater Degenerate Art Exhibition opened in the Munich Archaeological Institute.

This Degenerate Art Exhibition, which had over a million visitors in six weeks (or about as many as the London Tate Gallery in the whole year 1967-8) was rapidly organised by Ziegler on the basis of a decree signed by Hitler on 30 June, allowing him to

select works of decadent art in the sphere of painting and sculpture since 1910 from those owned by German State, Provincial and Municipal authorities ...

Among the 730 which he picked were some 25 apiece by Kirchner, Nolde and Schmidt-Rottluff, ten to a dozen each by Mueller, Beckmann, Rohlfs and Kokoschka, and work by Marc ('The Tower of Blue Horses'), Barlach, Chagall and virtually every other German twentieth-century artist mentioned in this book from Paula Modersohn-Becker on. The exhibition was hung to the maximum disadvantage of the pictures, with slogans on red banners, hastily scrawled derisory comments on the walls and insistent reminders of the prices paid out of public funds (possibly at the height of the inflation, when the figures naturally ran into millions). A more leisurely purge of museums throughout the country then followed, while the exhibition itself was shown in other German cities. This again was conducted under Ziegler's personal direction, and is reckoned to have led to the confiscation of about 5,000 paintings and

205

sculptures (of all nationalities) and 12,000 graphic works. It was legalised by a Degenerate Art Law of 31 May, 1938, which for some reason was not annulled after 1945, so that the confiscations remain valid today, together with any subsequent changes of ownership. Some of the more valuable works – such as three Van Goghs from the National-Galerie, Gauguin's 'Riders by the Sea' and one of the Cézannes from the Folkwang Museum – went into Goering's private collection or were sold for his personal benefit. One-hundred and twenty-five were sold for hard currency in an auction held in Lucerne by the Galerie Fischer on 30 June 1939, where Swiss, Dutch and Belgian museums bought a number of works. Others disappeared more or less mysteriously into private collections. The 1,000-odd paintings and sculptures and nearly 4,000 graphic works which had not been sold or looted by 1939 were burnt at the headquarters of the Berlin fire brigade. Many pictures remain

Hitler and Goebbels (front) going round the Degenerate Art Exhibition of 1937. The inscriptions and slogans are designed to make the exhibits look ridiculous.

lost, including some of those illustrated in this book.

That was that. By the end of 1937 Pechstein, Barlach, Rohlfs and Jawlensky were forbidden to exhibit, in addition to those who had already been banned. Feininger and Beckmann had left the country. Others were forbidden to work at all, notably Schmidt-Rottluff and Nolde in 1941. Kirchner killed himself on 15 June, 1939, after destroying the blocks of all his wood-engravings; 'the smear campaign broke him', wrote his wife. Barlach died of a stroke on 24 October, his funeral being attended by Kollwitz, Schmidt-Rottluff, Heise, Justi, and Hermann Hesse of the people mentioned in this book, and also a few others such as Max Planck, Benn, who had returned to the army medical service in 1935, claiming that 'the army is the aristocratic way to emigrate' was now forbidden to write, as also was Edschmid in 1941. Since Heynicke was concentrating on film scripts and light novels, and even Johst had fallen

207

The purge of 'Degenerate Art' from German museums, 1937.
Total of works confiscated, including prints and drawings

Listed by artists		Listed by cities	
Nolde	1052	Essen, Folkwang Museum	1273
Heckel	729	Hamburg, Kunsthalle and Kunstgewerbemuseum	1252
Kirchner	639		
Schmidt-Rottluff	608	Berlin, National-Galerie and Kupferstichkabinett	1152
Beckmann	509		
Rohlfs	418	Düsseldorf, Kunstsammlungen	900
Kokoschka	417	Dresden, Gemäldegalerie, Kupferstichkabinett and Stadt-museum	896
Barlach	381		
Feininger	378		
Otto Mueller	357	Chemnitz, Kunsthütte and Städt. Kunstsammlungen	641
Pechstein	326		
Hofer	313	Erfurt, museums	591
Corinth	295	Breslau, Schlesisches Museum	560
Grosz	285	Mannheim, Kunsthalle	584
Dix	260	Frankfurt, Städel and Städtische Galerie	496
Grossmann	206		
Felixmüller	151	Wuppertal-Elberfeld, Städtische Kunstsammlungen	403
Marc	130		
Nauen	117	Stuttgart, Staatliche Galerie	382
Lehmbruck	116	Weimar, Städt. Kunstsammlungen	381
Klee	102	Hanover, Landesmuseum and Kestner-Museum	375
Seewald	101		
		Cologne, Wallraf-Richartz	341
		Stettin, Städt. Museum	307
		Jena, Kunstverein and Stadt-museum	273
		Saarbrücken, Staatl. Museum	272
		Wiesbaden, Landesmuseum	231
		Königsberg, Kunstsammlung	206
		Hagen, Städtisches Museum	166
		Bremen, Kunsthalle	165

Note: The figures are naturally highest where there is a large body of graphic work, and lowest where an artist's pictures had scarcely begun to get into the public collections by 1933.

GEMÄLDE UND PLASTIKEN
MODERNER MEISTER
AUS DEUTSCHEN MUSEEN

Braque, Chagall, Derain, Ensor, Gauguin, van Gogh, Laurencin, Modigliani, Matisse, Pascin, Picasso, Vlaminck, Marc, Nolde, Klee, Hofer, Rohlfs, Dix, Kokoschka, Beckmann, Pechstein, Kirchner, Heckel, Grosz, Schmidt-Rottluff, Müller, Modersohn, Macke, Corinth, Liebermann, Amiet, Baraud, Feininger, Levy, Lehmbruck, Mataré, Marcks, Archipenko, Barlach

AUSSTELLUNG

IN ZÜRICH

Zunfthaus zur Meise, vom 17. Mai (Mittwoch) bis 27. Mai (Samstag) 1939

Eintritt: Fr. 3.—

Täglich geöffnet von 10—12 Uhr und von 2—6 Uhr (Sonntag nachmittag geschlossen)

IN LUZERN

Grand Hôtel National, vom 30. Mai (Dienstag) bis 29. Juni (Donnerstag) 1939

Eintritt: Fr. 3.—

Täglich geöffnet von 10—12 Uhr und von 2—6 Uhr (Sonntag geschlossen)

AUKTION IN LUZERN

Grand Hôtel National, Freitag, den 30. Juni 1939, nachmittags 2.15 Uhr

AUKTIONSLEITUNG: THEODOR FISCHER, GALERIE FISCHER, LUZERN

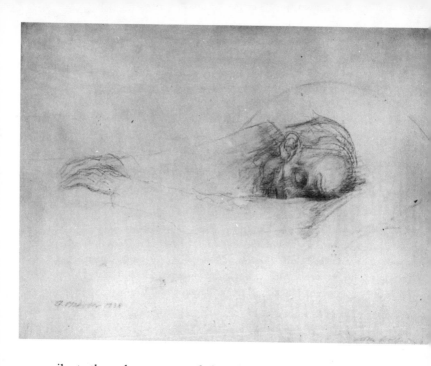

silent, the sole remnant of the whole Expressionist movement in Germany consisted of Heckel, Pechstein. Hofer and Dix, who could paint for their private customers or for sale abroad so long as they did not show in public; a few theatre people of non-Jewish origin, such as Werner Krauss and Heinrich George, who were prepared to perform the new repertoire; one or two artists like Klein (stage design) and Muche (textiles) who had taken refuge in other work; and a handful of minor Expressionists such as Otto Herbig and Willi Jaeckel who went on painting and even exhibiting in other, more acceptable styles.

The view from outside

Unlike the earlier reaction in 1920-2, this virtual extermination of the modern movement in Germany was not part of any wider European change of feeling. On the contrary, the continent now divided in a very odd way, with Nazi Germany on the same side as her proclaimed enemy Soviet Russia and, to a much more limited

The death of Barlach. Drawing of the sculptor on his deathbed by Käthe Kollwitz, signed 27 October 1938 and now in the Hamburg Kunsthalle.

degree, her ally Fascist Italy, and the rest of the artistic and intellectual world ranged against them. Just why this should have happened as it did has never been satisfactorily explained, but starting from the first Soviet Writers' Congress (at which Toller spoke up for Expressionism and Herzfelde for James Joyce) the Soviet Communist Party led by Stalin and Zhdanov pursued a policy of rooting out 'formalism' and 'cosmopolitanism' in the arts, which adopted similar jargon, set up similar structures, caused similar tragedies (such as the execution of Meyerhold after his arrest in 1939) and led to a very similar official naturalistic art. In the countries absorbed by the Nazis, starting with Austria in 1938 and Czechoslovakia in 1939, the same measures could be applied as in Germany proper, though there was not so much popular backing and less time in which to make them effective. In Italy, however, not only had there hitherto been no such interference, but the association of the Futurists with the Fascist movement meant that even the extreme avant-garde was covered by the official ideology and the Black Shirt. With the best will in the world not to lag behind his partner, Mussolini could make little contribution beyond a limited degree of racial discrimination.

In western Europe and the Americas the strong anti-Nazi feeling, particularly among artists and intellectuals, inspired a new sympathy with the kind of culture which the Nazis were trying to stamp out. This gave a second wind, as it were, to the scattered elements of Expressionism outside Germany, so that the earlier wave of foreign curiosity about the German movement around 1923 was succeeded by another after 1935. Three things combined to bring this about: the arrival in other countries of German artists, musicians, writers, theatre people and all sorts of cultural middlemen such as dealers and publishers; the natural association of left-wing political views (for the main opposition to the Nazis in those days was from the left) with Expressionism and its aftermath; and finally a certain instinctive sense that anything the Nazis rejected deserved support. The result was that indigenous expressionism in nearly every country was not only consolidated itself, but became informed by a much

Below The expressive Picasso of the anti-fascist 1930s. 'La Femme qui pleure', 1937, from Sir Roland Penrose's collection, London. *Right* An influential immigrant to Britain, Jankel Adler, whose mid-1920s portrait of Else Lasker-Schüler is now in the Wuppertal Museum.

better awareness and appreciation of what the German movement had been trying to do.

In France an Association d'Ecrivains et Artistes Révolutionnaires had been formed in 1932, with the Communist poet Paul Vaillant-Couturier as its moving spirit and such artists as Gromaire, Masereel, Edouard Pignon from the Pas-de-Calais, Edouard Goerg (mildly expressionist pin-ups of a stereotyped Parisian kind) and the young Francis Gruber (elongated misery, depicted with great skill) at one time or another among its members; another expressive painter of merit being the Alsatian Charles Walch. None the less it was the beginning of the Spanish Civil War in 1935 that really changed the face of art. This was above all on account of one picture, 'Guernica', which Picasso painted for the Spanish pavilion at the Paris International Exhibition of 1937 in memory of the (German) bombing of that town. This extremely expressive yet formalised masterpiece had been preceded by a number of studies and bull-fighting pictures which are perhaps the most expressionist things Picasso has ever done, and together, besides giving a decisive turn to Picasso's own work, they had a strong influence on painters everywhere who tried to tackle comparable subjects: the Czech Filla, for instance, in his 'Faëthon' of the same year, or the young Sicilian Renato Guttuso, whose 'Fucilazione in Campagna' in memory of Lorca was painted between 1936-8. A comparable approach can also be seen in Latin America, not only in the work of the Mexicans, who all returned to their country with the accession of President Cardenas in 1934, painting such frescoes as Orozco's 'The Outcasts' in Guadalajara (1937), with its similarities to Meidner and Gruber, but also in Segall's big paintings on the themes of racialism and emigration.

Both in the United States and in England the left-wing illustrators took a more or less expressionist direction: Richter and Gropper in *New Masses,* Boswell, Fitton and Holland in *Left Review.* Grosz, who emigrated to the United States in the winter of 1932-3, had an evident influence here, as also on the work of Ben Shahn, who had assisted Rivera on his Rockefeller Centre murals; though Grosz himself soon became restricted to an old masterly exactitude, alternating with fantastic romanticism à la Kubin. Other expressive artists came from the Federal Art Project set up by Roosevelt's Works Progress Administration in 1935, for instance Jack Levene, then in his early twenties, whose work sometimes looks like a cross between Grosz and Rouault, and has also been said to reflect

214

Soutine's influence. Of the Expressionists who settled in London, neither Meidner nor Kokoschka made any immediate impact upon the native scene; in fact Kokoschka had to wait twenty years to be acknowledged in his adopted country and Meidner remained in total obscurity till his return to Germany in the 1950s. The same was true of Schwitters in the Lake District. The two painters who were to prove most influential in Britain both arrived in Scotland with the Polish forces in 1940: Jankel Adler and Josef Herman. Adler had spent the 1920s mainly in Düsseldorf, while Herman had worked for two years in Belgium, where he seems to have learnt the monumental expressionism which he now applied to South Wales mining themes.

In America the first exhibitions of Kirchner, Nolde and Schmidt-Rottluff were given between 1936 and 1939, two of them at the Buchholz Gallery which had started up in New York; there was also a Kirchner show at the Detroit Institute of Art. In England a big exhibition of modern German painting was held at the New Burlington Galleries in 1938 as a demonstration against the Degenerate Art Exhibition. Herbert Read, who introduced Otto Bihalj-Merin's accompanying booklet (written under the pseudonym Peter Thoene), claimed that not only was the modern German school unknown to the public but 'even among those who are particularly concerned with modern art – art critics, collectors and dealers – it is almost entirely neglected': a situation which the exhibition failed to change.

Of the German Expressionist writers only Werfel and Toller now had a name with the foreign public, though the former's great American successes *Jacobowsky and the Colonel* and *The Song of Bernadette,* both totally un-expressionist in style and spirit, were still to come. Toller himself produced *Draw the Fires* at the Manchester Opera House in 1935, then in 1936 his new play *No More Peace,* with lyrics by W. H. Auden, had its première at the Gate Theatre in London with his wife in a leading part; it was also produced under the W.P.A.'s Federal Theater Project, though with little success. Auden, again, was one of Toller's co-authors in the cabaret programme *The Pepper Mill* which was put on by Klaus and Erika Mann in New York in 1937 (again without success) and later wrote his poem 'In Memory of Ernst Toller' after the latter's suicide, starting:

The shining neutral summer has no voice
To judge America, or ask how a man dies;
And the friends who are sad and the enemies who rejoice
Are chased by their shadows lightly away from the grave
Of one who was egotistical and brave.

A growing English awareness of the 1920s in Germany is reflected in Auden's own plays with Christopher Isherwood and in Isherwood's Berlin stories; their friend Stephen Spender likewise knew Germany and translated Toller's last play *Pastor Hall* (filmed in 1940 by the Boulting Brothers), collaborating also on a translation of *Dantons Tod* with Goronwy Rees. These were early symptoms of the change of temper which was to develop after the Second World War. For the moment it was confined to a mainly left-wing minority of the public, centred on the readers of John Lehmann's magazine *New Writing*, and it was blocked by a certain insularity on the part of the critics. Thus even J. B. Priestley's mildly expressionistic play *Johnson over Jordan* (staged in London in February 1939 with music by Benjamin Britten), with its Kaiser-like protagonist and its stylised subsidiary characters, was once again far from successful either critically or at the box-office. Its author later complained

that whenever I made an experiment I immediately lost all the older critics, who declared at once that it was pretentious and that they remembered something just like it in Berlin in 1923

– which they had greeted with just the same lack of enthusiasm, he might have added.

The Expressionist post-mortem

Within the scattered world of the German emigration the argument of the Goebbels and Rosenberg camps now repeated itself, though in rather more rational form. Had Expressionism in fact been the progressive and revolutionary movement it often claimed to be, or was it in fact a characteristic irrational piece of Nordic 'thinking with one's blood' which had objectively favoured the rise of Nazism, whatever the high intentions of its members? Starting in January 1934, and running through part of 1937 and 1938 this debate was pursued in the pages of the two Moscow émigré journals, *Internationale Literatur*, which Becher edited from that city, and *Das*

Wort. Two particular factors helped to unbalance it: first of all, it was sparked off by the situation of Gottfried Benn in the first three years of the Third Reich and took little account of the ensuing changes both in official Nazi policy and in Benn's own position; secondly, the Communist Party spokesmen who dominated the discussion, particularly Georg Lukács, were quite clearly influenced by their attitude to the parallel policy even then being put into effect in Russia. In Lukács's case this was one not merely of loyal acceptance but of genuine approval.

On 9 May 1933 Klaus Mann had written an open letter to Benn pointing out that he was the one reputable author who had not resigned from the Prussian Academy, and suggesting that this illustrated the 'virtually inexorable law that too much liking for the irrational leads to reactionary politics ...' He prophesied (all too rightly) that Benn's reward would be 'ingratitude and contempt'. Benn replied with a widely publicised 'Reply to the literary émigrés' expressing his support of Hitler's regime in almost Nazi terms ('Volk ist viel!'), citing Nietzsche on the fearful birth of a master race, repeating his call for 'the barbarians of the twentieth century', and claiming that History was about to 'produce a new human type from the inexhaustible womb of Race'.

Lukács followed this at the beginning of the next year with a long and reasoned criticism of the Expressionist movement, which he found too imprecise in its idea of 'bourgeois' and 'revolution', too clamorous in its language, too egocentric in its attitude and altogether too incapable of conveying any but a fragmentary view of the world to live up to its progressive pretensions and admitted achievements in stimulating opposition to the First World War. In his view it corresponded to the ideology of the USPD, a party which had helped betray the revolution of 1918. Thus it was perfectly natural that the Nazis should regard Expressionism as 'a heritage they could make use of' and give it an Aryan ancestry – he cited Schardt's concept of a 'Gothic-Faustian urge towards the infinite', traceable from Walther von der Vogelweide and Grünewald down to Barlach and Nolde – though because the conscious tendencies of the movement were anything but pro-Nazi it could only play a subordinate part in their cultural patchwork. No such allowances were made by the other party ideologist Alfred Kurella, Barbusse's sometime secretary and contributor of an article on erotic questions to *Die Erhebung* in 1919, when he renewed the attack in *Das Wort* in the second half of 1937. Using Benn as his main target he stated that it

217

was 'mandatory' that any wholehearted Expressionist should go over to Hitler. If most former members of the movement had not done so this proved nothing.

The flaw in such arguments was pointed out by Ernst Bloch: they were confined to literature, and took no account of Expressionism in the other arts. Over and above that, Lukács seemed to be paying too much attention to what the theorists of the movement had to say about it, and not enough to its original works, which contained an undoubted revolutionary and productive element. He had moreover made up his mind about the relationship of Expressionism to the Nazis at the time when that relationship was still in the balance, since when the Decadent Art Exhibition had shown only too clearly which way the balance had tipped. To Bloch therefore, who was later to be recognised as the outstanding Marxist philosopher of utopianism (*Das Prinzip Hoffnung*, 1954) it seemed that the Expressionists' humanitarian clichés were outdated, and therefore to be thrown on the scrap heap, but 'quite certainly not pro-fascist'. The trouble lay in Lukács's conception of the great classic tradition, which led him to see even Impressionism as a contributory element in the Decline of the West. This became still worse in the insensitive hands of Kurella, whose crude criteria of classicism, popular appeal, and the need to get rid of 'formalism' were extraordinarily close to the Nazis' own ideas.

What was at stake in such arguments, which were by no means restricted to Communists, was really the new Soviet policy towards the arts. Like the whole relationship between the Expressionists and revolutionary politics, they were to become important in determining the attitude taken towards the relics of the movement in eastern Europe after the Second World War.

9 Unresolved conclusions

Picking up the threads

It took five and a half years of bloody war for the world to rid itself of the Nazis, and their final collapse in 1945 left Germany deprived not only of government but to a great extent also of food, houses, industries, and raw materials. The mess was unparalleled. At the same time the country's living culture had been virtually extinguished and its sense of its own identity thrown into confusion. Bitter disagreements from the first prevented the four occupying powers from developing any co-ordinated policy or even setting up a central German administration. Yet the cultural problem was at first the same in each of the occupation zones: French, American, Russian and British, and likewise in the corresponding four sectors of Berlin: how could Germany's literary, artistic, theatrical and musicial life be reconstructed on non-Nazi and 'democratic' lines? Unfortunately not only was there wide difference as to the meaning of the word 'democratic', but much of the achievement of the 1920s in Germany was now ignored, whether by the occupation authorities, each of which was anxious to recommend its own often quite inappropriate cultural exports, or by the Germans themselves, who after twelve years of Nazi control had little clear memory of what went before and no idea where to find the books, pictures and scores which Goebbels had got rid of. The threads cut off after 1933 were thus not taken up in earnest until a new generation of intellectuals and students had become curious to know just what Hitler had so objected to, and set to work to find out.

By 1945 those former Expressionists who were not already dead were roughly between fifty and sixty years old, but from the first they did their best to fill the vacuum. Pechstein returned to his bombed Berlin studio that September, and became a professor at the Hochschule für Bildende Künste, where he was joined by Schmidt-Rottluff two years later; Hofer was made the school's director; Felixmüller took a job at Halle university in 1949; Heckel was a professor at the Karlsruhe Academy from 1949 to 1954. Dix came back from a French prisoner-of-war camp to resume painting in a placidly sub-expressionist style; by 1956 he had been elected to both East and West Berlin Academies of Arts. Becher and Wolf arrived in the wake of the Soviet occupying forces, after working for their wartime propaganda services and on the Free German Committee. Döblin reappeared as a French officer in Baden-Baden. Without official jobs but often with official encouragement, more and more of the exiles came back, if not to do significant original work at least to influence the younger generation by their presence – thus Günter Grass speaks of Döblin as his 'teacher' – and make them aware of the pre-Nazi heritage. This heritage of course was by no means purely or even primarily Expressionist, one of the most powerful examples for instance being that of Brecht. But because so much of the varied cultural development of Weimar Germany was in one way or another bound up with Expressionism – Brecht, for instance, had first-hand experience of some of its manifestations and a considerable respect for the plays of Kaiser – that movement was increasingly brought to people's attention.

The results differed in Western and Eastern Germany, and the two governments instinctively did their best to encourage this difference. That is to say that the West German department of cultural relations (quite rightly) came to see the work of the Expressionists, particularly of the painters and sculptors, as representative of their country's non-Nazi aspects, and accordingly promoted its showing abroad. This would have been less easy had there not at last been a considerable interest outside Germany in the movement and the whole period which it sprang from, while at the same time both academic study and the international art market began supporting it as never before. Thus there were Expressionist, Brücke or Blauer Reiter shows in Berne in 1948, St Gallen in 1949, Amsterdam in 1949 and 1951, Oberlin and Minneapolis in 1951, and at the Venice Biennale in 1952. Academic studies began appearing with such titles as *Georg Trakl. Strukturen in Werk und Persönlichkeit. Eine psychiatrischanthropographische Untersuchung* (1954) or *Das Phänomen der Menschenliebe im expressionistischen Drama als säkularisierte Form der christlichen Agape* (1952) – two examples taken from a random page of the nearest bibliography to the writer's hand. The awe-inspiring word *Expressionismusforschung* was coined. Of the many auction sales those of Mrs Walden's collection in 1954 (the Futurist pictures) and 1956 were of particular interest; Kokoschka's portrait of Walden, sold for 56,000 DM at the latter, being bought for the Tate Gallery five years later for 250,000

DM. Prices boomed as the museums stripped by Ziegler and his aides began to rebuild their collections (very few of the pictures were actually *given* back by those who had picked them up cheap in the 1930s); while for the West German new rich the Expressionists came to seem an attractive, sound and (in the occasional case of guilty conscience) thoroughly creditable buy.

What helped to emphasise this new-found respectability was the ambiguous status of Expressionism in the East. Here such returning expatriates as Arnold Zweig and Rudolf Leonhard, as well as far more politically-minded writers like Herzfelde, at first proved less influential than the party ideologists, who thought it necessary to import the Soviet doctrine of Socialist Realism (by which all distortion or stylisation was damned as 'formalist') and for the first nine or ten years after the armistice stuck closely to the interpretation put forward by Lukács, whose *Deutsche Literatur im Zeitalter des Imperialismus* (East Berlin, 1955), dismissed the whole movement as a paper 'revolution' (his quotation marks) confined to formal experiments and purely literary circles. Thus in 1952 Brecht, who was by no means sympathetic to Expressionism by nature but knew a major artist when he saw one, had to defend Barlach's work against the attacks of Wilhelm Girnus and others who found it uncanonically formal and too pessimistic in its view of the Russian peasantry. Even after Lukács's fall from grace in 1956 (after the Hungarian rising) Becher's deputy Alexander Abusch could still attack the Marxist critic Hans Mayer (an ally of Ernst Bloch's) as being over-indulgent to the literature of the 1920s, whilst an article by a certain Kurt Liebmann in *Bildende Kunst* (no. 8 of 1958) denounced Expressionism as 'a station on the road to "absolute" painting'. The result can be illustrated by the distribution of Kirchner's thousand-odd paintings. Roughly nine-tenths of them are in West Germany, Switzerland and the United States. East Germany has four.

Yet work apparently in the Expressionist tradition was once again produced in both halves of the country. In the West there was a double reason for this, since besides the indigenous writers and artists, like the short-lived Wolfgang Borchert whose play *Draussen vor der Tür* of 1947 was in neo-Expressionist style, or the painters Karl Kluth, Wilhelm Grimm and Werner Scholz who were all still in their forties in 1945 and could carry on much where they had been left twelve years earlier, there were also a number of new non-figurative expressionist influences from abroad. In particular the

221

Wolfgang Borchert

An diesem Dienstag

ROWOHLT

The Expressionist tradition
in the two Germanies.
Left Karl Staudinger's cover
for stories by Wolfgang
Borchert, 1948, (West).
Right Helene Scigala's 'Die Mahlu
a woodcut illustration to Zola's
Germinal, 1956, (East).

American Abstract Expressionists whose work will be discussed below were first shown in Berlin in 1951, their impact being reflected for instance in the work of K. R. H. Sonderborg and in the formation of the neo-Expressionist Quadriga group (K. O. Goetz, Otto Greis, Heinz Kreutz and Bernhard Schultze, all then in their late thirties) in Frankfurt in 1952. Even in the East, however, the strength of the 'proletarian' tradition deriving from Dix, Gross, Felixmüller and Kollwitz was enough not only to inspire but in the end politically to justify a form of socially-conscious art which differed from the Soviet model. The most important apologists of this trend, which can be seen in the work of honourable, if mediocre older artists like Nagel (president of the East German Academy in 1958 when Masereel was elected a foreign member) and the Grundigs, were the eminent Austrian Communist Ernst Fischer and the Halle art historian Wolfgang Hütt, author of several books and

223

articles tracing a specifically German tradition of 'committed' art. Nor should it be forgotten that Becher, who became Minister of Culture in 1954, had been a close friend of Ludwig Meidner's, while Kurella too, who was the party's chief cultural expert from 1957 till 1963, if always critical of Expressionism (and highly hostile to Kafka), was not unwilling to support the indigenous tradition against crude imitation of the Soviet pattern. The result is that mildly Expressionist influences of a strictly figurative (or Brücke) kind are to be seen in the work of many run-of-the-mill East German artists today.

The two outstanding survivors, epitomising the rival directions taken by the movement in 1933, were poets: Benn in West Berlin and Becher in East. Each in his way had a strong influence on the development of the country's culture after 1945, and they seem almost to have acknowledged the complementary nature of their different roles, respecting one another across the new barriers. Becher's function was public and to a great extent political; he was president of the official Kulturbund which worked under the Russians to reconstruct German cultural life, then head of the Writers' Section of the East German Academy on its foundation in 1950 and president of that body three years later; he also wrote the East German national anthem, a biography of the party secretary Walter Ulbricht and some atrociously sentimental pro-Soviet poems. Yet not only is the rhetorical phrasing of some of these poems reminiscent of his Expressionist work but his diaries too show him at times to have felt nostalgic about the early days of the movement, which he now applauded for its enthusiasms, right or wrong. He actually seemed closer to it than in his more restrained poetry of the 1930s, rejecting only the Expressionist assumption that new ideas had to be put in a new language. 'Therein lay the sacred mission of my work', he felt: 'To serve Mankind's future fulfilment'. It was almost as if he saw himself as an Expressionist who had got the forces of history on his side. As a verse of 1950 puts it:

Ein Ruf in der Nacht, ein Flüstern, ein Schrei
Und Jahre, Jahre wehen vorbei.
Ein jubelnder Chor nimmt auf mein Leben.

(A call in the night, a whisper, a cry
And years and years go drifting by.
A jubilant choir takes up my life.)

– the choir, to all intents and purposes, being the Song and Dance Ensemble of the Red Army.

Benn by contrast had been driven into privacy by the collapse of so many of his beliefs. He expected to be banned by the occupation authorities, and it was only in late 1948 that he could be persuaded to publish his backlog of works. True enough, his new story *Der Ptolemäer* frightened his prospective publisher, with its descriptions of post-war Berlin:

On the boulevards, the life of the steppes – uniforms and brothels in full swing. The Eighth Amurian Regiment – peacetime station Lo-sha-go – giving a band concert, their long trombones blaring. The bars fill up: polluted blood from Siberia and the scrapings of Hawaii ... The reconstruction of Europe is under way.

But just because he was not only a master of language but plagued, as the returning émigrés were not, by the same (unmastered) problems of conscience as so many other Germans, he now came to enjoy a unique reputation and influence, formulating in his lecture *Probleme der Lyrik* of 1951 a private, isolationist concept of 'absolute poetry' which was taken up with approval by Eliot and became a model for many younger German poets. In 1955, a year before his death, he too turned back to the Expressionist period and wrote a foreword for his publisher's anthology *Lyrik des expressionistischen Jahrzehnts*, itself something of a landmark in the movement's revival. Puzzling over the lack of common characteristics among the poets represented, he concluded that Expressionism had been the German term for that same fragmentation of reality that was known elsewhere as Cubism, Futurism or Surrealism. The task of a survivor like himself then must be the stoic one of

continuing to bear one's generation's and one's own mistakes and trying somehow to clarify them, to make a kind of swansong of them, leading them into that twilight hour when Minerva's owl begins her flight.

Widening possibilities

One of the stranger aspects of the whole quarter of a century since the war has been the growing acceptance in other countries of writers, artists, musicians and forms of art which in the past would have been dismissed as 'typically German'. In France, certainly, this was due most obviously to the strong German philosophical influence on such post-war intellectual leaders as Sartre (a pupil of

The aftermath of 'Guernica'. *Above* Plate by Renato Guttuso from the album
Gott mit uns, 1945. *Below* 'L'Ouvrier mort', 1952, a charcoal drawing by
Edouard Pignon from the collection of Myriam Prévot-Douatte, Paris.

Heidegger) and Merleau-Ponty (a follower of Husserl), together with
the Nietzschean Malraux – the second instance of an apocalyptic
believer in Man with a capital M who ended up as Minister of
Culture. Sartre's play *Les Séquestrés d'Altona*, like (on another
plane) Jean Cocteau's *L'Aigle à deux têtes*, is a good symptom of this
change in fashion. In England and the United States it was more
the result of the pre-war German emigration, which in two generations so leavened the whole apparatus of publishing, art dealing,
musicology, museum administration and art historical study that
the old mixture of ignorance and anti-German prejudice very largely
died out. Throughout the western world today the dominant
influences in such fields no longer come primarily from Paris: the
Bauhaus in design and art education, Brecht in the theatre, Schönberg and Webern in music, Miës van der Rohe in architecture and
(to a more limited extent) Kafka in the novel have now become the
outstanding models, even infecting the Communist countries.
Admittedly these particular examples are to a great extent non- or
post-Expressionist, but by simply making people aware of the
modern movement in Germany they have as it were dragged
Expressionism along in their wake. Never since the days of Wagner
and Nietzsche has the rest of the world been so open to German ideas.

There were also social and political reasons why this openness
should be exploited. First of all, the division of Germany put her
discordant occupiers in a position where each side had to conciliate
rather than control. The ensuing official tendency to flatter the
Germans, aggravated in the case of West Germany by that society's
growing economic wealth, increased until in 1966 we had the extraordinary sight of the Paris Musée de l'Art Moderne showing a mixed
exhibition of 'Le Fauvisme français et des débuts de l'Expressionisme
allemand', a correlation which it would hardly have occurred to any
pre-war French critic to make, not least because it would have
seemed presposterous so long as traditional painterly values were still
accepted; for by those standards the Expressionists (some of whom
now hang permanently in the museum) look terribly inferior. At the
same time there was also a less artificial motive for *rapprochement*

'Crucifixion', 1950, by the Italian-American Rico Lebrun, from Syracuse University, USA.

in the growing similarity between certain modern western societies and that of the Weimar Republic. All kinds of symptoms, both profound and superficial, go to indicate this: black clothes, the cult of violence, Brechtian haircuts, a growing disillusionment with parliamentary democracy, a concentration on sexual and artistic freedom at the expense of political awareness, and a general wish to polarise conflicts rather than resolve them by compromise. Though there are good reasons why this process (particularly visible in the case of England) should not lead to a repetition of 1933, it gives the younger generation of Europeans and Americans a natural sympathy with the culture of pre-Nazi Germany such as was conspicuously lacking before the war.

This new climate has contributed to a widespread expressionist revival. Partly this is a matter of themes: thus the cruelties of the war inspired not only such older artists as Marcel Jancu ('Genocide', 1945) but also the French Communist artist Boris Taslitsky ('Le Petit camp de Buchenwald en Février 1945'), Guttuso (the sequence *Gott mit uns* on the Ardeatine Caves massacre of 1944), Henry Moore (*Shelter Sketchbook*), Graham Sutherland and the Italian-American Rico Lebrun ('Massacre of the Innocents', 1948, and drawings of Buchenwald). Both Sutherland and Lebrun subsequently painted important 'Crucifixions' which develop a certain evident kinship between Grünewald and the expressive Picasso of 'Guernica' and after. The harsh impact of outer events may well be what turned the rather tame English romanticism of the 1940s into something tougher, inspiring Herbert Read (in his *Contemporary British Art* of 1951) to preach Expressionism rather than the Surrealism he used to favour, and identify it with a Northern Romantic tradition; the current vogue for the cruel cartoonist Gerald Scarfe, with his mélange of Grosz and Arthur Rackham, is perhaps characteristic. Partly however it was a simple matter of continuity, as for instance in the late work of Max Weber in the US, or Josef Herman and Jankel Adler and the artists influenced by them in Scotland, or the pupils of Beckmann and Kokoschka on both sides of the Atlantic, or in the growing reputation of an

228

independent like Bomberg, who had his English followers in the Borough Group in London.

In France too the rather mannered school of grey attenuated spikiness originated by Gruber and Giacometti was smartly exploited by such artists as Buffet and Jansem, with their mixture of the grotesque and the speciously 'compassionate'. There was however also a broad school of moderately expressionist French painting which came into greater prominence as the great men of the modern movement died off. 'It's as if expressionism were a means by which modern art is becoming somewhat more our own without losing anything of itself', wrote Jean Cassou in 1946. Strongest in the figure compositions of Bernard Lorjou, this tendency can be seen also in the figurative work of Edouard Pignon, Yves Alix, Mané-Katz and the painters associated with the annual exhibitions of 'Peintres Témoins de leur Temps'. Bridging the channel was another politically committed and basically expressionist painter, Peter de Francia, who was brought up in France but settled in London after the war. He had studied at the Brussels Academy and worked with Guttuso; in 1958 he did a big picture of the (French) bombing of the Tunisian village of Sakiet.

The same desperate intensity and passion as can be seen in the

English expressionism.
Left Joseph Herman's 'Miner
and Child', bought by the
Montreal Museum in 1953.

highly expressive paintings of Francis Bacon (whose screaming heads seem to echo the long succession of *Schreis* that began with Munch) is observable in the writings of Samuel Beckett. Not surprisingly, the whole movement of the Absurd Theatre has an expressionist irrationality which makes it particularly congenial to the German stage. This can be exemplified not only by the prevalence of Absurdist dramas in the West German repertoire since the late 1950s, but by the close parallels between Ionesco's *The Bald Prima Donna* and the faces of Iwan Goll some twenty-five years earlier. In poetry too there is the Anglo-Scottish movement of the 1940s called the New Apocalypse, which looked back to Blake and took the title of its anthology-cum-manifesto *The White Horseman* (1941) – cf. *Der blaue Reiter* – from D. H. Lawrence's *Apocalypse*:

The rider on the white horse! Who is he, then? ... He is the royal me, he is my very own self and his horse is the whole MANA of a man ... my *dynamic* or potent self.

230

Right David Bomberg's portrait of John Rodker, 1931, from Mrs Marianne Rodker's collection, Lestiou.

During that decade both Dylan Thomas and David Gascoyne were writing in an apocalyptic vein; thus the latter's 'Mountains' has the same 'cruel and jagged' images:

> Pure peaks thrust upward of mines of energy
> To scar the sky with symbols of ascent,
> Out of an innermost catastrophe –
> Schismatic shock and rupture of earth's care –
> Were grimly born.

In the 1950s the American 'beat' poets appeared, with the high Whitmanesque rhetoric of Allen Ginsberg's *Kaddish*, where Jewish mythology and oriental mysticism combine in a manner not unlike that of some of the utopian Expressionists. The need for a more or less Nietzschean philosophy to support such developments could be seen in the meteoric success of Colin Wilson's *The Outsider* (1956), which digested the ideas and lives of such forerunners as

Peter de Francia: 'The Bombardment of Sakiet', 1958–9. Tunisian Embassy, London.

Van Gogh, Barbusse, Nietzsche, Nijinsky and the French Existentialists, to justify its concept of the artist as ego-hero. With all its flaws this obsessively written book is directly in the Expressionist tradition.

In the Communist world there may not have been quite the same sense that 'God is dead', but the death of Stalin in 1953 likewise had an unsettling influence, introducing a cultural 'thaw' whose scope is still uncertain. The immediate effect was to modify the application of the doctrine of Socialist Realism while leaving the doctrine itself more or less untouched; thus once again there was room within the official canon for such figures as Meyerhold, Eisenstein and Lunacharsky, whose essentially romantic and at times expressionist concept of revolutionary art had long ranked as 'formalism'. The Soviet Academy's official history of the Soviet theatre (1966) even discusses the influence of Toller, Kaiser and Expressionism in general, com-

232

ing to the conclusion that it was largely the result of Lunacharsky's sponsorship and of the feeling that such writers symbolised the coming world revolution. The same year a symposium on Expressionism was published by the Academy for the Minister of Culture under the editorship of B. I. Singerman. This new Soviet climate of comparative tolerance has always seemed limited and conditional, but at least it has made possible a certain amount of individual divergence from the norm, sometimes (as in the cases of the sculptor Ernst Neizvestny and the painter Anatoly Zveryov) in a more or less expressionalist direction. At the same time those foreign expressionists whose political views do not conflict with Soviet policy are now once again accepted as contributing to a progressive 'realist' art: Masereel, the Mexicans, Guttuso (a member of the Communist Party) and the sentimental-expressive Chilean José Venturelli, who

Expressionism's centrifugal force.
Left Black Africa. Title page
from the Nigerian-based magazine
Black Orpheus, early 1960s.
Below left The USSR. Untitled
drawing by Ernst Neizvestny,
1964, from the Museum of Modern
Art, New York.
Right Chile. Jose Venturelli's
woodcut 'La despedida', 1942.

A JOURNAL OF AFRICAN AND AFRO-AMERICAN LITERATURE

has collaborated with the poet Pablo Neruda as well as with Siqueiros. Indeed once the bankruptcy of a purely literalistic 'socialist' art is admitted, however tacitly, a certain measure of expressionism is the obvious alternative.

The point is of relevance to the future of art in the underdeveloped and ex-colonial countries, where artists and writers alike seem to find expressionism, with its symbolist element, more accessible than most other modern European schools and a great deal more so than naturalism. This holds good not only for Latin America, where the indigenous expressionist tradition is now some forty years old, but also for the African continent and the Caribbean. In the visual arts there is already one obvious link in the contribution made by negro sculpture to the modern movement, which lies above all in its quality of expressive distortion, something that the Cubists soon lost sight of but the German Expressionists did not. There have also been influential teachers or *animateurs* from central Europe, such as Susanne Wenger and Ulli Beier in Nigeria, who have helped that

235

quality to find modern forms; the typography and woodcut illustrations of the magazine *Black Orpheus* under Beier's editorship provide good examples. The work of such widely dispersed artists, however, as the Rhodesian Thomas Mukarobgwa (whom Beier compares with Nolde), the Sudanese Ibrahim El Salahi, the Nigerian Demas Nwoko, the Angolan Valente Malangatana and the Guianan Aubrey Williams suggests a general and spontaneous expressionist tendency. Moreover, although there seems to be nothing much corresponding to this in English-language African or Caribbean writing, as soon as one turns to the French *négritude* writers there are some surprising expressionist echoes. Thus the Martiniquais Aimé Césaire's surrealist imagery cannot conceal his often Whitmanish message:

> mais moi homme! rien qu'homme!
> Ah! ne plus voir avec les yeux
> N'être plus une oreille à étendre
> N'être plus la brouette à évacuer le décor!
> N'être plus une machine à déménager les sensations!
>
> Je veux être le seul, le pur trésor,
> celui qui fait largesse des autres.
>
> Homme!
>
> (but me man! naught but man!
> Ah! to see no longer with one's eyes
> To be no longer an ear to stretch
> To be no longer a wheelbarrow for clearing away the scenery!
> To be no longer a machine for shifting sensations!
>
> I want to be the sole pure treasure,
> which gives generously of all the others.
>
> Man!)

– while President Senghor of Sénégal sounds like an African Claudel, as in his poem of 1940 to de Gaulle, 'le Guélowar':

> Ta voix nous dit l'honneur l'espoir et le combat, et ses ailes s'agitent dans notre poitrine
> Ta voix nous dit la République, que nous dresserons la Cité dans le jour bleu
> Dans l'égalité des peuples fraternels ...
>
> (Your voice speaks to us honour, hope and struggle, and its wings beat in our breasts
> Your voice speaks to us the Republic, the City which we shall build in the blue daylight
> In the equality of the brotherhood of peoples.)

The *ronflant* style that so easily seems ridiculous in English is immediately congenial to what Senghor calls

the language of the gods. Listen to Corneille, Lautréamont, Péguy and Claudel. Listen to the great Hugo. French is the great organ which can render every tone ...

– tones which certainly include that favourite Expressionist instrument, the trombone.

Finally Abstract Expressionism, whose impact on Germany itself has already been mentioned, developed during the second half of the 1940s, and by the middle of the following decade had become to most western art critics the dominant new school. Of the New York artists primarily associated with it, the Dutch-born Willem de Kooning also painted fiercely expressionist figurative pictures – such as the series of snarling *Women* of the 1950s – passing with no change of feeling from representational to abstract and vice versa. Jackson Pollock on the other hand worked a much narrower vein, that of a desperate but essentially graphological self-expression by means of marks on the canvas, many of which were more or less fortuitous drips. In the case of these two (though less so in that of other large-scale calligraphers such as Franz Kline and Robert Motherwell) there was an evident relationship to the non-figurative Kandinsky of some thirty years earlier, much of whose work is in the Guggenheim Museum in New York. Another influential figure whose age and early training had linked him to the German Expressionists, however he might disown them, was Hans Hofmann, who returned to painting in the mid-1930s after some twenty years as a pure teacher; he met Pollock in 1942 and seems to have inspired his drip technique. Both Pollock and De Kooning worked for the Federal Art Project in the 1930s (when Pollock also worked with Siqueiros), then made their New York reputations in 1948, and in 1950 were shown at the Venice Biennale with Lebrun and others, as a modern appendage to John Marin's retrospective. Two years later the name 'action painting' was coined to convey the new Klages-like conception of pictorial gesture, with its emphasis on the personal drama of the artist rather than on the quality of his work.

Almost simultaneously a comparable movement was evolving in northern Europe, where between 1941 and 1951 the COBRA group united Asger Jorn, Pierre Alechinsky, Karel Appel and other artists from *Co*penhagen, *Br*ussels and *A*msterdam. Of these the Dutchman Appel followed much the same approach as De Kooning,

The figurative side of Abstract Expressionism. *Below* Willem de Kooning's 'Woman IV', Nelson Gallery, Atkins Museum (gift of William Inge), Kansas City, Missouri. *Right* Asger Jorn's linocut 'Council for the propagation of Danish beauty in foreign lands', 1953.

while Jorn, despite a pre-war period of study with Léger, was a natural expressionist who now adopted a certain graphic primitivism and a dynamic ferocity of attack, calling his canvases by names like 'Despair' or 'Controlled Fury' (both 1952). Similarly Hofmann in the 1940s chose titles like 'Cataclysm', 'Ecstasy', 'Resurrection', 'Storm', before moving into a De Stael-like serenity after he had passed the age of seventy. Both schools were easily imitated in the years that followed, often by painters of no great technical brilliance, whether in the western or (more daringly) in the eastern spheres, eventually degenerating to the status of big-business office decoration and international hotel-art. At bottom this decline was due to a false relationship between passion and product, which neither a whole flood of mock-philosophising about the high moral qualities of non-figurative painting nor all the new resources for publicising artists' personalities could conceal for long. What can be said is that

239

abstract expressionism not only led to a fresh emphasis on the apocalyptic elements in the artist's pictorial handwriting (as found already in such figurative expressionists as Van Gogh, Meidner, Soutine and, at certain periods, Kokoschka) but stimulated figurative artists too to try some of its techniques, as seen for instance in some spectacular canvases by the Frenchman Paul Rebeyrolle.

A dynamic balance

What then *is* expressionism, as we now understand it? So far this book has aimed to do two things: first of all to trace the history of the German Expressionist movement as it is commonly understood, relating it as far as possible to its wider causes and effects; secondly to give some account of the many other works of art in our century which seem in the author's (subjective) judgment to be expressionist. In other words it has tried both to be the story of a movement in our time and a collection of assorted evidence which may help us to decide what we mean by that word. Of course we cannot at this point draw a neat line, as on a bank balance sheet, then tot up the results; the whole subject is still active and influential, with many new developments ahead of it. For expressionism in the larger sense, as Read saw, stands not for a mere stylistic school but for 'one of the basic modes of perceiving and representing the world around us'.

It is a fundamentally necessary word, like 'idealism' and 'realism', and not a word of secondary implications, like 'impressionism' ...

So let us first resume the characteristics of the German movement, then relate these to a wider kind of expressionism, trying to work towards a definition by seeing what they are *not,* and finally discussing why at the present moment these things seem to be worth investigation.

German Expressionism, which was a far more comprehensive movement than French Cubism, represented for some dozen years the united forces of the modern movement within a single language area. Though in style it was a ragbag, its spirit was remarkably coherent, and for many of those who became caught up in it it was an experience which marked them for life. To a great extent therefore it is associated with a particular generation: for though the leading Expressionists differed widely in age it is roughly true to say that hardly any German connected with (or even interested in) the arts born between 1880 and 1895 could escape being touched by the movement. Admittedly many of its concerns were shared with the modern movement as a whole or with its forerunners: for instance the imagery of the great industrialised city (including such phenomena as prostitution), the hopeful future of its inhabitants (the New Man, basically an urban creature), and, perhaps by contrast, a sense of individual isolation and a new fascination with sickness and death. But these had to be expressed in such a way as to communicate strong emotions, with something of the dynamism and vitality which Nietzsche proclaimed (and earlier generations rather took for granted, much as they took sex for granted before Lawrence). This primacy of active, restless emotion, affecting not only subject-matter but form, is indeed expressionism's most obvious feature. It is not, as is sometimes said, emotion as such, for relaxed emotions such as laughter or contentment are virtually excluded.

In the visual arts, where such characteristic concerns played a significant but by no means dominant part in determining subject-matter, the work's emotional charge took two forms. First of all there was deliberate distortion, which often made use of the visual discoveries of the Cubists and Futurists, exploiting their angularity, simultaneity and sense of disintegration or movement for expressive ends. Sometimes reinforcing that and sometimes in lieu of it (since there could not very well be any element of distortion in non-representational art) there was the actual violence and passion of the artist's handwriting, the force of his attack on his materials. At the same time the Expressionists for some reason tended, once the more or less Fauve period in Dresden and Munich had come to an end, to shun brilliant colours, sticking mainly to the browns and greens, dark blues and dull reds of the Grünewald 'Crucifixion' and the Greco 'Toledo'. In the theatre similar principles determined the usual Expressionist setting, apart from the special case of Jessner's steps (which became regarded as characteristic of Expressionism though their emotional function was slight), while a further element of distortion appeared in the stylisation of characters and acting. Dramatic structure disintegrated into a sequence of disconnected scenes, the psychology of the hero into different facets; other characters were presented mostly in the flat. Finally in writing, both of verse and of stage dialogue (more rarely of prose), the actual sentences were chopped up, telescoped or inverted not unlike the elements of a picture. Verse forms were manhandled for expressive ends very much as were visual ones; free verse accordingly was the

241

rule. Where Expressionism in the theatre was often used comically, with jerky effects like the silent cinema, the poets grew steadily more solemn and messianic. The intensest emotion to be expressed in this way was not so much the dynamic awareness of modern life that was typical of early Expressionism as the generalised hatred of warfare and love of humanity that characterised the utopians.

The German movement was so limited chronologically that it is not simple to establish clear relationships between it and the many non-German works of art of all periods which are commonly termed expressionist or strike the subjective judgment as being so. This problem can be approached in two different ways. One is to go by analogies: seeing where the same influences have been at work (e.g., Nietzsche, Whitman, Strindberg, Gauguin), attributing a common awareness of them to men who were between twenty-five and thirty in 1910, and looking for characteristics such as we have attributed to the German movement, while realising that they are found in rather different combinations outside it. Though this helps to clarify the expressionist affinities of men like Gaudier-Brzeska or Maya-kovsky or O'Neill, it makes for a much narrower area of search than the second approach, which is to decide what one really means by expressionism with a small e, then see how far the answer relates to our analysis of the movement. The value of doing this is that by eliminating everything ephemeral, like its borrowings from its immediate forerunners or from other parts of the modern move-ment, we are brought back to the basic question of emotion, which in any expressionist work has got to emerge as the ruling force, spontaneously dictating any formal distortion or morbidity of theme.

Not all who worked within the ambit of German Expressionism meet the definitions we have given. Klee for instance was concerned with quite different spheres, while some of the best-known Expres-sionists only met them during a given period. Thus Kokoschka's Dresden landscapes, which are sometimes cited as his most Expres-sionist works because of their brilliant colouring (far subtler, how-ever, than that of the Brücke) and flat areas of paint, have a new serenity which is quite un-expressionist, and really mark his turn away from the movement. For expressionism is not just colourful primitivism, which is something much more characteristic of the Fauves, but primarily a question of distortion, while even distortion is not expressionist unless it is directed above all, consciously or not, to the communication of some intense emotion. Lehmbruck and the

242

sculptress Renée Sintenis, often grouped with the Expressionist movement, are quite alien to its spirit because their distortions are calculated to sentimentalise; Epstein because he sentimentalises in his bronzes and monumentalises in his carvings; Hodler because he is not so much concerned with emotions as with symbols for ideas, or in his later works, again, with monumentality. Nor can anybody rank as an Expressionist whose distortions are primarily naive, or even *faux-naïf,* aping the naive artist's innocence (as in the cases of Rousseau on the one hand and Modigliani on the other), or fail to convey any strong emotion at all. Yet another distinction – often a much more difficult one – has to be made between Expressionism and the merely grotesque, with which, as in the case of the Prague circle, it often overlaps. For grotesque art is concerned less with expressing the emotional tensions within the artist, or between the artist and his surroundings, than with making the reader's or spectator's flesh creep, or more often just tickle; and to achieve this it has no need of new formal means but can rely on a long tradition of the conventionally 'uncanny'. Admittedly there are Expressionists who can be related to this tradition, but its purer exponents, like Kubin and Meyrink, are not by any means expressionist. Such distinctions, which seem subjectively obvious, are not easy to establish objectively since so many of the people we have just named were interlinked with the German movement. But it was possible to contribute to and associate personally with German Expressionism without really being an expressionist. In such cases the spirit was weak, though the factors of time and place were willing.

There are also the questions of national temperament and political commitment. It is common to hear expressionism described, out of pride or repugnance, as a particularly German or Germanic or Northern or Nordic tendency; and of course there is something in this, or the movement would not have taken root where it did. On the other hand once one starts trying to distinguish between big-E and small-e expressionism one finds that some of the movement's purely German features are peripheral to the wider trend: the element of cruelty, for instance, or the special brilliance of Expressionist wood-engraving, or the whole tradition of the grotesque; you will look in vain for any of this in say, Rouault. Again, expressionism, particularly in the visual arts, is often treated as specially prevalent among those of Jewish origin. In Germany, as we saw, this was just not true, though a number of the poets were Jewish and Jews were prominent among the painters' patrons. If expressionist

243

artists elsewhere on the other hand were often Jewish it was not their Jewishness that was the crucial factor so much as their understanding of central Europe. As for the political element, it was undoubtedly present in the movement proper, and it reappears in Guttuso and the Mexicans and the expressionist Picasso, and even in the young O'Neill and Elmer Rice (an opponent of the First World War who was, incidentally, of German descent), while Césaire is a Communist and Senghor was a member of the French Socialist Party till the late 1940s. Certainly there were exceptions, ranging from Claudel among the movement's forerunners to Hans Hofmann among its heirs, but generally expressionism in this century has been most congenial to people of left-wing views. From Van Gogh on, its dynamism, and even its madness, were partly due to a wish to change mankind.

The story has many lessons, above all because there are so many analogies with the present day. Fifty years after the turning point of the Expressionist movement the climate in many western countries is in one way and another extraordinarily similar. We have had (and are still having) an Art Nouveau revival, followed by a still slightly tentative disinterment of Arts Décoratifs 1925; we have resuscitated *Dracula* and the whole apparatus of *fin-de-siècle* horror; much of our humour has become morbid and cruel. Anarchism, if still a negligible force compared with what it was before 1900, plays a more important part in Europe than it has done for many years. At the same time, particularly in California and New York, there is a recrudescence of the kind of orientally-based mysticism that interested men like Itten and Kandinsky; it only seems strange that Ginsberg, Timothy Leary and its other prophets have not yet brought back Rudolf Steiner. Steiner's architecture on the other hand *has* been the subject of renewed interest, and even the fantasies of a man like Finsterlin seem relevant now that we have the techniques to carry them out; they are not all that remote from Sydney Opera House. On the political level too the Left's slightly desperate search for a revolutionary, even Marxist ideology which shall not be dominated by the ageing Communist hierarchy makes any kind of militant utopianism seem attractive. The pacifism of the German Expressionists, their boundlessly hopeful ideals and their intense sense of mission are absolutely in line with the feeling of young people in many countries today. Thus the Munich Soviet (though not, nb. its repression) was echoed in Paris in May 1968, where Toller, himself the subject of a topical new German play by Tankred

Dorst, would have understood the students' feelings, together with many of their slogans.

Read in this light, the history of our century suggests all sorts of conclusions, at least to those who do not automatically dismiss such quests and the spirit which they represent. Here I can only underline one or two that strike me as important. Personally I am in every way mistrustful of Johannes Becher's middle-aged nostalgia for the movement; the climate of excitement and heightened living which is generated at such moments may be unforgettable to the participants, but enthusiasm notoriously can do more harm than good, and the only way to judge it is by results, of which one, certainly, was Becher's own ambiguous career. Seen thus, it is odd how differently Expressionism affected poets and artists. The artists, who on the whole seldom dealt with directly political themes though often feeling strongly about them, tended to be raised above themselves by the movement; it somehow stimulated good work from those of naturally mediocre talents. The poets, from Werfel's *Der Welt-freund* on, were on the contrary corrupted by it. Writers of great facility and skill, like Werfel himself and Becher, because they were too gullible (possibly also too vain) about their public function, uncritically inflated their talents and wrote like windy, at times even burst, balloons. That temptation is still there for those like Senghor or Ginsberg who seem to take a similar view of themselves. One can see the movement's strengths and weaknesses illuminatingly combined in the theatre, where some really terrible writing (e.g. in *Der Bettler* or *Masse-Mensch*) was saved by the stimulus of a new dramatic form, then brought to life by brilliant productions and an intense relationship with the audience. For Expressionism was good for the framework, apparatus and conventions of the arts. It was fatal for the artist's judgment of himself.

And was it not in the long run also fatal for many of the artists? Today, when several formerly indifferent countries, like England, have developed an immense public or official concern with culture, so that more or less avant-garde work in the arts is encouraged as never before, it is worth recalling what happened in Germany after 1933. The modern movement in that country (as also in Russia) was suppressed all the more brutally because it had been promoted above the public's level of tolerance (which is always well above its level of understanding). Of course history never repeats itself exactly, particularly when it involves so special a phenomenon as German National Socialism. But once such disastrous possibilities have been experienced they ought at least to be borne in mind. Indeed the whole relationship of Expressionism to Nazism is something that deserves further study, however easy it may seem to dismiss the arguments of men like Lukács as an old-fashioned Stalinist aberration. For there *was* a potentially Nazi element in its ideology; it *was* rooted in much the same irrationalism and agnostic mysticism; it *was* to some extent deliberately barbarian. To admit this is not to condemn it, and of course the idea of a purely rational art is an absurd one. But if the Expressionist movement is a live enough example today to be worth studying at all we must try to understand the dangers of expressionism as well as its achievements. To do anything else is to treat it as a museum piece.

Acknowledgments

Many thanks are due to Hans Hess and Michael Hamburger for advice and comments. Denis Bablet, Peter de Francia, Pierre Garnier, John Golding, Pierre Vorms and Frank Whitford answered queries; Mrs Marianne Rodker and F. S. Booth helped with pictures; S. S. Prawer kindly allowed his lecture on *The 'Uncanny' in Literature* (1965) to be quoted. The author is also grateful to Jean Jacquot and Roger Bauer for inviting him to the conference on 'Expressionisme dans le théâtre' at Strasbourg University in November 1968, which yielded a number of interesting papers and conversations, notably with Lotte Eisner, Pierre Halleux and Kurt Pinthus.

Every effort has been made to trace the copyright owner of each illustration in this book. However, in a number of cases the publishers have had no reply to their enquiries, or even have not known where to enquire. They apologise in advance for any unauthorised use thus made of copyright material. Acknowledgment – further to any made in the captions – is due to the following for illustrations (the number refers to the page on which the illustration appears): frontispiece Pierre Vorms; 15 Photographic Giraudon, Galerie Mouradiau; 18 (*top*), 166, 167 copyright A.C.L. Brussels; 22 Metropolitan Museum of Art, New York (bequest of Mrs H. O. Havemeyer); 26 Bibliothèque Nationale, Paris; 27 (photo Bulloz), 43 (*right*), 162 SPADEM, Paris; 30-1 Musée d'Unterlinden, Colmar; 29 (*below*) (Mrs Simon Guggenheim Fund),176 (Acquired through the Lillie P. Bliss Bequest),234 (*below*) (Gift of Olga A. Carlisle), The Museum of Modern Art, New York; 37, 41 (*right*),

Books and Sources

Publications already mentioned in the text are not listed unless there has been a recent reprint. Cheap paperback editions are distinguished by small capitals.

1 General studies of Expressionism

The most useful are Bernard S. Myers's *The German Expressionists* (New York 1957; shortened edition 1963), Michel Ragon's *L'Expressionisme* (Lausanne 1966), Richard Samuel and R. Hinton Thomas's *Expressionism in German Life, Literature and the Theatre 1910-1924*, (Cambridge 1939), Peter Selz's *German Expressionist Painting*, (Berkeley 1957) and Walter H. Sokel's *The Writer in Extremis* (Stanford 1959). Of these Myers, Ragon and Selz deal predominantly with the visual arts, the others almost entirely with writing. Ragon alone goes outside the German movement, though the curious might care also to look up Sheldon Cheney's *Expressionism in Art* (revised edition, New York 1948) which cites many American examples and uses the term 'expressionism' to denote almost any modern trend; originally based on some lectures of 1932, it was influenced by the teaching of Hans Hofmann.

Of more specialised works, Karl Ludwig Schneider's *Zerbrochene Formen* (Hamburg 1967) is unusual in linking the visual and literal aspects, while Armin Arnold's *Die Literatur des Expressionismus* (Stuttgart 1966) gives an account of the movement's origins on which that in the present work is largely based.

2 Documentary and reference works

Four essential publications have been edited by Paul Raabe: *Expressionismus. Literatur und Kunst 1910-1923*, the catalogue of an exhibition at the Schiller-Nationalmuseum, (with Ludwig Greve, Munich 1960); the bibliography *Die Zeitschriften und Sammlungen des literarischen Expressionismus* (Stuttgart 1964); *Expressionismus. Aufzeichnungen und Erinnerungen der Zeitgenossen* (Olten 1965); and EXPRESSIONISMUS. DER KAMPF UM EINE LITERARISCHE BEWEGUNG (DTV, Munich 1965). Another selection of documents is Paul Pörtner's *Literatur-Revolution 1910-1925*. Some of the movements' proclamations are reprinted in Kasimir Edschmid's *Frühe Manifeste* (Hamburg 1957) and Dieter Schmidt's *Manifeste Manifeste* (Dresden n.d.), while a wide range of material is drawn on in Paolo Chiarini's *Caos e Geometria* (Florence 1964), which summarises the main theoretical essays and articles bearing on all the arts.

For the theatre Günther Rühle's *Theater für die Republik 1917-1933* (Frankfurt 1967) gives well-indexed excerpts from contemporary criticisms of the main German plays, with an informative commentary. For literature

248

Expressionismus als Literatur edited by Wolfgang Rothe (Berne 1969) contains essays on some forty writers, with bibliographies and biographical notes. Details of others can be found in Hermann Kunisch's *Handbuch der deutschen Gegenwartsliteratur* (Munich 1965), which also includes a comprehensive essay on the movement by Günther Erken. An earlier standard work on the writers of the period was Albert Soergel's *Dichtung und Dichter der Zeit* (Leipzig 1925).

3 Precursors

Leaving aside obvious and well-documented figures (Nietzsche, Gauguin, Van Gogh and Strindberg, for instance), it is worth mentioning such less-known works as Fritz Burger's *Cézanne und Hodler* (Munich 1913), Paul Haesarts's *Laethem-Saint-Martin* (Brussels 1965), Marcelle Kemp's *Romain Rolland et l'Allemagne* (Paris 1962), Meier-Graefe's *Entwicklungsgeschichte der modernen Kunst* (two editions, 1903 and 1914; English translation 1908), Schuré's *Précurseurs et révoltés* (Paris 1904), Van de Velde's *Geschichte meines Lebens* (Munich 1962), Paul Vogt's *Das Museum Folkwang Essen* (Cologne 1965), Walter R. Volbach's *Adolphe Appia* (Middletown 1968) and Stefan Zweig's biography of Verhaeren (English translation 1914).

For contributory or overlapping movements see Christa Baumgarth's GESCHICHTE DES FUTURISMUS (Hamburg 1966), John Golding's *Cubism. A History and an Analysis 1907-1914* (London 1959. Second edition 1968), Miroslav Lamač's *Modern Czech Painting 1907-1917* (London 1968), Lajos Nemeth's *Modern Art in Hungary* (Budapest 1969), and Camilla Gray's *The Great Experiment in Russian Art 1863-1922* (London and New York 1962). The Cassou/Langui/Pevsner *The Sources of Modern Art* (London 1962) is also very relevant.

4 German groups, magazines and anthologies

There are useful illustrated volumes on the Brücke and the Blaue Reiter by Lothar-Günther Buchheim (Feldafing 1956 and 1959). For the Sturm see Nell Walden and Lothar Schreyer: *Der Sturm* (Baden-Baden 1954) and the former's *Herwarth Walden* (Mainz 1963). For the Neuer Club and the Neo-pathetisches Cabarett see Günter Martens's account in volume 6 of Heym's collected works (Munich 1968), on which the present book has drawn. For the Novembergruppe see Helga Kliemann: *Die Novembergruppe* (West Berlin 1969).

Kraus of Leichtenstein have reprinted twenty-four magazines including (of those referred to in this book) *Revolution, Das Tribunal, Die Weissen Blätter* (1913-21) and *Zeit-Echo*. Paul Raabe has edited a photo-reprint of *Die Aktion* and a paperback selection of items from it ICH SCHNEIDE DIE ZEIT AUS (Munich 1964). Other reprints include *Menschheitsdämmerung* (Hamburg 1959), *Der Blaue Reiter* (Munich 1965), *Neue Jugend* (East Berlin 1967) and Bruno Taut's *Frühlicht 1920-1922* (Berlin 1963). The series *Der Jüngste Tag* (reprint in two volumes announced by Scheffler, Frankfurt), is invaluable as a source for authors not otherwise republished.

Newer Expressionist anthologies include Karl Otten's two volumes *Schrei und Bekenntnis* (plays) and *Ahnung und Aufbruch* (prose) (Neuwied 1959 and 1957), and the selection LYRIK DES EXPRESSIONISTISCHEN JAHRZEHNTS (Munich 1962).

5 Individual German artists

Certain artists have been dealt with in solid monographs and/or biographies. The following shows the authors' names, with * indicating oeuvre-catalogue and † a catalogue of graphic work:

Barlach F. Schult*†. *Beckmann* Peter Selz; Gallwitz†. *Campendonk* Paul Wember; Matthias T. Engels†. *Dix* Fritz Loeffler; Florian Karsch†. *Feininger* Hans Hess*. *Grammaté* Ferdinand Eckhardt†. *Heckel* Paul Vogt; A. and W. Dube†. *Jawlensky* Clemens Weiler. *Kandinsky* Will Grohmann*. *Kirchner* Donald E. Gordon*; A. and W. Dube†. *Kokoschka* Hans M. Wingler*; Wilhelm Arntz†; Edith Hoffmann; J. P. Hodin. *Kollwitz* August Klipstein†. *Kubin* Paul Raabe†. *Macke* Gustav Vriesen. *Marc* Alois Schardt†. *Masereel* H. C. von der Gabelentz†. *Meidner* Thomas Grochowiak. *Modersohn-Becker* Gustav Pauli†. *Mueller* Florian Karsch†. *Nolde* Gustav Schiefler†; Werner Haftmann. *Pankok* Rainer Zimmermann. *Pechstein* Paul Fechter†. *Purrmann* Gotthard Jedlicka and Wilhelm Weber†. *Rohlfs* Paul Vogt†. *Schmidt-Rottluff* Rosa Schapire†; Will Grohmann. *Schwitters* Werner Schmalenbach*. *Segall* P. M. Bardi.

A number of other artists were dealt with in brief monographs in the *Junge Kunst* series (Klinckhardt und Biermann, Leipzig, 1919 ff.)

6 Individual German writers

Since 1945 Collected (unless otherwise stated) or Selected Works of Expressionist and related writers have appeared as follows:

Barlach (Piper, Munich 1956-9). Benn (Limes, Wiesbaden 1958-61). Bloch (Suhrkamp, Frankfurt 1959). Däubler (Kösel, Munich 1956). Döblin (Sel., Walter, Olten 1960-4). Ehrenstein (Sel., Luchterhand, Neuwied 1961). Einstein (Limes 1962). Frank (Aufbau, East Berlin 1957; new edition announced by Nymphenburger, Munich). Goering (Langen-Müller, Munich 1961). Goll (Poems only, Luchterhand 1960). Hardekopf (Die Arche, Zurich 1963). Hasenclever (Sel., Rowohlt, Hamburg 1963). Herrmann-Neisse (Sel., Langen-Müller 1961). Heym (Ellermann, Munich 1960-). Kafka (Fischer, Frankfurt 1948-58). Kaiser (Sel., Kiepenheuer & Witsch, Cologne 1966). Kokoschka (Langen-Müller 1956). Lasker-Schüler (Kösel, 1959-). Lichtenstein (Die Arche, 1962-6). Loerke (Suhrkamp 1958). Mühsam (Sel., Volk und Welt East Berlin 1958-). Sack (Langen-Müller 1962). Schickele (Kiepenheuer, Cologne 1960-1). Sorge (Christiana-Verlag, Zurich 1962). Stadler (Ellermann 1954). Sternheim (Luchterhand 1963-8, Aufbau 1965-). Stramm (Limes 1963). Toller (Sel. Rowohlt 1961). Trakl (Variorum edition, Otto Müller, Salzburg, 1969). Unruh (Sel., 1961). Van Hoddis (Die Arche

1958). Werfel (Fischer 1948-). Wolf (Aufbau 1960-). A. Zweig (Sel., Aufbau 1957-). On Wolfenstein see Peter Fischer's critical study (Fink, Munich 1968).

Of cheap paperback editions, DTV (Munich) has published a selection of poems by LASKER-SCHÜLER; also Barlach's DER TOTE TAG/DER ARME VETTER, a selection of Döblin stories DIE ERMORDUNG EINER BUTTERBLUME, Goering's SEESCHLACHT, Kubin's novel DIE ANDERE SEITE and Heinrich Mann's essays GEIST UND TAT. The Fischer-Bücherei (Frankfurt) publishes paperback selections of poems by Heym, Loerke, Stadler and Trakl, also Kafka's AMERIKA, DER PROZESS, DAS SCHLOSS and DAS URTEIL.

7 The other arts

On the theatre: Bernhard Diebold's *Anarchie im Drama* (Frankfurt, 1921), H. F. Garten's *Modern German Drama* (London 1959) and Horst Denkler's *Drama des Expressionismus* (Munich 1967). On music: Luigi Rognoni's *Espressionismo e dodekafonia* (Turin 1954). On architecture: U. Conrads and H. Sperlich's *Fantastic Architecture* (London 1963), Denis Sharp's *Modern Architecture and Expressionism* (London 1966) and Barbara Miller Lane's *Architecture and Politics in Germany 1918-1945* (Harvard 1968). On cinema: Lotte Eisner's *The Haunted Screen* (London 1969), Rolf Hempel's *Carl Meyer* (East Berlin 1968) and Siegfried Krakauer's *From Caligari to Hitler* (Princeton and London 1947).

8 Autobiographies

Relevant memoirs (M), letters (L) and diaries (D) have been written by Ball (L), Barlach (L), Becher (D). Beckmann (L), Benn (M, L), Brod (M), Dukes (M), Edschmid (M), Goll (L), Grosz (M), Guilbeaux (M), Kafka (D), Kessler (D), Klee (D), Kollwitz (D and L), Kortner (M), Loerke (D), Marc (L), Modersohn-Becker (D), Nolde (M, L), Pechstein (M), Rice (M), Rolland (D), Toller (M) and Wolff (L).

9 English translations

Aside from scattered items in magazines, not much by the German Expressionists has appeared in English. The principal poets are included in Michael Hamburger's and Christopher Middleton's anthology *Modern German Poetry* (London 1962) and Patrick Bridgwater's TWENTIETH CENTURY GERMAN VERSE (Harmondsworth 1963), while there are poems by Trakl and Benn in MODERN EUROPEAN POETRY edited by W. Barnstone et al. (New York 1966). Patrick Bridgwater has translated *Twenty-two poems* by August Stramm, Brewhouse Press, Wymondham, 1969. *Twelve Poems* by Trakl in Michael Hamburger's translation appeared under the title *Decline* (Latin Press, St Ives 1952); Trakl's *Selected Poems* edited by Christopher Middleton (London 1968) and Benn's *Primal Vision* edited by E. B. Ashton (London 1961) include work by the same translator. *Poems* by Werfel have been translated by Edith Abercrombie Snow (Princeton 1945). A story by Heym is in GREAT GERMAN SHORT

STORIES edited by Stephen Spender (New York 1960). Some late poems by Goll appeared in English during his US exile in the Second World War: e.g. *Fruit from Saturn* (Brooklyn 1946). *Seven Plays* by Toller were published by John Lane, London in 1935, and there were also translations of *The Swallow Book* (verses from prison) and *I Was a German* (memoirs, 1934). Kaiser's *Gas* and *From Morn to Midnight* appeared in the 1920s. Recently a new series has been started by Calder and Boyars, London, edited by J. M. Ritchie under the title 'German Expressionism', beginning with *Seven Expressionist Plays* (1968) and *Vision and Aftermath. Four Expressionist War Plays* (1969); volumes of five plays apiece by Kaiser and Sternheim have been announced. An ANTHOLOGY OF GERMAN EXPRESSIONIST DRAMA is edited by Walter H. Sokel (New York 1963).

Klee's diaries and Grosz's autobiography (somewhat abridged) have been translated. Of Expressionist prose writers Ehrenstein's *Tubutsch* (New York 1946) and Unruh's *The Way of Sacrifice* (*Opfergang*) may be relevant. Otherwise, apart from Kubin's early novel *The Other Side* (London 1969), it is mostly their post-Expressionist works that have been translated: e.g. Döblin's *Berlin Alexanderplatz* (London 1931), Kokoschka's *A Sea Ringed with Visions* (London 1962) or the novellas of Leonhard Frank. Kafka's works are published in English by Schocken, New York and Secker and Warburg, London. THE CASTLE, THE TRIAL, THE METAMORPHOSIS and THE DIARIES are available in paperback.

10 The Nazi reaction

See Paul Ortwin Rave: *Kunstdiktatur im Dritten Reich* (Hamburg 1949), Hellmut Lehmann-Haupt: *Art under a Dictatorship* (New York 1954), Franz Roh: *Entartete Kunst* (Hanover 1962) and the five volumes of Joseph Wulf: KUNST UND KULTUR IM DRITTEN REICH (Hamburg, 1966). 'Lebensweg eines Intellektualisten', a section from Benn's *Kunst und Macht* (Stuttgart 1934), has been republished in slightly embellished form in his DOPPELLEBEN (Munich 1967).

11 The wider scene

Of the non-German authors cited, Apollinaire, Cendrars, Johnston, Jouve and O'Neill have all appeared in collected editions. Other relevant works include Bernard S. Myers: *Mexican Painting in Our Time* (New York 1956), Antonio Rodríguez: *A History of Mexican Mural Painting* (London 1969), André de Ridder: *La littérature flamande contemporaine 1890-1923* (Antwerp and Paris n.d.) and Peter Bauland: *The Hooded Eagle. Modern German Drama on the New York Stage* (Syracuse 1968). There are monographs and/or catalogues devoted to several of the artists referred to – e.g. Burliuk (K. S. Dreier), Chagall (Franz Meyer), De Kooning, Gromaire, Hartley, Hofmann, Jorn, Neizvestny (John Berger: *Art and Revolution*), Permeke, Pollock, Soutine and Weber – and Ulli Beier's *Contemporary Art in Africa* (London 1968) is also recommended.

Index

This index is necessarily selective. Bold figures refer to main entries, italic figures to illustrations, and figures in brackets to quotations.